Cat/pol[?]
20.

On a Killing Day

On a Killing Day

Dolores Kennedy
with
Robert Nolin

Bonus Books, Inc., Chicago

96 95 94 93 92   5 4 3 2 1

Library of Congress Catalog Card Number: 91-77989

International Standard Book Number: 0-929387-75-9

Bonus Books, Inc.
160 East Illinois Street
Chicago, Illinois 60611

Printed in the United States of America

Composition by Point West, Inc.

"On a killing day, those guys always wanted to go
way, way back in the woods."

—Aileen "Lee" Wuornos
January 1991

For Kathy Kennedy, Wendy Battistone and Rich Krepak—with gratitude and love

and

In memory of my friend and fellow writer, Paul D. Sweeney, whose death has left an empty space in my life.

Contents

Acknowledgments

C rime destroys lives and inflicts irreversible tragedy on the families of victims. It defies our understanding and overpopulates our prisons. It also seems to bring out the worst in almost everyone.

Prosecutors shriek "Death," the public cries "Vengeance," the news reporters proclaim "Exclusive," television advertises "Movie of the Week," the system announces "Control," the politicians request "Votes," and the elements of politics, power and greed converge in a mighty eruption known as criminal justice.

Before Aileen Wuornos had even been identified as a suspect in the murder of seven men across central Florida, contracts on the story abounded, hindering investigation, undermining witnesses, hampering defense. And so to tell her story became a challenge, not of investigation, but of determining who was under contract to who and, therefore, what information had already been signed, sealed and delivered.

I was fortunate. I became friendly with a tiny wonderwoman named Arlene Pralle, who guided me through the morass of "unavailable" and introduced me to the inner workings of her relationship with Aileen Wuornos.

And so I wish to thank Arlene Pralle and, through her, Steve Glazer and Aileen Wuornos, for their contributions to this tale. I also wish to thank Robert Nolin, of the *Daytona Beach News-Journal* for his assistance and for being there when I could not be.

My appreciation to Robert Pralle, Assistant State Attorney David Damore, Deanie Stewart, Dawn Botkins and Assistant Public Defender Billy Nolas for their willingness to share their thoughts, and to my long-suffering family and friends for their support and patience—Mary Hodges, Jim, Karen and Sean Kennedy, Angie DiMaso, Bill Heirens, Patricia Vader, Michele DiMaso, LouAnn DiMaso, Emily Ray, Rev. Jack Nordgaard, Michael Arabshian, Barbara Fasano, Edward Baumann, Jennifer and Eric Battistone, Donna Smolak, Delores Caliendo and Marvin Youngerman.

And a "thump on the head" to the Florida Department of Corrections, who allows reporters and television personages, but not book authors, to interview death row inmates.

Prologue:
Daytona Beach is a State of Mind

Getting to Daytona Beach is easy. Just run away from home.
Leave your parents, leave your wife, quit your job, jump parole,
wipe the grease off your hands and hit that Jersey state line. Go south on
Interstate 95, then take a quick left past Florida.

Welcome to paradise. There's sunshine, jobs, cheap living and babes
in bikinis. You can even drive your car on the beach. Sea, sex, prosperity
and exhaust fumes. An American illusion served up on a beach so ex-
ploited it's become no more than a sandy parking lot.

Getting out isn't so easy. There's never enough money to get to Miami. Jobs aren't that plentiful after all. Living is cheap, but so are wages.
Once you've blown your wad getting to Daytona Beach, it's hard to re-
build your traveling roll.

That's when the dream fades into desperation, with temptation
quick on its heels. Temptation means crime. Those who succumb end up
bleeding into the gutter after a drug deal, or starring in a videotaped
murder, or getting carved up or burned as a sacrifice to Satan, or suddenly finding themselves shotgunned or stabbed for some small-time insurance payoff.

Crime has a special flavor in Daytona Beach, a bent toward freaki-
ness. Whether the city grows its own grotesqueries or the freaks flock to
its agreeable shore is a matter of genetics vs. environment. Even the experts can't agree. Listen to the chatter around courthouse and cop shop:
"What is it about this burg? What breeds such hinky crime?"

Well, Daytona Beach is a hinky place. A palm-fringed backdrop for
tawdry intrigue. The Casablanca of cheap, where Bubba plays Bogart.

Penthouse magazine once labeled Daytona Beach "the summit of
sleaze." Hardly a shocking appellation to real Daytonans. They yawn at
mere sleaze, having been weaned on the truly bizarre.

This is a land where bodies bloom in the jungle each spring. Banner
planes could headline each day's violence: Bikers settle score with kick,
body lands in garbage bin. Tennessee drifter guns down popular ball
player who had the audacity to offer a beer. Maniac runs screaming

across four lane highway to slice open stranger's belly. Fourteen-year-old shoots mother, stashes corpse in car trunk. Woman on trial for torching trailer to collect insurance on two toddlers' deaths. Boat salesman stops to take piss, stabbed to death by a Chicago hitman. Suburban teen ices drug dealer lover, confesses, walks free after confession is excluded from trial.

People get murdered here, as in any city, for the usual reasons. Money, revenge, sex, business. But Daytona Beach seems to elicit a unique end-of-the-line dementia.

Look at the city, what it has to offer, who buys what it's selling. The gritty beach town lies about sixty miles east of Orlando. A good bet for a cheap, workingman's vacation. Redneck tourists from all over the Southeast know this. So do outlaw bikers. Desperate blue-collar workers flee dead-end jobs in the urban north to follow the good life...and the myth of plentiful jobs...in Daytona Beach.

Teenage runaways from every hamlet and crossroad along the East Coast gravitate to the city's glitzy waterfront, where they sell drugs, stolen property or themselves.

Daytona Beach is a place of muscle and road dust, a dirt-under-the-fingernails resort. If it's money and a modicum of elegance you want, try Miami...the streets are clogged with Mercedes and Jaguars. In Daytona Beach you'll find RVs, pickup trucks, low-slung Harley choppers and souped up greaser cars with New Jersey tags. It's the beat-up station wagon of Florida vacation spots.

The Halifax River, a wide stretch of the Intracoastal Waterway, divides the Mainland from the Beachside, a subtropical peninsula. The Rockefellers used to vacation here. The reigning entreprenurial nobleman now is Big Daddy Rat, who makes his fortune selling T-shirts that offer such witticisms as "Blow Me."

The Beachside is the province of people like the Spider Lady, whose face is tattooed with, what else? a spider web. You can get one of your own at any of a dozen tattoo parlors, legit or otherwise. Or leather underwear, complete with hidden zipper pocket. You can even get your genitals pierced.

The Beachside's architecture is quaint waterfront bungalow gone to seed. The decrepit yet picturesque little houses provide low-rent hidey-holes scant blocks from the Atlantic Ocean. They form a waterbound warren of bikers, thugs on the lam, juvenile desperadoes and embastioned retirees.

In one cramped house, two decades past, a trio of teenagers built a basement altar and tortured a boy nigh unto death. The house stands the same today; nor have the neighborhood denizens changed.

Along Main Street, dirty little bars march to the sea. The kind of bars where men shout, "Show your tits!" and the women cheerfully oblige. Daytona Beach's most famous bar sits across from the weedy and sagging cemetery. A biker joint called the Boot Hill, bras festoon its ceiling and blow jobs are administered in shadowy corners.

Crowning the Beachside is the Boardwalk, a drab concrete promenade of carnival rides and penny arcades. Here the desperate pilgrims seek out their own, homing in on the rusted, clanking apparatus, the bells and whistles, the gaudiness graced by a dishwater sea.

In great part, the city can thank the automobile for what notoriety it has. Its specious clutch on fame is a beach whose hard-packed sands can support traffic. Greedy tourism boosters (unmindful of the Riviera or Malibu) unashamedly bill Daytona as "The World's Most Famous Beach."

The beach is a strong draw for the kind of people who find it a thrill to drive their cars on sand. A reeking miasma of exhaust stench and pungent suntan lotion fills the air. People actually jog on it, and tourists idiotically wash their cars in the salty water.

A forty-mile-long coastal highway, the beach is a marriage of those oddly American ideals of tropical sun and the automobile. A convertible sports car kind of feeling.

The reality is that on any given summer Sunday, virtually tens of thousands of Central Floridians jam the shore, turning it into one immense gridlock...cars crawling through a mass of near-naked bodies. The unforgettable scene is underscored by pounding rock music from car stereos and boom boxes.

Sunbathers, of course, are routinely run over. And on this beach, instant kharma is delivered by both God and man. One spring afternoon a lightning bolt struck and killed a young vacationer as he waded in the surf with his fiancee. There wasn't a cloud in the sky.

In the 1920s, cars were raced on that beach, but ever-increasing speeds made the sands impractical. So in the fifties, the Daytona International Speedway was built some seven miles west of the Atlantic. The Speedway's twice yearly racing season provides the only national significance Daytona Beach has ever achieved.

In recent years the city has gained a different kind of renown. Daytona Beach's murder rate sometimes surpasses that of Orlando, a city three times its size. Rapes have tripled in ten years. Tabloid TV shows, which thrive on mayhem, find fertile ground here.

The city's sizable transient population forms a ready-made corps of criminals. The Boardwalk is their turf.

Crime on the Boardwalk is petty...transients work any scam, however minor. Teenagers on skateboards peddle joints, motel maids rifle tourists' rooms, daylight burglars rip off cars on the beach while their owners frolic in the surf.

But the transients are easy prey too. Chicken hawks...older men who lust after young boys...prowl the Boardwalk, tempting their victims with money, drugs, or simply a place to stay. Teenage girls in bikinis display their supple bodies, ready to do anything for a couple of bucks, a change of clothes or a night in a warm bed.

Roadside prostitutes are everywhere, ugly and cheap. Often they are transvestites. A favorite trick is to pilfer the john's wallet while he's intent on a blow job, his pants sagged around his ankles.

Daytona Beach's Boardwalk produced one of the four women on Florida's Death Row.

Deidre Hunt was an attractive young transient from New England who worked the Boardwalk as a prostitute and bartender. She wasn't in town six months before she began to kill.

The linchpin in a murder plot that left two young men dead, Hunt was captured on a fifty-seven-second videotape coldly firing four shots into a teen bound to a tree.

The man behind the camcorder was Kosta Fotopoulos, a wealthy Greek Boardwalk pool hall owner. He videotaped the murder to ensure Hunt's complicity in a scheme to kill his rich wife.

Fotopoulos, an international counterfeiter, was a gun freak who lived in a world of secret agent fantasy. Hunt, through his connections, became the darling of Daytona Beach's elite. She attended parties at politicians' homes, as well as City Commission meetings.

Kosta and Deidre accounted for two deaths. Both are now awaiting execution.

The Fotopoulos case is the best-known of Daytona Beach's grotesque murders, but even it may be outstripped by the city's most recent high-publicity homicide.

The Larzelere case boasts patricide, incest, drugs, homosexuality and high living.

Virginia, thirty-nine, and her son, Jason, eighteen, were lovers. They were wealthy and exotic uptown dopers in a grand, yet ill-kept mansion. For $2.1 million in insurance, they plotted the death of Norman Larzelere, Virginia's dentist-husband and Jason's stepfather.

Norman was shotgunned in his office. Jason is under prosecution for being the triggerman. Virginia, convicted of being the mastermind, was condemned to death. She joined Deidre Hunt and Aileen Wuornos in Florida's exclusive female Death Row sorority.

Imagine the local coffee shop chat: three out of four of the state's female killers came from Daytona Beach.

Apart from greed or sex, Satanism, too, has been a theme in Daytona Beach's directory of death. Belief in the darker side may be more prevalent than most here suspect: spates of area cemetery ransackings periodically occur. One season, decomposed heads began turning up in gutter and riverside. Teenagers on a lark had uprooted them from graves.

In 1987, two teenage couples led by Bunny Dixon, an ardent devil worshipper who communicated with the spirit of a dead ten-year-old named "David," kidnapped a Vietnamese immigrant from Orlando.

The victim was taken by night to woods north of Daytona Beach, where Dixon took a knife and carved a large inverted cross on his chest to brand him as a sacrifice to Satan. He was then shot to death.

At trial, the defense tried to mount a "devil made me do it" case. The killers, they said, acted under the direct influence of Satan. It didn't wash. Dixon pleaded out and got life; her youthful triggerman was sentenced to death.

Within three years the town experienced another satanic killing.

This time, two seventeen-year-old boys, one a confirmed satanist, raped and strangled to death a fourteen-year-old runaway on a railway track. They burned her body while chanting satanic verses. One killer kept a beaded braid of the victim's hair as a souvenir.

Both teens pleaded to life sentences. One still scrawls "Satan Lives!" on his prison cell wall.

More pedestrian murders, yet each with its particular element of strangeness, routinely occur.

Domestic slayings happen in every town, yet those in Daytona Beach seem to carry their own special twist.

A Tennessee exterminator, fresh from a prison term for killing his fourth wife, honeymooned in Daytona Beach with wife number five, a striking blonde. During the week the bride made love with three men, strangers from the beach. The husband found out and shot the woman in her sleep.

Another husband nearly hacked off his wife's head with a steak knife during a domestic dispute. He argued a "battered husband" defense: the heavyset wife had been beating him for years and he finally retaliated. He was convicted.

Senseless and baffling assaults are on the rise everywhere. Daytona

Beach is no exception. Here, it seems, you take your life in your hands by simply strolling down a Beachside sidewalk.

A young sailor was doing just that several years ago when a bearded, wild-eyed biker burst raging from a driveway. For no apparent reason he smashed the sailor to the pavement. The sailor died, his skull cracked open. No arrest was ever made.

The Outlaws, one of the top four criminal bike gangs in the country, recently moved into Daytona Beach in a big way. This will be their Southeast showcase headquarters. Dressed in suits, or fronting straw men, they bought up legitimate businesses. They plot their moves in a sprawling clubhouse behind a stockade fence.

Bikers belong in Daytona Beach. For one week every March, bikers numbering in the hundreds of thousands descend upon the city to drink Bud beer, shock the citizenry and indulge in this mysterious fellowship of being a hairy, leather-clad, crusty character who likes fat and sloppy women second only to riding American-made Harley-Davidson motor-cycles.

It's called Bike Week, and the civic boosters, sniffing tourist dollars, love it. The party-line myth, scoffed at by most residents, is that these foul and obnoxious "motorcycle enthusiasts" are in reality all doctors and lawyers playing dress-up for a week's fun in the Daytona sun.

Fact is, most are working-class types who saved up all year for their fling. They spend freely and tip well. But swollen coffers aren't the only thing they leave behind.

There are the bodies. Every year you can count on some hunter or hiker discovering a decomposed corpse in the bush. Clothing and accoutrements define the victim, a casualty in some bike gang feud. The various panhead tribes find Daytona Beach's Bike Week a convenient venue for settling old scores.

Given the nationwide demographics of the visitors, Daytona Beach's killings often go unsolved. The killer, like his victim, was here one day and gone the next.

Besides, in a city where truly innocent people are routinely victimized, why waste police talent on some out-of-state dead creature whose rot-fuzzed skull is crowned by a leather cap that reads, "Fuck the World"?

Another aberration in Daytona Beach crime comes with Spring Break, the annual invasion of beer-swilling, sex-starved collegians. Most recently their numbers hit 400,000, more than twice the city's normal population jammed into three miles of Beachside motels.

Spring Break crime is minor, yet it still plays a role in the criminal character of Daytona Beach. The college kids are preyed upon by more worldly transients, ripped off in fake dope deals, or light muggings. But the kids are generally vacationing on the cheap, and don't have large sums to tempt truly vicious criminals.

The exhuberant collegians themselves, though, enjoy their own brand of childish crime. They dash with the immortal impugnity of youth across the four lanes of A1A, the main oceanfront artery. Police call it the "dance of death." Accidents claim one or two every year.

More spectacular are the balcony falls. There are a handful every season, and rare is the Spring Break without a fatality. The kids, drunk as a rule, climb from room to room on highrise hotel balconies, usually a male seeking entry into a coed's domain. Or they lower sheets and grip their desperate way from floor to floor.

Of course, they plummet to the pavement below. The wonder is so many survive. The city eventually passed an ordinance outlawing balcony monkeyshines; now squads of cops, like a SWAT team assaulting a target, charge into rooms to arrest violators. One hotel owner even considered caging his balconies.

If any man personifies the character of Daytona Beach crime, it's Gerald Stano. The serial killer lived a grimy blue-collar existence as a laborer and short-order cook. He loved his blue car and drove it endlessly across the state. He picked up prostitutes and hitchhikers and murdered them by strangling, drowning or shooting. He was forced to do it, he said, because they were acting "bitchy."

Stano confessed to more than thirty murders in Florida, New Jersey and Pennsylvania, but he is a true child of Daytona Beach. He stands convicted of killing ten women, is under three death sentences and seven sentences of life in prison.

Stano, who was impotent, killed young women out of some kind of sexual rage.

Aileen Wuornos, prostitute, hitchhiker, lesbian, said she killed older men, also during sexual episodes.

Twin manifestations of murder, mirror images of madness, they worked the same turf: Daytona Beach.

So what is it about this city? There's an edge-of-the-world desperation, overlaid with a mythical patina of tropical sex and carefree abandon. Yet the dream goes unfulfilled, the ticket to paradise goes unpunched. It's the frustration of bitter and grubby existence pushed to one final limit, then mocked by the purity of the sea.

Bikers, like carrion crows, flock to such a scene. College students, the consummate dilettantes, thrill to dip their toes in its scary depths.

Stanos, Wuornos, and all those lesser-known opportunists of murder, know well this terrain.

Daytona Beach is not just a place. It's a state of mind.

—Robert Nolin

1

Way Out in the Woods
. . .I Don't Know Where

A maid whom there were none to praise, And very few
to love...

"She Dwelt Among the Untrodden Ways"

William Wordsworth

Chapter One

Richard Mallory liked women. He liked the way they looked and smelled and moved, the way their hair clung damply to their necks, and the warm moistness of their skin when he made love to them. He liked the way he felt when he was with them—powerful, controlling, sensuous.

He was comfortable and aggressive with women, seeking them out on the dance floor, suggesting intimacies and striking bargains for favors. But, in all other areas of his life, Richard Mallory was a private man, noncommunicative, a mystery even to those who should have known him best.

"I was the closest thing to a close friend he had," said John Townsley, a former employee of Richard's television repair shop, Mallory Electronics, "and I never really knew him. He told so many stories, I was never sure whether he was telling the truth.

"He had a way of upsetting people on purpose," said Townsley. "If he liked you, fine. If he didn't, he'd find a way to get to you."

Mallory lived alone in a multi-family apartment complex in Clearwater, Florida, called The Oaks. Few people in the complex knew him and, because of his erratic lifestyle, no one missed him when he disappeared. The only thing the manager could recall about Mallory was that he had asked to have his lock changed on his apartment seven or eight times during the three years he had lived there.

At Mallory Electronics, Richard's absences were frequent and unexplained. He would simply not show up and the shop would remain closed. "He always paid his employees for the days he was gone," Townsley remembers. "He was having a hard time of it financially, especially since he had no credit. Richard had taken off for several months, lived off his cards and neglected to pay them back."

At the time of Mallory's final disappearance, Townsley no longer worked for him. "I was one of the few people he didn't fire," he said, "because I quit." It was apparent that Mallory would hire people when he had a backlog of work, wait until the work was caught up and then let them go.

Investigator Lawrence Horzepa of the Volusia County Sheriff's Department was assigned to follow up on the Mallory disappearance. Bespectacled and earnest, Horzepa looked more like a graduate student than an investigator.

"We found that in doing a search of the business that he appeared to be heavy in debt," he reported. "He owed several thousand dollars for the rental of the store-front property that he had. We found hostile notes from customers who had dropped off items to be repaired, which he apparently never did, and they were calling back or writing notes— apparently he wasn't returning phone calls—asking when they were going to get their items back.

Mallory had been married once, some years ago, and his ex-wife, Linda Mallory, remarked that "he could be sweet as anything and then, ten minutes later, he would scare the heck out of you."

His most recent girlfriend, Jacqueline Davis, an insurance broker, described Richard as a man who liked to drink, enjoyed the strip bars, and was into some pornography. She would also tell Horzepa that Mallory was an ex-convict with a history of mental problems, had severe mood swings and could be abusive to women.

Jackie did not share Richard's desire for nightlife and so, when he felt the need, Richard Mallory would throw his bag into the back seat of his 1977 Cadillac and head for the Tampa/Clearwater nightlife, or, more recently, Daytona Beach, where the bars were exciting and dangerous and the women were plentiful. He reputedly had relationships with some of the dancers at those bars and on the last day of November, 1989, as he headed out of Clearwater via I-4 toward Daytona Beach, he looked forward to a weekend of hard drinking and hard lovemaking.

Mallory was lean with a carefully cropped mustache above his upper lip, "a good-looking man," according to Townsley. His full head of dark hair was combed back from a high forehead, and he thought of himself as fifty-one years young. The women he sought simpered and purred when he was with them and undulated slowly before his eyes when they danced for him, and it was a heady experience to which he had long since become addicted. He had no problems with his women. He could handle them all. He thought.

Aileen "Lee" Wuornos did not like men. She was blond and husky, with tousled hair and a defiant expression which seemed to have settled permanently on her wide Nordic face.

Off and on for more than twenty years, Lee had been supporting herself through prostitution, roaming Florida's highways in search of men who would offer her a ride and with whom, frequently, she would have sex. She stated her rates at "head for $30, $35 straight, $40 for half and half, a $100 an hour." When they wanted something more than "head," "that's when we would pull off the road and go into the woods," she told investigators.

Sometimes she would say that she enjoyed the sex, and was often fond of her clients. And the money was good.

Lee was tough and overweight, and Sgt. Bruce Munster, who headed the task force at the Marion County Sheriff's Department, would say of her later: "She was often described to us as obnoxious, aggressive, not sexy. Most men put her out without any money at all."

Lee's relationships with men had always been disastrous. Deserted by her mother before she was six months old, she was adopted by her grandparents. Her grandfather abused her emotionally and physically.

She was raped by a friend of the family, found herself pregnant at age thirteen, and sent to a home for unwed mothers. When the baby was born, he was removed for adoption. Shortly thereafter, she was kicked out of the house by her grandfather.

With no home, she slept in abandoned cars, and turned to prostitution, and men had used her and discarded her and cheated her and mocked her.

At age twenty, seeking security, she married a man three and a half times her age. They were divorced after one month. She says he beat her with his cane. He says she had an uncontrollable temper.

Shortly after that there was a new man in her life and one night they argued. In order to test his love, she had held up a convenience store and been arrested. If he loves me, he'll get me out of this fix, she thought. She was sentenced to three years for armed robbery and sent to prison. When she was released he refused to take her back.

And there had been other men who had taken her in and quickly thrown her out. To survive, she had forged checks and stolen property and with each demeaning experience, the anger inside Lee Wuornos bellowed and roared and clamored for release.

And so, over the years, she had grown hard, and the need for love had burrowed under the anger, deep within her, unfulfilled and frustrated by her relationships with men.

And then, in her late twenties, she met Tyria Moore, product of a middle - class, respectable family, and she beckoned up that need and thrust it, insatiable, on the unsuspecting young girl from Cadiz, Ohio.

"It was love beyond imaginable. Earthly words cannot describe how I felt about Tyria," Lee said.

Tyria must be taken care of as she, herself, had never been.

"The only reason I hustled so hard all those years was to support her. I did what I had to do to pay the bills, because I didn't have another choice. I've got warrants out for my arrest. I loved her too much," Lee would say later.

And so she put more hours into prostitution—widening her field, taking more chances, disappearing for days at a time in order to sell herself repeatedly before returning home to the woman who had become her friend, her family and her security.

But something unexpected happened. Lee, having experienced the affection of the plump, pink-cheeked Tyria, who encouraged her to expand her trade so that they could live more comfortably, and having pronounced to all those who would listen that "we are lesbians," became unable to contain the anger inside her. She became less willing to service the men whose attentions she solicited, and she began to draw a line over which they could not pass. On one side of the invisible marker stood Lee, the invincible prostitute, offering all things sexual. On the other side crouched the anger, seething, roiling, out of control, detached from her persona and waiting to strike.

"They were crossing my line as far as like, they were going to rape me, kill me, I don't know if they were gonna strangle me, uh, if they had a gun I had no idea if they had a gun or anything. . . ."

Richard Mallory knew nothing of the line and would, no doubt, have scoffed at it had he been told.

He also did not know that a few months earlier, his passenger had stolen a .22 caliber handgun—"for protection."

And so, on the evening of November 30, 1989, under an overpass outside Tampa, Richard Mallory, who liked women, picked up hitchhiker Aileen Wuornos, who did not like men. And they drank and talked and pulled off into the woods for sex. Before the night was over, Mallory had crossed the line of which he knew naught and lay dead deep within the wooded area, covered unceremoniously with a dirty piece of ragged carpet. Four bullet wounds, three in his chest, and one in his neck, evidenced his encounter with the anger of Aileen Wuornos.

The following day, Mallory's Cadillac Coupe de Ville was found abandoned just off John Anderson Drive in Ormond Beach. Blood was on the front backrest of the car behind the steering wheel, but the body from which the blood had escaped was nowhere in sight. Horzepa reported that "no keys for the car were found. Numerous items were located just east of the vehicle, lying in the sand, which were Mallory's wallet containing his Florida driver's license, miscellaneous papers belonging to Mallory, two plastic tumbler type glasses, half empty bottle of vodka, along with several other items. The driver's seat of the car had been pulled all the way to the front, and Mr. Mallory was a little larger than that unless he liked to drive in what I would consider an uncomfortable position."

Further examination of the car revealed a pair of prescription eyeglasses under the front seat and, in the trunk, the impression left by a tool box which had apparently been removed.

The car was dusted unsuccessfully for fingerprints by the Florida Department of Law Enforcement, and then towed into the Volusia County Sheriff's Office compound. All the items found in the area were placed into safekeeping.

Investigators began immediately to question anyone who might have had contact with Richard Mallory prior to December 1. They found that he had been seen at his shop on November 30 by Jeffrey Davis, the son of Jacqueline Davis, and were able to locate a customer to whom Mallory had confided his plan to visit Daytona Beach for a couple of days. Notes and phone numbers in Mallory's apartment led investigators to two dancers at local strip bars, Chastity Marcus and Kimberly Guy, and Doug Lambert, Chastity's boyfriend.

Horzepa talked to Chastity Marcus. "She [Chastity] told us that she had had a date with Mr. Mallory, her and Kimberly Guy. And I asked her what 'a date' meant, and she told me that 'a date' to her and Kimberly Guy was that they went back to his place of business and had sex with him." And then, Chastity told the investigator, she and Kimberly had sex with each other.

As payment for their services, Kimberly Guy received a 19-inch color television and a VCR, undoubtedly the property of Mallory Electronic customers. The young women believed this had taken place on the night of November 30.

Two buzzards first discovered the body.

On December 13, twelve days after Mallory's Cadillac had been found abandoned, James Bonchi and Jimmy Davis from Ormond Beach were scrapping for metal in wooded areas off U.S. 1. Bonchi turned onto a trail that he had wanted to follow for "years and years. On this day I just decided to turn off in there. It was a well-worn trail because, you know, any trail like that probably people will be dumping garbage.

"Okay so we went back in there. We were walking all around and, you know, we would check the north end of the woods where we were tracking, just tearing the woods apart to see what we could find. And so when we first pulled out there, we seen two buzzards in the tree. And I just kidded with Jimmy, I said, 'Oh, no, a dead body,' you know. And sure enough, it was by the time we left, you know.

"Okay, so we had looked all through the north side of the woods. And then we were just about ready to leave, and he said, 'Let's go, let's go.' And I said, 'Let's look on the other side of the woods, too.' I walked right by the body thinking it was just deer or hog guts. And he thought it was, too, at first. I walked by, and there is like a set of car tracks going by the body. And I was following that.

"Then Jimmy hollered, 'Bonchi, Bonchi,' he said, 'Open this tarp.' And he didn't realize what it was, until at the same time I am looking at it. And you could just see the body, you know, it was laying down with a hand sticking out as if like somebody was sleeping under a blanket.... From the look of just the hand itself, I just determined that it had probably been there at least a week, because you could tell it was like all, you know, sunk in."

Without removing the carpet cover from the body, Bonchi and Davis called the sheriff's office and then returned to the scene. When the investigators arrived, the men were removed from the area.

"They didn't let us look," recalled Bonchi.

Volusia County deputies answered the call from Bonchi and Davis. Removing the carpet, they found a badly decomposed, fully dressed male body in jeans and pullover shirt, the belt slightly askew. The pockets of the jeans had been turned inside out. Partial dentures lay on the ground next to the body.

Charles James Lau, investigator with the Volusia County Sheriff's Department, oversaw an immediate autopsy of the unidentified body, which recovered four bullets from its torso. The hands of the victim were transported to the crime lab for latent prints because, as Lau explained, "When we have an unidentified body, you can't roll the fingerprints because of the decomposition."

Horzepa recalls his reaction when the body was identified as Richard Mallory.

"I was fairly convinced that there was only one person that was more than likely involved with Richard Mallory. That was based on the information given to me from the people that knew him, from his ex-girlfriend, from the fact that he was extremely nervous and leery of people. I didn't believe that Richard Mallory would—if he did pick up a hitchhiker—pick up more than one person because he seemed to me to be the kind of person who always wanted to remain in control. And my opinion of him was, if he felt it was a one-on-one with a female, that he would have control of the situation.

"Jackie Davis had just basically said that he didn't trust men. He would probably trust a woman. I asked her if he would ever pick anybody up as far as like hitchhikers or have anybody go with him anywhere, and she said to her knowledge that he would never pick up a man, but there was a possibility that he would go ahead and pick up a hitchhiker.

"I spoke to the ex-Mrs. Mallory, and she also advised that there would be a possibility that he would stop for a female hitchhiker and pick one up."

Investigators returned again to the Marcus, Guy, Lambert trio. Disappearance had now become murder and Chastity Marcus and Kimberly Guy seemed to have been two of the last people to see Mallory alive.

Further interrogation of Chastity's boyfriend, Doug Lambert, revealed him to be a highly nervous man, who admitted his fear of Chastity Marcus because of her relationship with Robert John "Bruiser" Carrier, the forty-one-old president of the Indianapolis Chapter of the Sons of Silence, a well known motorcycle gang. He described Chastity to investigators as schizophrenic.

"One minute she was, uh, 'I love you.' She was the nicest person in the world. The next minute she was 'I hate you.' " He added that she had a violent nature and would often hit him. He feared retaliation from her, through Carrier, if she became angered.

Under pressure, Lambert admitted that Chastity had spoken about the murder of Richard Mallory. It had happened after a particularly violent scuffle during which Lambert was attempting to kick her out of his apartment and out of his life.

"She goes, 'I'm just gonna call those cops and tell them that I did do those murders,' " Lambert recalled.

A warrant for the arrest of Chastity Marcus was immediately issued, but Chastity, who had confided to the manager of the strip bar where she worked that she was "hot as a firecracker" and had to get out of town, had disappeared.

Two months later she was located just outside New Orleans, Louisiana, brought back to Daytona Beach and arrested June 29, 1990, on a warrant signed by then-Circuit Judge Uriel Blount, Jr. Lack of evidence forced David Damore of the Seventh Judicial Circuit's State Attorney's Office to drop charges on July 11, 1990.

Kimberly Guy agreed to take a lie detector test and passed it.

Mallory's sister in Texas and brother in New Jersey wanted no involvement with the remains of Mallory Electronics.

"There was nothing to probate," John Townsley shrugged. Townsley took over the repair equipment that had been abandoned, moved the shop several doors from the original site and Mallory Electronics became Johnny's TV & VCR of Palm Harbor, Florida.

Despite the fact that she had broken up with Mallory before his death, Jackie Davis took charge of the cremation of the body, scattering his ashes in a nearby wooded area.

The murder of Richard Mallory seemed an isolated, if curious, homicide, and with no further clues from which to develop a case, the investigators were dead-ended.

Chapter Two

Aside from Lee Wuornos and the late Richard Mallory, one other person had knowledge of the killer.

Tyria Moore had been Lee's roommate, lover, best friend for more than three years when Richard Mallory was killed. The two women had lived capriciously, moving from place to place and job to job. Tyria worked periodically, depending on the current situation, but it was Lee who met their financial needs by leaving for several days at a time to hustle.

Tyria knew about the murder of Richard Mallory because Lee told her. She later explained to the police:

"She [Lee] came home early one day in December of 1989 with a two-door Cadillac with tinted windows and a gator plate on the front. We used this car to move from the Ocean Shores Motel to [an apartment on] Burleigh Avenue.

"Later that night after I came home from work, Lee told me she had shot and killed a guy that day. She later told me she had covered his body with a piece of carpet...and left the car in some woods off John Anderson.

"When we moved in on Burleigh, she had gotten some things in which she showed me something with the name 'Richard' on it. She gave me a gray jacket and scarf, which I believe she had gotten from that car."

But, at the time, not sure what to do with the information revealed to her by her lover, Tyria put it out of her mind.

"There was a time between Ty and Lee where no matter what Lee did, Ty filtered out the bad and only saw good," Sgt. Jake Ehrhart of the Volusia County Sheriff's Department later told reporters.

"She had a choice between her loving relationship with Lee and going to the police. Her emotions won."

James Albert Legary remembers the two young women who moved into the efficiency apartment on Burleigh Avenue and became his neighbors.

"Her [Lee] being there was grossly unpleasant," Legary said.

"The first time that I saw her, I pulled into the driveway and she was leaning against something and staring....the expression on her face was like I will kick your ass."

During the next weeks, Lee accused Legary's fifteen-year-old son of stealing her cat, stealing her hubcaps and dousing her garage with paint.

"On all three of these occasions, she was going to either kick my ass or shoot me or something of that nature," Legary said.

He also remembers that, "On several different occasions, if I was in my yard, she would toss firecrackers out the window and then cackle like the Wicked Witch—it was very strange, but the cackle sounded exactly like the witch from the Wizard of Oz."

Acknowledging that he never had a problem with Tyria Moore, he was, nonetheless, relieved when his neighbors moved away.

According to friends of Lee Wuornos and Tyria Moore, it had been love at first sight in June of 1986, when the two met at the now-defunct Zodiac Bar in South Daytona. Lee was in the area after fleeing the law on charges of forged checks; Ty had received an insurance settlement resulting from an automobile accident and broken away from her hometown of Cadiz, Ohio.

It was Lee's second lesbian attachment, her first having occurred with an Italian woman named Toni in the Florida Keys during the previous year. The passionate relationship between the two women was enlivened by frequent jealousies and physical violence.

Toni and Lee had returned to Orlando and purchased equipment to begin a pressure steam cleaning business. Lee says it was her money that allowed the purchase.

"Toni, she was like a really good friend," Lee recalled. "I wasn't alone anymore. I wanted to stay with her."

After several months, Lee came home to find Toni, the cleaning equipment and all her possessions gone. The only items left behind were a fan and a phone bill for $485.

"She was using me. I was so upset about losing a business that I'd have had the rest of my life."

With Ty things were different. Unlike the feisty Toni, Ty was quiet and often shy. This time Lee considered herself married and she liked to refer to the young woman as "my wife."

Tyria Moore, who, according to Lee, had always preferred women over men, had been "born again" in 1984 and had developed close ties to the Calvary Baptist Church where she had recently been baptized. She attended Bible study sessions and sometimes babysat for the Rev. David Laughner, who had become her friend as well as her minister. She met with limited success in sharing her religious beliefs with Lee. Lee knew the Bible and could recite scripture, but her actions were often in conflict with Ty's more traditional background. And Ty had her own departures from scripture. She was living in a homosexual relationship. As the months passed, Ty's religious associations diminished. When they met, Ty was working as a maid at the El Caribe Motel on A1A and living on Halifax Drive with her friend, Cammie Greene, who had taken her in after she was evicted from her apartment.

"We were friends, at least until she met Aileen," Mrs. Greene told reporters. "My husband and I finally asked them to leave because we didn't want their lifestyle in the house.

"We all knew, including Ty, that Lee was probably prostituting herself out on the road," Mrs. Greene added.

On the day that Lee left the Greene household, she took with her the driver's license and other identification belonging to Cammie Greene. Unbeknownst to the woman who had given them shelter, Cammie Greene was about to become one of several aliases for Aileen Carol Wuornos.

For a while Lee and Ty lived together at the El Caribe Motel, but money was scarce, and in the spring of 1987, Ty approached a friend she had known from church and asked if she could rent a room.

The Daytona Beach News-Journal reported the friend's recollections:

"She said, 'I need a place to stay.' Then she brought in Lee. Lee strutted around, stuck out her hand and said 'Hello.' She didn't smile. She began talking quickly about how she had heard good things about Ty's friend and about how she and Ty had met. Then she said, 'Well, did Ty ask you?' "

Because she was fond of Ty, the friend agreed to rent the two women a room if they slept in separate beds. The scriptures, she said, explicitly forbade homosexual relationships.

"The Lord," she recited to the two women, "wants you to be with a man. That's why they're here."

The friend recalls that Lee's natural intensity turned to rage. "Don't you try to force me to be with a man! I was married to a man and he beat me! I can't even talk about my father! That's why I am this way—because of a man!" She glowered at the woman in front of her.

Regretfully, the friend asked the two to leave. She genuinely liked Ty, who she remembered as being "all sweet, all smiles, real soft," and wished she could help her.

"I'm not holding Lee responsible for what happened to her," she confided to Ty before they parted, "but I think you should tell her to go her own way."

In March of the following year, Ty and Lee bought a 1968 Corsair trailer. Lee says that she financed it. Ty says she borrowed money from a friend to buy it. Soon the two women had moved the trailer to the Ocean Village Camper Resort in Ormond-By-the-Sea.

According to Lee, Ty did not like trailer life. "She always wanted a luxury motel or a plush apartment," Lee said.

Lee enjoyed the privacy and country surroundings afforded by the trailer park, but their residency was short-lived.

One of the desk clerks described that period to reporters: "They got one of their wild hippy friends to drag that trailer in here. They always had junk sitting out. And we were trying to improve the image of the park."

The employee recalls that the women became the talk of the park, exploiting their relationship, wearing white T-shirts with the sleeves cut out and no brassieres.

Billy Copeland, another employee of the resort, rented the trailer space to Ty and Lee.

"Lee had some cruel eyes—death row eyes I call 'em. I don't even know what that means—that's just the way they make you feel. I know that girl could kill you in a heartbeat, but I always liked her."

Their situation at Ocean Village Camper Resort became increasingly tenuous and ended at about three o'clock one morning when a mixture of gunshots and loud country rock proved to be the final insult and they were told to leave.

Back in Daytona, Ty returned to work—this time as a maid at the Casa Del Mar Motel. And, once again, the likeable Ty found a place for the two of them to live.

Alzada Sherman, Ty's friend at the motel, was later questioned by both defense and prosecution about that period:

"Now, you indicated before we went on the record that Lee and Tyria stayed with you for a month?"

"Uh-huh."

"And is that at the address that you gave at the beginning?"

"Exactly."

"Did you live at the motel that you were working in?"

"No."

"What was the name of the motel?"

"Casa Del Mar."

"But they stayed in your apartment?"

"Yes. I have a two bedroom apartment."

"They shared one of the bedrooms?"

"One of the bedrooms. It wasn't supposed to be that way."

"How was it supposed to be?"

"It was told to me that Lee was going away for a year and a half and she wouldn't be back. And Tyria needed a place to live. I liked Tyria. So I needed a roommate at the time to share with the rent. So I offered her the room. To share the rent," Alzada told the attorneys.

It had been a very unpleasant period in her life and she didn't like having to go over it.

"Did she initially move in by herself?" the questioning continued.

"Yes."

"How long was it before Lee moved in there?"

"Well, she [Ty] moved in on Friday. Lee moved in on Sunday. She left and I thought she was gone. But she showed up Sunday."

"Was there any conversation between Friday and Sunday about her possibly moving in?"

"No."

"What happened on that Sunday?"

"I confronted Tyria about it," Alzada sighed. "And she said, let her spend the night and she will be gone in the morning, which she was. But then she shows back up Wednesday. It was like every other day she would come back."

"And did that routine go on throughout the month?"

"Yes. And I told them they had to move."

"What would be said to you, typically, each time she would come back to spend the night?"

"She had no place to go."

"And did you ever ask them where she was during those days that she wasn't there?"

"Yes. Their answer was working."

"Did she say where she was working?"

"Lee said she was working in Orlando. She did floors with those big machines."

"Pressure cleaning type things?"

"Yes."

"So she would be gone for a day or two and show back up?"

"Then she showed back up. Sometimes she will come at night in a cab."

"During that time frame when Lee would come back in would she ever have anything with her that she didn't have when she left?"

"No. She always took a bag, like a—when you go to the gym, you know, gym bags. That's the kind of bags she would leave with. And she would come back with the same bag."

"While Lee was in your home, how did she act?"

"Very difficult. When she wasn't drinking she was calm. But when she drinks she was loud, obnoxious."

"How often would she be drinking?"

Alzada grimaced at the recollection. She had been uncomfortable in her own house while Lee was there.

"During the time she stayed there that's all she did mostly."

Busch and Budweiser beer were Lee's favorites, Alzada recalled, and drinking bouts were usually followed by loud arguments behind the closed bedroom door.

"Ty would say, 'Shut up, Lee, I don't want to hear it,' " Alzada remembered.

"Can you estimate when she was there drinking about how much she might drink in an evening or a day?"

"Normally, she would either come in with a 12-pack and maybe drink two or three 12-packs in a night and a day. She is a heavy drinker."

In the end, unwilling to tolerate her houseguests, Alzada Sherman insisted that they move out.

Even at work, she recalled, Lee would often arrive drunk to pick up Ty. Scenes inevitably followed and Ty would complain that her relationship with Lee was "not so good. She is so bossy."

In spite of her reputation for being quiet and shy, Ty lost her job in the laundry at the motel when, during an argument with her supervisor, she hurled herself at him, fists flailing.

The anger of Lee Wuornos was legendary among local bus drivers who transported her to and from areas where she began her hitchhiking forays.

Terry Adams, operations supervisor of Votran, the East Volusia County Transit, was swamped with reports from his drivers that Lee was "nasty mostly and threatening them with bodily harm, cursing at them because of certain situations."

Driver Richard Loomis had attempted a conversation with the blonde woman.

"She started screaming and hollering. 'I am not going to tell you where I am going or my name or where I live or anything,' " he said.

"If she had her way, she would sit down and just ignore everybody. If for whatever reason she got on and started, which was frequent, it would be like she was trying to find a way to argue with you...She always mentioned men. I don't know of a woman driver in the place that ever had trouble with her."

Loomis recalled hearing that a black bus driver picked Lee and Ty up near I-4 and 92 and commented to Ty that she was "looking good."

"Well, Aileen didn't care for this," Loomis said. "She punched him right in the mouth, and he knocked her through the door, I think."

Driver Dennis Metcalf was another victim of Lee's behavior: "Well, when she was at the bus stop, say you would pull up and the buses have kneelers on them. And she would say 'kneel the mother fucking bus you asshole or you nigger, you cock sucker'...She was just mean as a rattlesnake."

Chapter Three

B y the middle of May 1990, the murder of the hapless Richard Mallory had been all but forgotten by the Volusia County Sheriff's Department. There was, seemingly, no reason to believe it was anything but an isolated incident.

And then began a series of disappearances of middle-aged men, whose journeys from various beginnings to various destinations were intercepted by death.

On May 20, the truck of forty-three-year-old David Spears was found, abandoned, near County Road 318 and I-75 in Marion County.

A construction worker who lived in Winter Garden, Spears commuted each day to Sarasota to work.

A blond hair was visible on the steering wheel of the truck and a torn prophylactic package was found on the floor of the vehicle. All personal property, including mechanics' tools, clothing and a one-of-a-kind ceramic statue of a panther, was missing from the truck. The truck seat was pulled close to the steering wheel.

Two weeks later, the decomposed body of the missing Spears was located off U.S. 19 in Citrus County. He had been shot six times with a .22 caliber handgun, and was nude except for the baseball cap which sat jauntily atop his ravaged head.

On the ground near the body was a used prophylactic, a torn prophylactic package and empty cans of Busch and Budweiser beer.

Within the next week, forty-one-year-old Charles Carskaddon was on his way from his mother's home in Prairie, Missouri, to Tampa to pick up his fiance.

His body was found, nude, off S.R. 52 and I-75 in Pasco County. Grass and foliage covered the body, along with a green electric blanket. He had been shot nine times in the chest and abdomen with a .22 caliber handgun.

On the following day, his car was located near I-75 and County Road 484 in Marion County. Carskaddon's mother stated he left with a blue steel .45 caliber automatic pistol with pearl handle, a Mexican blanket, stun gun, flip-top cigarette lighter, watch, tan suitcase, black T-shirt, gray snakeskin cowboy boots. Carskaddon, she said, had removed the pin from the handgun. None of the items remained in the car.

The next Florida man who did not reach his destination was sixty-five-year-old Peter Siems, a part-time missionary on his way from Jupiter, Florida, to visit relatives in Arkansas.

Neighbors observed him placing luggage into his Pontiac Sunbird early in the day on June 7. Relatives reported his failure to appear and the body of Peter Siems has never been found. His credit cards have not been used, nor has money been withdrawn from his bank.

The Fourth of July dawned hot and sunny that year and Lee and Ty had loaded the red and white cooler into the trunk of the Pontiac Sunbird and spent the afternoon at an Indian Reservation near Orange Springs.

Lee had been drinking all day and, on the way home, Ty drove the car. The dirt road she chose was skiddish, and she lost control, slamming into a fence.

Residents of the area observed the two women, who they later described as a short, heavy brunette, and tall blonde, park the severely damaged car in front of their homes.

As they watched, the blonde walked to the front of the automobile and tore the license plate from the front bumper. The dark-haired woman withdrew a red and white cooler from the back seat and the two walked off together south on C.R. 315.

The witnesses noted that the women, at the approach of an automobile, would dash into the woods and hide, only to reappear after the car had passed by. They continued to do this until they were out of sight.

A motorist, thinking that the women might need help, pulled over to assist. He noticed that the tall blonde was bleeding on her left arm. The blonde asked for a ride, but he refused. She became angry and began to verbally abuse him.

The motorist drove off, but contacted the Orange Springs Fire Department and notified them of the injured woman.

The paramedics located the women, pulled over, and asked the blonde if they could help. She said, "I don't know anything about an accident and I want people to stop telling lies and leave us alone."

The paramedics observed that the women's shirts were wet and the blonde's arm had been injured. The blonde was described as very angry and aggressive, while the shorter woman stood away from the conversations and said nothing.

When it was reported that the damaged silver Pontiac had been abandoned by the women and the rear license tag and keys had been removed, the identification number was checked by police and found to belong to the missing Peter Siems. Latent prints, cast in blood, were removed from the vehicle, as well as bloodstained fabric from the seats and door handles.

Property recovered from within the automobile included Busch and Budweiser beer cans as well as Marlboro cigarettes and two beverage cozies. Underneath the passenger seat lay a bottle of Windex window spray with an Eckerd Drugs price label affixed to it, easily traceable to the store on Gordon Street in Atlanta, Georgia.

By now a police artist had drawn composites of the two women, based on the memories of the paramedics and other witnesses to the episode with the Pontiac Sunbird.

Armed with the sketches and the bottle of Windex, the investigators travelled to Atlanta to question the manager of Eckerd Drugs. Viewing the sketches, he recalled the two women entering his store late on a Friday night.

"The store is in a bad part of town in a predominantly black area and white people do not venture into this area after dark," he said.

The manager recalled that the women purchased cosmetics and a black box of Trojan prophylactics, the same brand found near David Spears' body and inside the trunk of his car. A beverage cozy was also traceable to the Speedway store in Wildwood, Florida, near the entrance/exit ramps of I-75.

Peter Siems and his wife were missionaries and neither drank nor smoked cigarettes. Relatives stated that Siems had never travelled to Atlanta. Mrs. Siems had been in Europe for some time, completing her missionary work.

Troy Burress drove a truck for Gilcrest Sausage Company of Ocala, where he also lived. On July 30, he travelled the Daytona route, which took him to several locations throughout central Florida. His last stop was to have been Salt Springs in Marion County.

When he did not arrive back at the Gilcrest Sausage Company that afternoon, employers began to trace his movements and discovered that he had made a stop in Seville, Florida, before continuing on to Salt Springs.

Between Seville and Salt Springs, death hitched a ride with Troy Burress. His truck was found later that day off S.R. 19, but his body was not discovered until August 4 on S.R. 19 about 40 miles northeast of Ocala. He had been shot twice with a .22 caliber handgun. The clipboard and receipts, which had been removed from the truck, were found near the body, but the money was missing.

Seven gunshots, six to the torso and one to the head, had been pumped into the body of fifty-six-year-old Charles Humphreys of Crystal River, Florida, before it was located off C.R. 484 near I-75 in Marion County on September 12, 1990.

A former Alabama police chief and current child abuse investigator, the luckless Humphreys was on his way home when he picked up a blond hitchhiker.

His money and wallet were missing.

His car was found September 19 backed into a space behind an abandoned service station at the intersection of I-10 and S.R. 90 near Live Oak in Suwannee County. The vehicle tag, keys, and bumper stickers were removed from the automobile. One can of Budweiser beer was found under the passenger seat. The vehicle had visible marks on it indicating that someone had wiped all fingerprints from the inside and outside of the car.

A close examination of the car's contents revealed a cash register receipt for beer or wine from EMRO store #8237, a Speedway truck stop and convenience store located at S.R. 44 and I-75 in Wildwood. The receipt was dated 9-11-90 at 16:19 hours (4:19 p.m.)—the exact date and time of Humphreys' disappearance. The clerk who had been on duty that night could not identify a picture of Humphreys, but did recognize the composites of Lee and Ty. They had entered her store and walked out the back early in September. She thought they were prostitutes, but believing they had left the area, had not called the police.

Nearly a month later, personal effects of Humphreys were located in a wooded field off Boggy Marsh Road in southern Lake County near U.S. 27. A search of the area had revealed ownership papers for his car, his pipe, tobacco, a Sumter County map, HRS paperwork, and ice scrapers from his glove box. A yellow bumper sticker was found crumpled on the ground and Miller Lite beer bottles and Budweiser beer cans surrounded the items. Still missing were his briefcase, police badge and wallet.

Walter Gino Antonio, sixty-year-old Cocoa, Florida, resident, was driving to Alabama to look for a job. Recently engaged, he wore a gold and silver diamond ring on his hand, a gift from his fiance.

Antonio's body was found, nude except for tube socks, on November 18 near the intersection of U.S. 19 and U.S. 27 in Dixie County. He had been shot four times with a .22 caliber handgun, three times in the torso and once in the head.

His car was found a week later parked in a wooded area near I-95 and U.S. 1 in northern Brevard County. The vehicle tag and keys were missing and bumper stickers had been removed. A piece of paper covered the vehicle identification number and the doors were locked. Empty Budweiser beer cans were found on the ground near the vehicle, which had been wiped clean of fingerprints.

A list of possessions in his car, supplied by his fiance, included handcuffs, reserve deputy badge, police billy club, flashlight, Timex wristwatch, suitcases, tool box and a baseball cap. None of the items remained in the car.

Personal identification and clothing were discovered in a wooded area in Taylor County, approximately thirty-eight miles north of the body location. The luggage was missing, but clothing had been dumped by the side of the road. Credit cards and identification were intact inside his wallet.

Within a thirteen-month period, a trail of middle-aged male corpses had been scattered across the highways of central Florida.

Chapter Four

It is clear that Tyria Moore was content to allow Lee to support her without questioning the means of that support. What is not clear is how much she knew.

In an affidavit given to the police following Lee's arrest, Ty described the next months.

"She came home with an older pick-up truck approximately late May or early June 1990, and a day or two later came home with an older brown big car.

"The next car she came home with was a Pontiac Sunbird, which she told me a couple of stories of where she had gotten it approximately in June of 1990. At that time, she showed approximately $600 in cash in $100 bills. She later took myself and my sister to Sea World.

"She kept that car until July 4, when I was driving it back a dirt road to see an Indian Reservation. On the way back out, I lost control and rolled the car through a gate and fence. We got out and Lee told me to run. At that time, I thought the car may blow up.

"A couple of people came out and Lee told them not to call the cops because her father lived just down the road. We then returned to the car and Lee tore off the license plate from the back and threw it in the field. She then got in the driver's seat and I got into the back seat and she drove until the tire went flat. When we got out, she tore the plate off the front of the car and threw it into a field. We then ran to the wooded area and at that time I knew the car must have been stolen.

"In the wooded area, Lee washed some blood off of herself which she had gotten when the car rolled and had got cut on some glass on her right arm. We then went on down the road and at some time she threw the keys and the registration into a field or woods.

"We were approached by a couple of people whom I believe were with a fire department or something like that. They asked if we were the ones in a wreck and Lee said no and I agreed.

"We then went down the road to a house where a gentleman gave us a ride to State Road 40. We were then picked up by a lady with kids and she gave us a ride to what I believe was a store. That was as far as she was going. There was a road that went back off of 40.

"We were then picked up by a gentleman who took us to some kind of military base where we all went in. We had to give our names. Lee said a name for me and I gave my last name. After leaving there, the gentleman gave us a ride all the way to Daytona Avenue behind our house in Holly Hill.

"The next car I saw Lee with was a 4-door small blue car in approximately late August to early September 1990. I came in from the Casa Del Mar and Lee was on the bed with a couple of briefcases and some boxes going through it. We later drove to the Bellair Plaza where we threw something away in a dumpster.

"A day or two later, I heard the news of a murder and they showed a picture of the man's car, which was the same one Lee had."

The pick-up truck was no doubt the property of David Spears. The "older brown car" was the 1975 Cadillac belonging to Charles Carskaddon, the small blue car had sped away from the body of Charles Humphreys, and the ill-fated Pontiac Sunbird had been on its way to Arkansas when its owner, Peter Siems, picked up a hitchhiker.

"Whenever money got tight, she would leave," Ty remembered. "I knew what she was doing. I just chose to ignore it."

On the days when Lee took to the road in search of customers, she would pose as a hitchhiker or disabled motorist at highway entrance or exit ramps. Later, she was to become known as the "exit to exit" prostitute.

Following her arrest, several men came forward in defense of the woman they had picked up by the side of the road.

On December 11, 1991, a man named "Tom" wrote to Lee in jail:

"This has got to be the most difficult letter I have ever written."

Tom reminded Lee that he had picked her up on I-95 outside of Daytona over a year ago.

"I was driving an old '72 Ford and we drank several beers in the car while we were together," he said. "Then we sat by the St. Johns River talking about nothing in particular.

"I had naturally heard on the news about this lesbian serial killer, but I really didn't pay that much attention to it until I saw you on TV ...I saw the pain on your face and I only wish I was smart enough to say something to help erase some of it.... I know you have a phone and I would love to talk with you, but am in between jobs and don't have much loot."

Another "Tom", Tom Evans, a songwriter from Nashville, called Lee's defense counsel to tell them that he and Lee had been together for five days and five nights in Tennessee. He said that he had been ill and she had taken care of him, even buying him the medicine he needed. They did not have sex during that time, he added. The attorneys took a statement from him and promised to call him as a witness.

"She could do eight guys in one day and seven could get away," said Cpl. Bob Kelley of the Sheriff's Department in Volusia County.

"Then one would do something that made her decide, well, he doesn't need to live."

"She had a profile of the men she was looking for, and she was very picky," Sgt. Munster told a reporter. "She would only 'date' decent people. They had to be older—no drugs. On many occasions there was an offer of sex for thirty dollars. Sometimes she would jump out of the bushes and flag people down. The ruse was 'the kids are sick,' or 'the car's broken down.'

"Some didn't go into the woods. No one who went into the woods came back and lived to tell, as far as I know."

"They all deserved it," Lee reportedly told a friend. "They all asked for it. I feel sorry for the families, but those men shouldn't have been out there doing what they were doing. Everything I did was in self-defense."

In a sense, Lee Wuornos had been defending herself all her life. She was born on leap year, February 29, 1956, in Clinton Hospital, Detroit, Michigan, to sixteen-year-old Diane Wuornos and nineteen-year-old handyman Leo Pittman.

The tumultuous marriage had ended a few months before her birth, leaving the young Diane to raise Lee and her older brother, Keith.

Lee never knew her father, who was jailed on charges of kidnapping, rape and child molestation. When Lee was fifteen, he formed a noose from a bedsheet and hung himself in his cell. Her young mother was unable and unwilling to cope with childraising. When Lee was six months old, Diane went to dinner and never came back. She did, however, call her parents to tell them to pick up the children.

Lauri Wuornos, a Ford factory worker, and his wife, Eileen Britta, adopted Aileen and Keith, and brought them to live in their home on a tree-lined street in Troy, Michigan. For many years, Lee believed that her aunt and uncle, Lori and Barry, were her sister and brother. She did not know that her grandparents were not her real parents.

During her ninth year, a chemical explosion, which she and Lori accidentally set off, resulted in severe burns on Lee's face and arms. She was hospitalized for several days and confined for months afterward. The burns healed slowly, but Lee worried that she would be deformed and scarred for life. Today, faint scars on her forehead and her arms remain.

When Lee was ten, says Lee's mother, Diane Wuornos, now Diane Tuley, and living in Texas, she learned the truth about her parents from gossip at school. Diane, when questioned by reporters, recalled: "She was always a bad girl."

School reports indicate that during the early years Lee was a good and conscientious student, but by age ten she was often given a mild tranquilizer by school doctors. She had obvious problems seeing and hearing. Numerous requests were made to Eileen Britta Wuornos to meet with school authorities to discuss treatment for Lee's hearing problem. They were ignored.

"She told me that there was nothing wrong with my hearing, that I just didn't want to take directions," Lee recalled.

Class photos located in Troy, Michigan, show a series of pictures of the young Aileen Wuornos, evolving from a bright young face, to a sad, dejected teenager.

According to Lee, her grandfather was both physically and verbally abusive when she was a child, and she was beaten many times with his belt while her grandmother looked on, helpless and crying.

Although it has been suggested that she was sexually abused by her grandfather, she now says she has no recollection of it.

A former classmate, Dawn Botkins of Lapeer, Michigan, remembers going home with Lee after school one day.

"Keith, Lori, Lee and I went to her house. Her grandfather was there and he and Lori greeted each other affectionately. He said nothing to Lee.

"You could see the hate when the two were in the same room."

Both Lauri and Eileen Britta were alcoholics and Eileen Britta died of cirrhosis of the liver when Lee was fifteen. At the time, she was on medication for a thyroid condition.

Whatever her grandmother's failings as a mother, Lee loved her and still refers to her as a heavenly angel. Lee blames her grandfather for her death. She remembers that Eileen Britta was not supposed to have alcohol, but she asked for beer to ease the pain and her grandfather gave it to her with her medication. "He shouldn't have let her have it," she says.

Before her grandmother died, Lee had already begun to run away from home, truant from school for long periods of time, and living in abandoned cars. In her young mind, the fears of the unknown were preferable to the constant abuse in her home. By the time she was thirteen, she had been raped by a friend of the family and was pregnant. The man, in his forties, offered Lee a ride home. Instead, he drove into the woods where he threatened her with a weapon. If she did not cooperate with him, he would kill her, he said.

For six months, she kept her pregnancy a secret. When it was revealed, Lee was sent by her grandparents to a home for unwed mothers. The baby, named by Lee for her brother, Keith, was put up for adoption.

Lori Grody, who lives in a small rural community 40 miles east of Traverse City, is the natural daughter of Lauri and Eileen Britta Wuornos. She and her brother, Barry, were part of the household in which Aileen Wuornos grew up.

After intensive questioning by Jackelyn (Jackie) Giroux, a Hollywood producer interested in Lee's story, Lori admitted that "Lee, if she didn't answer 'Yes, sir' [to her grandfather]—when Lee would not do that she would be hit with a belt."

Lori also recalled that Lee was not allowed to receive Christmas presents.

"I was told one story Lori remembered was Diane used to send Christmas presents and the father would take them away," said Jackie. "I was led to believe that Lee never really discovered who her mother was until she was about twelve years old. And it's not totally clear to me whether she learned in school or whether she actually learned from one of the neighborhood kids, but it was definitely not from her family."

Interviewed by the press, Lori had second thoughts: "We had a normal family life. That's what I want to tell the jury. My parents were strict, but never abusive. She was rebellious and wouldn't follow rules.

"She's trying to blame our parents, but it's not true. It was her. Something was always wrong with her. It still is."

When Lee's pregnancy became known, "they swept the whole thing under the rug," Lori said. "They never tried to find out the truth, who was the father or what really happened.

"After that she always said, 'All men are out to use women,' " Lori recalled. "She said she hated men. She was very angry."

Barry Wuornos was older than his sister, Lori, and left home to join the service when Lee was nine. He says that the adoption of Lee and Keith was "a sore point" in the family, but described the family as having a "normal lifestyle. We were a pretty straight and narrow family."

Lori Grody had told Jackie Giroux about her brother.

"Barry was in the home until he went in the service," said Jackie. . . . "And he was kind of a quiet guy, liked to golf, liked to stay . . . did not like to make waves, liked to stay out of people's way." And Lori contends she didn't know Barry very well. "There seems to be an age difference there that they seem to use as a factor of not knowing each other."

In her deposition, Jackie Giroux told both prosecution and defense what she had learned from Lee Wuornos about the relationships within the Wuornos family.

"She told me that her brother, Barry, had hit her as well."

"When? They were what age?"

"When? I believe she was around fourteen, thirteen or fourteen."

"Did she discuss with you the details of that incident?"

"That he hit her, that Barry had hit her with his hands outside. He had beaten her up."

"Did she say why, what her version was why they had gotten in a fight?"

"She felt that she had said something to Barry that angered him. I don't remember what it was."

"Did she indicate this only happened once, that he had struck her?"

"I believe only once, that I recall."

"Did she indicate to you whether or not she harbored any ill will towards Barry because of this other incident or are there other occasions?"

"No," replied Jackie. "There was no hard will she's indicated."

"How about any other family member, Lori or Keith?"

"No. She seems to have really adored Keith."

"But she hated her grandfather?"

"Yes, her grandfather."

"But she adored Keith?"

"That's what I remember her saying. Yes."

"I thought you said also her grandfather sexually abused her."

"That's what she told me in January, then she said, no," Jackie stated.

"She changed her story?"

"Yes."

"How did she change that story?"

"Well, at first, she told me in January that if she didn't do what her grandfather asked her to do, which is go out and get him cigarettes or cigars—one time she went out to get the cigarettes and cigars and took too long because the bicycle broke and that he would strike her and that he would have sex with her. I think she said—she had the choice is what I recall."

"Of having sex with her grandfather?" the prosecution asked.

"Or being beaten."

"Or being beaten? Which did she choose, when given the choice. Did she tell you?"

"That she did. On occasion she did have sex with him. I don't know how many times or whatever."

"But later on you said that she changed that and denied having sex with her grandfather?"

"Yes. She said she didn't remember that any longer, right."

"She denied it. She said, I don't remember it occurring. Is that correct?"

"That is correct."

"Did she change her story about anything else her grandfather did? That's a pretty serious allegation, to say you're having sex with your grandfather, then deny having it. Did she say anything else about denying him having beaten her?"

"No. She said he still beat her."

"The beating with the belt, that stuck?"

"That's correct."

"But, she changed the story about the sexual abuse?"

"Yes."

"Did she also change that about Keith, whom she told you she adored?"

"No. She kept to the facts. She adored Keith."

"Even though she had intercourse with him, her brother?"

"Yes."

"She claimed she had intercourse with Keith?"

"Yes."

"Did you ask her about that, when she denied having intercourse with her grandfather, if she still had intercourse with her own brother?"

"Yes."

"What did she say?"

"She did have intercourse with her brother."

"Did she say if it was consensual or how old she is?"

"She said it was consensual and I believe she said, she was fourteen, thirteen or fourteen."

"Did she indicate whether or not . . . how many times they had intercourse together?"

"No. I never asked her."

At fourteen Lee quit school and ran away. Two weeks later her grandmother died. She returned, but her grandfather threw her out of the house.

"I saw her hitchhiking on Rochester Road when she was about twelve or thirteen," a neighbor told reporters. "She looked like a lost child. She always had a bag over her shoulder, like an overnight bag . . .

You didn't dare look at her... 'Don't mess with me' was the message she gave... She had the look of death in her."

Lee showed up at neighbors' doors when she was hungry or needed a place to sleep. Another woman remembers: "She didn't have the confidence of anyone—no teacher, no friend. Some people pick the darkness. She was like that."

A friend during that period recalls: "I know she hated men.... she had no dates, no major crushes. If she was with a boy, it was always for the money. She had no close friends. And not a single adult ever helped her, absolutely not one."

"I always thought Aileen would be involved in something like this, but I figured it would have been her who would have been the one killed, not the other way around," Dawn Botkins said.

"After I heard, I just lay awake, thinking about all the hate in her life, about all the times she tried to be accepted but wasn't, about all the terrible things that happened to her.

"She was a good person at one time, but no one really let her be good," Dawn concluded. "She was hurt physically every day."

In her deposition, Jackie Giroux remembered Lori Grody telling her about Lee's relationships with her peers.

"She was not well liked by her schoolmates. She always seemed a little different and fought with people a lot. In the middle of being with kids she would start laughing. No one understood why she laughed. Or she would start to become argumentative. When she was asked why, she would just say, this is just the way it is."

And while Lee was protective of Lori, telling her that "You shouldn't be dating. You shouldn't be going out with men," there were incidents of violence between the two girls.

Her grandfather sent her to a detention home in a nearby community, but to Lee it was a prison, and she continued to run away at every opportunity.

At seventeen, she was hitchhiking around the country, taking odd jobs, but supporting herself mostly through prostitution.

In Colorado, Lee was arrested for drunken driving, weapons offenses and disorderly conduct. She served time only once—ten days for driving under the influence.

She claims that she was raped numerous times while on the road.

In 1976, when Lee was twenty, her grandfather died. Whether or not it was suicide remains unresolved. Lauri Wuornos was found in the garage with the car running. Authorities could never determine whether the diabetic man had an attack in the car, or intentionally killed himself. The death was officially listed as accidental carbon monoxide poisoning.

That was also the year that Lee married a man from an old and highly respected Philadelphia family, Lewis Gratz Fell. Her union with the seventy-year-old Fell lasted one month, after which Fell filed for divorce. The judge issued a restraining order against Lee because of her "violent and ungovernable temper."

Lee was married to Fell and living in Florida when her brother, Keith, died of cancer. He had requested cremation and he wanted his ashes scattered in Florida. Lee returned to Florida shortly after his funeral and fulfilled his wish.

In 1978, despondent and with no support from friends or family, Lee shot herself in the abdomen and was hospitalized for two weeks. She told doctors she had tried to kill herself six times between the ages of fourteen and twenty-two, but admitted the attempts were not all serious.

Life became a series of short-term relationships with men.

For a while, in 1981, she lived in a mobile home with a retired businessman who was separated from his wife. Lee was quick-tempered, he said, but he found her warm, loving and resourceful. She strove to please him and he remembers the day that the vacuum cleaner broke. By that evening, it was replaced with a new one. She had stolen it from a nearby hotel.

Her lover also found her to be a bright, willing student who, with his encouragement, became an excellent golfer.

One night they quarreled. Lee awakened the next morning still angry and feeling that this man might be just like all the others who had taken advantage of her over the years. She took the car, bought a six-pack of beer, then stopped at a pawn shop to buy a pistol and some bullets. She drove for hours, despondent and contemplating whether or not to shoot herself.

Late in the afternoon, clad only in shorts and a bikini top, Lee entered a Majik Market in Edgewater, Florida.

"I was fed up with living," she said. "I had no car, no money, no family. I had nothing. Struggling seemed senseless. I even tried to join the service—the army, navy, air force—but you needed forty-two points to pass, and I always missed by exactly five points. So I was going to kill myself.

"I drank a case of beer and a quarter pint of whiskey. I also took four reds. Librium. I got my boyfriend's car and went to this store. I grabbed a six-pack of beer and two Slim Jims. I had $118 on me.

"I walked up to the counter and put my purse on it. The handle of my gun was sticking out, and the woman started screaming like hell about how I was going to rob the store. She freaked out, and I said, 'What the hell, you want a robbery, then I'll rob your store. Give me your money.' "

The clerk handed her $33 from the cash register.

"I walked out of the store real slowly, cause I was so drunk and I couldn't find my keys. I sat in that car for three minutes looking for them. Then I drove away and started hauling ass down the highway. Then the radiator blew and I had to stop, and these kids helped me push to a gas station. I was wearing one of those country hats, and I took that off, and the shorts, so I was just in my bikini. I was trying to alter my description, and that's when the cops arrived."

Lee saw the robbery as a test of her boyfriend's love. She reasoned that if she were caught and sent to prison and he found a way to have her released, it would prove his love for her. A father to growing children, one of whom bears his name, he found the heat generated by Lee Wuornos was quickly becoming an inferno.

Russell Armstrong, a criminal defense attorney in Daytona Beach, represented Lee Wuornos on the charges of armed robbery.

"I felt from the beginning that she was dangerous to herself, but I never suspected she was capable of hurting others," Armstrong remembered.

The middle-aged Armstrong is an Abraham Lincoln buff and a Florida Gators fan. Leaning back in his office chair, he was surrounded by artifacts of both.

Armstrong's pretty, dark-eyed secretary delivered some files and reminded him of a court date. He ran his fingers through his thinning, sandy hair, glanced at the files, and turned his attention back to the subject of Lee Wuornos.

He found the twenty-five-year-old Lee bright, but suicidal in 1981, and asked Circuit Judge Kim C. Hammond to order a psychiatric evaluation prior to trial.

"I liked Lee and I was worried about her," said Armstrong. "She obviously needed someone to care for her."

Dr. George W. Barnard, who frequently serves as an expert witness for the courts, examined Lee and arrived at the following conclusion:

The prisoner is a 25-year-old white divorced female who has an appreciation of the charges against her and says she does not know the range and nature of the possible penalties. She understands the adversary nature of the legal process and has capacity to disclose to attorney pertinent facts surrounding the alleged offense, to relate to attorney, to assist attorney in planning her defense, to realistically challenge prosecution witnesses, to manifest appropriate courtroom behavior, to testify relevantly, to cope with the stress of incarceration prior to trial and is motivated to help herself in the legal process. It is my medical opinion the defendant is competent to stand trial, was legally sane at the time of the alleged crime and does not meet the criteria for involuntary hospitalization.

According to Barnard, Lee told him she had never been a slow learner in school and that she had worked as a waitress, cashier, cook, maid, prostitute and pool hustler. Her longest job had been seven months and she had been fired many times.

Her ability to maintain jobs, as well as personal relationships, was negligible.

Lee was given a three-year sentence. She served eighteen months.

Marty Roland, records supervisor at Florida Correctional Center in Lowell, Florida, said: "There were three of us who must have dealt with Lee Wuornos when she arrived here. I was the one who fingerprinted her. But I don't remember her. If she had been a particularly difficult inmate or a particularly outstanding one, I would remember her. Some you remember, and some you don't."

Lee was disciplined six times for fighting and disobeying orders. She later told a friend she spent her prison time studying theology.

She also began a correspondence with Thomas Shelton, a middle-aged man living in the east. When Lee was released from prison in early 1983, she said she was going to Maryland to live.

Shelton immediately recognized that Lee had problems. He attempted to obtain help for her, but the clinic he contacted declined to admit her. After several months, he sent her back to Florida.

Russ Armstrong, realizing her dilemma, asked her former boyfriend to take her back. He declined.

In January of 1984, Lee moved on—this time to New Smyrna Beach, where she lived with a retired truckdriver for several months.

"Two men came and dropped her off one day," he told reporters. "She needed a place to stay. She cleaned and cooked. I wanted somebody quiet, because it's a quiet neighborhood. She seemed bitter somehow, but she always put herself together. She could have taken advantage of me if she had wanted. She did have a temper, but was a pretty girl."

Sometime during 1984, Lee met Toni in Key West. When that relationship ended, she had lost her money and her possessions. And she had suffered yet another rejection.

When Lee returned to Daytona Beach, she continued to claim that she owned a steam-pressure-cleaning business. It explained her absences to others when she disappeared for days to "go to work."

Chapter Five

Marion County Sheriff Sergeant Brian Jarvis had, within five years, risen through the ranks of the department from traffic patrol to supervisor of the Major Crimes Unit. Darkly handsome, Jarvis, in his 1989 evaluation report, was described as "the glue that kept the division together." He was also the brains behind the arrest of Aileen Wuornos.

In August 1990, Jarvis and an investigator sat in the Sheriff's Office in Ocala puzzling over the recent death of Troy Burress, whose body had been found August 4, forty miles northeast of Ocala.

"We really didn't have any leads," Jarvis told reporters. "And then I received a bulletin from the Florida Department of Law Enforcement that Citrus and Pasco counties had found two bodies in remote areas with .22 caliber slugs, and there were a lot of similarities."

Further investigation showed the method of operation was the same.

Lt. Horzepa remembered that "the victims all appeared to be at least middle age or above. They appeared to have been traveling alone. All the victims had been robbed of their own personal property. The victims' vehicles, when they were found, they were found abandoned, and it was from where the body was actually located. The bodies were normally found off of an interstate, close to an interstate, but right off in a concealed area. All the cars appeared to have been wiped down of the prints. Seats in the cars had all been moved up to the front.

"Also, the majority of the victims' pants pockets were turned inside out."

"It looked like a serial killer," Jarvis said. "It was a first link."

By this time, a task force had been formed among those counties in which bodies had been located or missing persons had been reported.

When the incident concerning two women and a wrecked Pontiac Sunbird was reported, Jarvis sensed something more.

"That stuck in our minds," he said. "And the victims were shot with .22 caliber shells—a woman's gun. These things together suggested we had women murderers."

With the media publication of the composite sketches, the investigation surged ahead. The role of Jarvis became more pronounced. He developed a computer program to coordinate the leads which were beginning to pour into the Sheriff's Office. In the middle of December 1990, leads no. 5, 243, 297 and 361 identified the sketches as two women, lesbian man-haters, capable of violence.

Those faces, they said, belonged to a short, hefty twenty-eight-year-old former motel maid, Tyria J. Moore, and a tall, aggressive blond hooker known variously as Lori Grody, Cammie Greene, Susan Blahovec, Lee Blahovec and Aileen Wuornos.

There had been more than 900 leads. But these, ultimately, were the ones that mattered.

A statewide investigation produced surprising results. Investigators found that Lee Blahovec served as an alias for Aileen "Lee" Wuornos, a drifter who was wanted in southern Florida on a warrant for check forgery. Cammie Greene's name appeared on a Daytona pawn ticket which represented items belonging to Richard Mallory.

Horzepa explained the process:

"In Volusia County, there is a transaction made in a pawnshop where somebody sells something—i.d. has to be obtained and a thumbprint is also given on this particular pawn ticket and then the originals from all the pawn shops in Volusia County are sent to the sheriff's office."

The thumbprint on the pawn ticket belonged to Aileen Wuornos.

Ordinarily, Jarvis, in his capacity with the Major Crimes Unit, would have followed up the investigation into the potential killer of seven Florida men. And so he was surprised when the investigation was suddenly taken over by Capt. Steve A. Binegar, Jr., the sheriff's Criminal Investigation Division commander, and Major Dan Henry, the department's second-in-command.

"These men are administrators," he told reporters. "They don't do investigations. Prior to identifying the girls, it was a team effort that I was supervising. After identifying them, it became a close-knit group that I was being excluded from."

Tyria Moore was growing increasingly nervous. After telling Ty her role in the murder of Richard Mallory, Lee never again mentioned killings, but the cars kept appearing. Lee passed them off as loans from customers or payment for services, but Ty wondered. Richard Mallory's car had come home with Lee and Richard Mallory was dead.

In the fall of 1990, Lee and Ty moved into room number 8 of the Fairview Motel, just south of Daytona Beach in Harbor Oaks.

Lee told reporters that: "If I made $130, I'd take $30 and give her the rest to pay bills. She always told me, 'Get a motel with a swimming pool, 'cause it's so boring here all day long.' So I found a place with two swimming pools, a shuffleboard, a lounge, and a store with beer.

"The problem was I wasn't supporting her as richly as she wanted. She always wanted a brand-new car or a rented one. She wanted clothes, she wanted an apartment with plush furniture. 'I've got to have my things,' she said. So materialistic. I brought home about $300 every two weeks, but it wears you out, constantly talking to all those men, staying up."

In Daytona Beach, $300 represents ten blow jobs. Not counting the ones who refuse to pay.

The Fairview Motel is a run-of-the-mill motel on U.S. 1, just outside Daytona Beach. It offers modest housing, and proximity to three bars and a convenience store. Lee and Ty would visit the store daily, buying as much as two cases of beer at a time.

Brenda McGarry, the clerk at the convenience store who often checked out Lee's purchases, remembers that Lee would approach men in the fifty to sixty age range at the pumps.

"She was physically very aggressive," Brenda said, "flexing her muscles and carrying herself with a masculinity."

Sometimes the two women would make small talk.

"She would talk about her mom," the clerk recalled. "And she kept saying, 'the pain, pain, it gets like this (indicating size), and the only thing that gets rid of the pain, slams it, is the hate.'

"This girl went back to the age of twelve and told me extensively how her mother died and how it was her father's fault and what he did to do it! . . . She would bad mouth her father and then she would glorify her mother."

Lee Wuornos, who never knew her father, and had been abandoned by her mother, was talking about her grandparents.

"I was so stupid," admitted Brenda. "Lee kept saying that she needed to get over to 92 to make some money. I thought 92 was a bar. It never registered to me that 92 was a highway."

During the fall of 1990, Lee was a regular customer at the convenience store.

"She needed her coffee, Marlboro lights and 12-packs of Busch," said Brenda.

Sometimes Ty would be with her.

"Lee always took the lead, going through the door, holding the door, holding the beer. I thought Ty was shy and timid, you know. Maybe she was shy. Or it was just that Lee was dominating.

"I watched the two girls manipulate each other, trying to pick up men in front of my place of business. One threatened the other. Ty would tell Lee, 'No, let's go home.' Lee would say, 'No, we need some money.' In her own words, 'Need the money.' "

One day, Lee came into the store to ask Brenda McGarry for a job.

"I gave her an application and told her to fill it in truthfully," Brenda remembered. It soon became obvious that Lee was going to falsify her last employment and the people needed for references.

"She came out and said she made $2,000 to $3,000 a month doing what she did," Brenda said.

But apparently Lee wanted to change her life.

"She thought I was going to hire her right there," said Brenda. When she didn't, Lee took the application, but never returned it.

Shortly before Thanksgiving, Ty and Lee came into the store.

"Oh, it was a joyous occasion," Brenda said. "They both came in. They were both very happy. Ty was talking quite a bit for a change instead of Lee. Very happy. She hadn't seen her parents or her home. She was going to go down for a vacation. Usually Ty stood behind Lee. Lee was behind Ty this time. She stood back. You could see that she was withdrawn. . .I asked how she was going. She said that she was sent a ticket to fly."

By this time, Lee and Ty had been forced to move from the Fairview Motel because they could no longer afford the rent. Ty was not working and their only source of income was Lee's prostitution.

Just down the street from the Fairview Motel, Velimir Isailovic and Vera Ivkovich serve up good food at an unobtrusive, white frame Yugoslavian restaurant called the Belgrade. Vera operates the restaurant, buying, preparing and serving Yugoslavian dishes. She makes it clear that there is no alcohol. Velimir does machine repair in their garage.

A native of Yugoslavia, Vera survived World War II with the help of rations from the United States. She has not forgotten what it's like to be hungry and she knows how it feels to need a place to stay. And so when Lee and Ty appeared at the restaurant in October of 1990 and asked if they could rent the small room adjoining the restaurant, Vera said yes, for $50 a week.

Vera Ivkovitch is weathered and slightly stooped. She has been cooking all her life, having been trained in New York after arriving from Yugoslavia as a young woman.

"I knew Lee from the early eighties," she says, apologizing for her accent as she serves steaming bowls of bean soup and salads dripping with homemade dressing.

"She was a good working person and always dressed nice. She and her friends, both men and women, would come into the restaurant to eat. When she disappeared, I wondered, 'Where is Lee?', and I was glad to see her when she came to my restaurant. She said, 'Vera, I am back,' and I said, 'Welcome home.' "

Lee, suitcase in hand, told Vera that Ty was her "friend," but the relationship was clear.

"I don't judge them," said Vera. "This was the first time I was stupid."

It was an uncomfortable month for Vera and Velimir.

"When they would go to the gas station next door to buy beer, they would never cross through the parking area," Vera remembered. "Instead, they would sneak back through the bushes on the far end of the property. Now I know they were afraid of being seen from the street."

And Lee's hours were strange.

"One day she would leave in the morning, the next she would sleep all morning, the next she would go and come back. She kept telling us how hard her life was, and I would say, 'Why tell me? Look, I'm in here at 6:30 a.m. and I stay until 9:00 p.m., every day, seven days a week,' " says Vera.

The women invaded the quiet dignity of the Belgrade Restaurant. Night after night, loud music reverberated from the small bedroom. Velimir remembers saying to them on several occasions: "Hey, here is no bar. Turn down music, it's middle of night.

"We are not nosy. We don't see nothing," Velimir says, "but she (Lee) start to fight with me. She start argue with me, very bitter."

In his deposition, Velimir Isailovic told his story:

"Two, three days after she check in she said, 'Can you give me ride to my job.' I said, 'Okay.' Because she don't have car. She don't have nothing. She stay in the room. She gave money if she go to work. Put her in my pickup truck...Say, 'Which way are you going to go?' She says, 'Going south to the New Smyrna Beach.' I go to the New Smyrna Beach. And I ask her, 'Do you know where you going to go, do you know street address?'

"Because she tell me she got cleaning business. I think she is going to go somewhere to clean house or something like that. She say, 'Keep going.' I start to laughing, I say, 'I think, you don't know where you are going to go.' She say, 'I know, turn right to the 95.'

"I say, 'Why you don't tell me, I don't have gasoline to go too far'... She say, 'Okay, if you catch 95, exit south and stop.' Again, I don't have in my mind nothing wrong. I ask, 'How are you going to go from here?' 'Don't worry, I'm walking.'

"I drop her on 95 exit south. I come back home and I tell me wife, 'Look she don't have any business. She does not work anywhere. You know where I put her? Right on 95. Some kind of monkey business, yet.' But what kind we don't know, I don't know. I don't know how long she going to stay that day, that time. Probably several hours. Not too long.

"Three, four, five hours she come back. She bring—give my wife very small money, $30, $40. I don't know. Not too much. She go in the room, buy beer, drink beer all night long. I say, 'I don't know how come she has got money to buy beer, but she don't have money to pay the rent and food.' Start to make me really mad and confused.

"But, anyhow, I quit to give her any favor. She say, 'What's wrong with you?' I say, 'Nothing at all, you start to lie, you don't have any job, you don't have any business.' 'Oh yes, I got good business, good this and that, can you give me ride.' I say, 'No. I told you no any favor for you anymore.' She say, 'Can you give me ride to Winn-Dixie Store?' Said, 'No.'

"She start to bring $10, $20 to my wife. I say, 'That's enough. Better tell her to go out.' That's three weeks. Two or three days before Thanksgiving, I think."

Vera recalls that the two women ran up a tab in the restaurant for almost $100. "When someone would come in the restaurant, they would pick up their food and take it to their room," she says.

It was not until later that Vera understood why Lee and Ty did not want to be seen.

Shortly before Thanksgiving, Lee and Ty moved out of the small room. They had grown to like the three dimensional portrait of "The Last Supper" which hung beside their bed and Lee offered to buy it from Vera. Vera refused to sell.

"Several times, she try to give me things," Vera recalls. "Once it was an electric shaver, and, again, a gold chain."

In the end, the two women left owing $34.

"Quickly after that the other one—fat—Ty, disappear—disappear from two or three days later we don't see. Usually they go to gas station, next door to gas station to buy newspaper, buy beer, buy coke," Velimir said.

"But Lee stayed a little longer," he said. "I don't know how long. One day in gas station, I pick up gas for me. She is running in the gas station to buy something, newspaper. Just make joke, I say, 'Hey, when you bring me my money?' Because she owed $30 or $34.

"And that time she say, 'I'm sorry, you are son of a bitch, you are lucky you are still have life.'

". . . Couple days later see sketch on TV first. Sketch on TV, I tell my wife, 'Look, does it look like these two girls who live in house, our place?' She said, 'Oh, no, come on.' After, these polices come to show sketch. Yes, that's exactly. That's all I know about her, these two."

Chapter Six

The composite sketches of the tight-lipped blonde with the stringy hair and the dark-haired moon face under the baseball cap plagued Ty's days and haunted her nights. She was glad to leave Daytona Beach and go home to Ohio for Thanksgiving. She had a lot of thinking to do.

Lee Wuornos had no family with whom to share Thanksgiving. During Ty's absence, Walter Gino Antonio's body, clad only in tube socks, was recovered from the wooded area off U.S. 19, eight miles north of Cross City. His maroon, two-door Pontiac Grand Prix, with the permission of manager Rose McNeill, was parked by Lee Wuornos in the lot behind the Fairview Motel.

"Lee asked me if she could park her boyfriend's car behind the motel," she remembered.

She was told that the boyfriend was married and he did not want to have his wife drive by and find his car parked at the motel. Mrs. McNeill recalled that Lee kept the car there for only a few days.

Donald Willingham met Lee at a bar during the previous year. They shared a game of pool and went their separate ways. On the day after Thanksgiving, Willingham was driving on Spruce Creek Road in Daytona Beach when he saw Lee walking down the sidewalk.

"I thought I recognized her," he said. "I was just out driving around. I have a girlfriend that lives down on Spruce Creek Road and I was going that way. I was just out. And I happen—I thought I recognized her.

"And I turned around and I went back up. And it was her. So I pulled over and asked her where she was going. And she said, 'I'm trying to get to the airport.' I said, 'To the airport? What are you going to the airport for?' She says, 'My girlfriend is coming in.' I said, 'Who?' And she said, 'Ty.' That was all she said.

"I said, 'Well'—she said, 'Would you do me a favor and take me out there?' And I said, 'Yes, I will take you out there.' Because I wasn't doing nothing. And so later—she was supposed to come in at 12:30 that day, I think, is what she said. And I says, 'Yes, I will take you out there.'

"So she got in the car and we went down Taylor Road back up Clyde

Morris. And she said, 'Well, I need a beer.' I said, 'We can't get no beer here, it's Port Orange.'

"And so I stopped and I got her a beer. And we rode around until the plane came in. And I took her to the airport and picked this heavy-set girl up that she said was Ty."

Lee had waited impatiently at the gate for Ty to disembark the plane bringing her back from her home in Ohio. She had missed her and was anxious to give her the present she was carrying in her pocket—a man's ring, size 10 3/4, yellow gold with a diamond set in a field of white gold. The ring Walter Gino Antonio's fiancee had bought for him a short time ago. As the two women greeted each other, Lee slipped the diamond on Ty's finger. At last she was able to give her wife an appropriate symbol of her love.

Outside, Lee and Ty climbed into Donald Willingham's truck. He remembers that: "From there I took her to—she said, 'Well, stop up here and let us get some beer and you can take us to the motel where we are living.' I said, 'Okay.' And I took her up on U.S. 1 and Nova Road at the—Fairview Motel was the name of the motel. And she asked me if I could come back and pick them up, that they had to move out. And I said, 'If I'm not doing nothing I will come back and pick you up and move you.'

"And so later on I did. And I said, 'Where are you going with it?' She said, 'I guess we will have to put it in storage.' And I said, 'All right.' She said, 'My girfriend is going back up north.' Said that they were splitting up.

"And from there I took them. I took them up there and they put the stuff, whatever they had—I don't know even what all it was. It was all boxed up and everything when they loaded it in the car. They had a couple suitcases. And so she was catching a Greyhound bus out of Daytona going back up north. And we took her to the bus station. Well, we took the stuff to the storage which was up there on Nova Road. I went later and found out what the name of it was. I didn't even know what the name of it was....Later I went up there and it was Jack's Mini-Warehouse."

Tyria Moore was bailing out. As she stepped into the bus station with Lee, she removed Walter Gino Antonio's ring from her finger and gave it to the woman she was leaving behind. Ty had confronted Lee with her suspicions and Lee had thrown the .22 caliber gun into Rose Bay near the Fairview Motel in Ty's presence. But Ty was through taking chances with Lee. She knew that eventually Lee would be caught, the composites were everywhere, and if Lee had to answer for what she had done, Ty did not want any part of it.

Willingham testified that at the bus station, "I didn't go with them. I sat in the car. And they got out and, I guess, she went in and got her tickets and whatever. And she was in there five or ten minutes or so and then came back out and got in the car and said, 'Let's go'. . . She seemed upset at the time. And she had got some beer. There was some beer in the car. And she was drinking beer. And she got to crying about, you know—mumbling to herself more or less. In a little bit she—it passed over. And she started talking about something else. And then Ty wasn't mentioned no more."

Lee and Willingham returned to his house, where she cleaned up and they went to bed.

"In going to bed with her did she charge you money?" Willingham was asked during his deposition.

"No. She didn't charge me any money. I had been hauling her around. As a friend, really. I mean, just by knowing her. Because I wasn't even drinking," Willingham said.

"She could have got me," he added.

After Ty's departure, Lee went alone regularly to the convenience store near the motel. Brenda McGarry remembered Lee's behavior during that period.

"She came into the store. She needed a cup of coffee. She was extremely tense. She said she couldn't eat. She needed that cup of coffee. . . .she had tears in her eyes. I asked her what was wrong. Basically, she said that Ty came back just to get her stuff and is going back—her mom promised her two cars, a good paying job that she needed to get away from [Lee]; that she had been doing what she had been doing for the last six years because of her, because she loves her, because she wants to take care of her.

"She opened up and told me that Ty was her lover, that she loved her and that she couldn't live without her, you know, in that respect.

" '[Ty] made me do these things,' Lee told Brenda. 'There is so many times I nearly got caught.'

" . . . She also made the statement that if she gets caught, '[Ty] is going to pay also for the things that she did. She thinks she is so slick. People think she is quiet, that she is shy. She is not shy,' " Brenda said.

Without Ty, Lee was lonelier than she had ever been. She had returned to the Fairview Motel, but asked to move from room no. 8. It had, she told Rose McNeill, too many memories.

Her possessions now had dwindled to a tan suitcase and the single silver key which opened the storage locker at Jack's Mini-Warehouse. She had even hocked the diamond nugget ring that Ty had returned to her.

Without Ty, Lee was no longer motivated and often went for days without "doing" any men. She was tired and despondent and felt much older than her thirty-four years. Soon there was not enough money to stay at the Fairview Motel and she took to the streets, sleeping where she could, when she could. If business was good and she had money, she would get a motel room.

But business was not always good. She was reminded of the younger Lee, who slept in abandoned cars. And she wondered why people kept leaving her behind.

Just before Christmas, Lee met a paunchy ex-marine named Dick Mills at Wet Willie's, a hard-edged hole-in-the-wall biker bar on U.S. 1. Mills told reporters that Lee was "getting trashed beyond belief and howling and singing. . . and driving everyone nuts."

Mills and his wife had just separated after a few months of marriage and he understood Lee's grief because he shared it.

"We were both in the pits of hell," Mills said. "She was blown out over Ty and I was blown out over wanting Connie back. . . She kept going over how I. . . reminded her of Ty. She was totally fascinated at how much we looked alike.

"We talked about a lot of things—from art to parapsychology to ancient history. I couldn't believe I'd met another human being that had such awesome comprehension and knowledge," Mills recalled.

He found Lee to be a "wild, savage party animal" with an insatiable desire for sex and alcohol.

"There's only two people I've ever met who have met the devil and shaken his hand," said Mills extravagantly. "The one is me and the other is her."

After five days together, Mills left Lee on Christmas Eve to return to his wife. On parting, he said he handed her $50.

Nearly a year later, he told the *Globe* a different story.

"It all started so innocently. But it turned into a nightmare. If I'd known what I was getting myself into, I would have run for my life.

"But I didn't have a clue. On that first day, I was trying to drown my sorrows in beer at Wet Willie's in Daytona Beach, Florida.

"And I saw this woman doing exactly the same thing down at the other end of the bar...

"That night, her troubles made her all the more appealing. We were both pretty down and out, and we desperately needed each other.

"Suddenly, she turned, looked deep into my eyes and said, 'Dick, you and I are one—aren't we?'"

Several days later, Lee offered: "Dick, I'll be your wife if you pay me $500 a month."

"I was stunned," said Dick. "She was telling me she'd have sex with me if I paid her. I was really smitten and thought we might eventually marry, but no way would I do that."

According to Mills, Lee revealed her secret fantasies. One of her favorites entailed having a black hood placed over her head while she was tied to a tree in a forest.

"Then a guy would come up to her, rape her and then shoot her in the head.

"She said the killing would make her climax."

The final straw, said Mills, came when he took Lee to a party at the home of his daughter, Raveshia, in Ocala.

"Lee got blind drunk and insulted everybody....She was like an animal and drank us completely out of beer....The next day, I packed Lee's bags, drove her to a motel and told her I would give her $500 if she stayed out of my life."

According to Lee, Mills was very depressed over the loss of his wife and she counseled him.

"You're such a good counselor. Where did you get so much insight?" he asked her.

Mills invited her to the Christmas party at his daughter's house. She had not wanted to go, but he insisted. When she got there, Mills' family was not receptive to her and she got drunk and retaliated. It ended their relationship. She denies ever wanting to marry him. And, she says, the only thing he ever gave her was a pair of L.A. Gear gym shoes.

After her experience with Mills, Lee spent the remainder of the holidays in bars, hustling pool, guzzling beer, beating out rhythm on jukeboxes and wailing the songs that reminded her of Ty. Randy Travis, accompanied by a mellow guitar, said it best:

Diggin' up bones, diggin' up bones
Exhuming things that's better left alone

I'm resurrecting memories of the love
   that's dead and gone
The other night I sat alone diggin' up bones.

Down the street from the Fairview Motel, a squat brick building stares out at U.S. 1 through dirty plate glass eyes. The front door yawns widely, revealing a dim and empty interior. Ivy climbs its walls and its roof. Among the myriad of bars, third-rate motels and used car dealerships that line the highway, it is noticeable only through the protruding sign that announces "The Last Resort Bar."

Inside, panties and bras dangle from the ceiling. They tremble and age in the grimy air. Of particular interest is the dingy white bra that belonged to Lee Wuornos. The one with the safety pin attached.

Lately, there have been fewer customers and the bar often stands empty. The story of Lee Wuornos has made The Last Resort famous, but Cannonball, the 6-foot-6, 320-pound bartender, says it has hurt business. People don't want to "hang around with murderers."

Cannonball, three quarters Indian, one quarter Scandanavian, ("When the norsemen came to Florida, they left behind a lot of blue-eyed Indians"), runs The Last Resort. He could not own it, even if he wanted to, because Indians are not citizens. He scorns society and says that by the time he is fifty (he is forty-one), he wants to disappear into the backwoods of Florida and live quietly. In the meantime, he, the two pool tables and the jukebox are the staples of the bar.

Cannonball says that since the arrest of Lee Wuornos, he has seen a steady stream of women wondering if she had anything to do with the disappearances of their boyfriends or husbands.

"One lady offered $700,000," Cannonball told a reporter shortly after Lee's arrest. "Who knows if it was a serious offer? But I didn't know anything about their husbands. The truth is, I only saw Wuornos come in here three or four times. She'd get drunk, but she wasn't an alcoholic. She was boisterous, she played pool. But she didn't associate much. You could see right away she was a flat cracker." A flat cracker, explains Cannonball, is a lesbian.

Even before Lee Wuornos entered his life, Cannonball had plenty of offers. These were offers for sex from both men and women. "I mind my own business and don't get involved," he says.

A notice behind the bar reflects its clientele's philosophy: "All you need in this life is a tremendous sex drive and a great ego—brains don't mean a shit."

The backyard of the bar is filled with curiousities. Numerous motorbikes adorn a tree; an open coffin boasts a sign offering "a little peace at the Last Resort." The stage which juts from the back of the building is used by The Last Resort Productions to sponsor, among other things, wet T-shirt contests. The contests invariably degenerate into spontaneous nudity, by spectators as well as participants. Sex is not uncommon in the backyard of The Last Resort—beer-glutted couples indulge in hurried couplings or surreptitious blow jobs.

"We tend to get a lot of people in here who are running from one thing or another," stated Cannonball.

As recently as last year, The Last Resort was just one of many biker bars that line Highway 1. But now the The Last Resort is famous. It is inextricably tangled with the story of Lee Wuornos—because it was here that detectives arrested her on the evening of January 9, 1991.

"She didn't seem at all the type to kill anyone. She never picked up anyone in the bar and came in a few times with another woman, who didn't appear to me to be Ty Moore, but maybe it was," says Cannonball.

On the morning of her arrest, Cannonball came to work to find Lee asleep under the tin overhang on the side of the building on the yellow vinyl seat which had been dislodged from an old Dodge pickup truck. She hadn't hooked for days now and the money had run out. She was unaware that a team of investigators had tracked her every move for more than forty-eight hours.

According to investigator Bruce Munster of the Marion County Sheriff's Department, they had followed her from one bar to another, hoping that she would lead them to Tyria Moore.

Police reports describe the events:

A surveillance team was dispatched to the Daytona Beach area in search of Aileen Wuornos and Tyria Moore. On 01/08/91 a team of Officers inside the "Port Orange Pub" on Ridgewood Avenue, Daytona, spotted Wuornos at that location. Undercover Officer Mike Joyner observed her with a tan suitcase which she carried from one location to another. Conversations with her and the observations of the undercover team were that she has mood swings from friendly and congenial to aggressive and abusive and is known to consume both Busch and Budweiser can beer and smoke Marlboro cigarettes. She told Mike Joyner that everything she had was in the suitcase and showed a key to him which she said was her life. She then walked to the Last Resort Bar. She spent the night in the bar with this suitcase. She hadn't any place to stay and told Joyner that she had broken up with her girlfriend Ty and missed her.

The surveillance continued until the evening hours of 01/09/91 at the Last Resort Bar. Intelligence revealed a large party was to occur at the bar that evening. Because of this, a decision was made that surveillance would be almost impossible.

Late in the day on January 9, 1991, Lee Wuornos stepped outside The Last Resort with two men who offered to buy her a motel room for the night.

"I woke up around eleven [that morning]," recalled Lee, "and went back to The Last Resort and started drinking. There were two under-cover cops. One of them gave me twenty dollars, and they bought me a motel room. I called to check it out, and there was a room under my name. I told them I wasn't hooking, but I wouldn't mind giving head for the twenty dollars, though I'd rather just pay it back. One of them wanted me to step outside to give some directions. A couple bikers walked out with me, and then there were these six guys in suits."

Sgt. Brian Jarvis was not among them.

"I was in charge of the investigation," he said, "and I was the only guy at home."

Lee was arrested by Bernie Buscher and Larry Horzepa on an out-standing failure to appear warrant out of Volusia County. Their investi-gation had revealed a history of Lee's trouble with the law.

In May 1984, she walked into Barnett Bank in the Florida Keys and forged her employer's signature on two checks—one for $5,000 and the other for $595. She was arrested that same day. Two years later, she pleaded guilty to forgery after the prosecution agreed to drop related charges. Sentencing was set for April 30, 1986. She did not show up. A warrant was issued for her arrest. In June of that year, she was appre-hended in Volusia County on a driver's license violation—in a stolen au-tomobile. A loaded .22 caliber revolver was hidden under the front seat and she was carrying twelve rounds of ammunition in a bag. Lee was charged with grand theft and carrying a concealed firearm. Again she failed to appear in court and another warrant became outstanding.

Late that year, she was arrested in Dade City for grand larceny and resisting arrest. Eventually, the charges were dropped.

The Volusia County warrant gave the investigators what they needed—the ability to collar the woman they suspected of murder.

Buscher remembered arresting Lee outside The Last Resort Bar:

"She appeared confused...why generally she was being arrested," Buscher said.

"It is really not that unusual for an individual who is not aware that he or she is going to be arrested. Other than that, at least in my contact with her, she didn't appear to be distraught or anything of that nature. She was in possession of her faculties. I don't recall if she was intoxicated. If she was, she certainly didn't appear to be to me."

Both men noted that her main concern while being booked at Volusia County Detention Center was: "Where's my key? Where's my key? My life is that key."

Buscher recalled that she was afraid the key would "turn up missing." The key, he added, was found in Lee's purse attached to a brass ring key holder. The purse also contained a business card from Jack's Mini-Warehouse on Nova Road.

Chapter Seven

Karen Collins, an undercover detective with the Pasco County Sheriff's Department, was investigating the murder of Charles Carskaddon. The opinion of those at the department was that Aileen Wuornos was a suspect. On the day of her arrest, Karen approached Lee at the Volusia County Detention Center where she was being processed.

Perhaps because she was a woman, Lee began to tell her about her life. Karen remembered Lee stating that she had lived in the area for approximately seven years and had recently lost her lover and her home. Since then, she said, she had been living on the streets. All her possessions were in a storage unit. Lee admitted to hitchhiking around town and "doing men" for money. During her booking procedure, including fingerprinting, she worried that police suspected her of killing the men whose bodies had been found near the interstates.

"It was her belief that the police believed she looked like the girl in the pictures being circulated in the newspapers," Karen remembered.

On the following day, Bernie Buscher traveled to Jack's Mini-Warehouse and talked with Alice Colbert, who with her husband, Melvin, owns the warehouse. She pulled out records for the investigator showing that a storage bin had been rented on December 3, 1990, by Cammie Greene. The cupboard, in building 43, hall number 1, bin G, was paid up until February.

On January 14, Circuit Judge S. James Foxman issued a search warrant for bin G. As investigators had suspected, it was filled with items stolen from the men who had been found dead throughout Central Florida.

A check of area pawn shops revealed that Richard Mallory's 35mm camera and radar detector had been pawned for $30 at the O.K. Pawn Shop. The items had been sold and police were attempting to locate the owners. At the same shop, the diamond nugget ring that had been stolen from the body of Walter Gino Antonio was recovered. All items had been pawned under the name of Cammie Greene.

Although the police had found Lee, they were frustrated in their attempts to locate Tyria Moore. For several days following Lee's arrest, they maintained constant surveillance at bin G of Jack's Mini-Warehouse, hoping to flush out the woman they considered to be Lee's partner in crime. The press pronounced the two women an updated version of "Thelma and Louise."

Learning of Lee's arrest, Ty fled from her parents' home and went into hiding at her sister's in Scranton, Pennsylvania. It was there that Major Dan Henry of Marion County Sheriff's Department found her. In her possession were, among other things, a briefcase and clock radio identified as the property of Charles Humphreys, Lee's fifth victim.

Henry checked Ty into a local motel and summoned Bruce Munster to interview her.

The offers made by the investigators to Tyria Moore, and exactly what transpired in that motel room, may never be known. In the end, the woman who had known about the death of Richard Mallory for more than a year was not charged. She was not granted immunity and she did not plea bargain. She did agree to testify against Lee Wuornos at trial and it was rumored she signed a contract with Munster, Henry, and Binegar to sell her story, along with theirs, for a television movie.

Munster and Henry brought Ty back to Florida, where they kept her in a motel room under twenty-four-hour surveillance. As part of the deal she had made with them, she was to persuade Lee to confess.

Ty sent a note to Lee at Volusia County Branch Jail requesting that she call her collect at the motel. Over four days, Ty had eleven telephone conversations with Lee. Excerpts follow:

Operator: We have a collect call to Room 160 from Lee.

Moore: Uh, yes, go ahead.

Wuornos: Hey, Ty?

Moore: Yeah.

Wuornos: What are you doin'?

Moore: Nothin'. What the hell are you doin'?

Wuornos: Nothing. I'm sitting here in jail.

Moore: Yeah, that's what I heard.

Wuornos: How...what are you doin' down here?

Moore: I came down here to see what the hell's happenin'.

Wuornos: Everything's copasetic. I'm in here for a...a...vi...uh...

con...carryin' a concealed weapon back in '86...and a traffic ticket.

Moore: Really?

Wuornos: Uh huh.

Moore: 'Cause there's been officials up at my parents' house askin' some questions.

Wuornos: Uh oh.

Moore: And I'm gettin' scared.

Wuornos: Hmmm. Well, you know, I don't think there should be anything to worry about.

Moore: Well, I'm pretty damn worried.

Wuornos: I'm not gonna let you get in trouble.

Moore: That's good.

Wuornos: But I tell you what. I would die for you.

Moore: Would you?

Wuornos: Yes, I would. That's the truth. I'll gladly die for you. And I'll just wait to see you on the other side. But you didn't do anything.

Wuornos: Are you really by yourself?

Moore: Yes, I really am.

Wuornos: Aw, I'm so proud you work in a factory.... What do you make?

Moore: Buckets.

Wuornos: Is it...is it boring?

Moore: No, not really.

Wuornos: Good. How much you makin' an hour?

Moore: Time goes by pretty fast. $4.55.

Wuornos: Oh, that's cool. Good. I'm so happy for you. When I get this thing cleared out, I can't wait to get outta here and get me another job and everything.

Moore: I know.

Wuornos: It really is mistaken identity. I'm tellin' you it is. I know it is. And I know it's one of those girls or somebody at work must have said, Hey, those look like...that looks like Lee and Ty and everything else, you know.

Wuornos: God, Ty, I miss ya so much. I'm sorry that, you know, I knew that...we couldn't pay the rent no more and everything. We had to...that you had...it would...it was best for you to go back up and get...'cause I knew, I told ya if you go up you'd find a job in a heartbeat...and I was thinkin' about goin'...gettin' up there but I said, shit, it's snowin' and stuff and there's no sense in me goin' up there in the snow and everything when I didn't really have any real good, you know, help or anything like that.

Moore: They're comin' after me. I know they are.

Wuornos: No, they're not. How do you know that?

Moore: They've got to. Why are they askin' so many questions then?

Wuornos: Honey, listen...do what you gotta do, okay?

Moore: I'm gonna have to because I'm not goin' to jail for somethin' that you did. This isn't fair. My family is a nervous wreck up there. My mom has been callin' me all the time. She doesn't know what the hell is goin' on.

Wuornos: I...listen, you didn't do anything and I'm...I will definitely let them know that, okay?

Moore: You evidently don't love me anymore. You don't trust me or anything.   I mean, you're gonna let me get in trouble for somethin' I didn't do.

Wuornos: Tyria, I said, I'm NOT. Listen. Quit cryin' and listen.

Moore: I can't help it. I'm scared shitless.

Wuornos: I love you. I really do. I love you a lot.

Moore: I don't know whether I should keep on livin' or if I should. . .

Wuornos: I'm not gonna let you go to jail. Listen, if I have to confess, I will.

Moore: Lee, why in the hell did you do this?

Wuornos: I don't know. Listen, did you come down here to talk to some detectives?

Moore: No. I came down here by myself. Just why in the hell did you do it?

Wuornos: Ty, listen to me. I don't know what to say, but all I can say is self-defense.

Wuornos: Don't worry. They'll find out it was a solo person, and I'll just tell them that, okay?

Moore: Okay.

Wuornos: And you'll be scot-free. You didn't do anything. All you did was work, eat, and sleep. You never were around.

Moore: But, Lee, I knew for a year about the first one, at least. I mean, that's a hell of a long time.

Wuornos: I don't know. I think that you didn't know. I think that I pretty much left you out of that.

Moore: No, you didn't. You came right out and told me about that one, and then I saw it on the news.

Wuornos: Ty, what do you wanna do? Go to prison?

Wuornos: Tell 'em everything. Although. . .it. . .I told you everything just before you left. You were thinking about turning me in.

Moore: When you did it the first time, I should've said somethin' and. . .

Wuornos: Well, you were confused and scared, Ty.

Moore: I know I was.

Wuornos: You're not the one and I'm not gonna let you go down on something you didn't do. I love you too much to do that. I love you more than...I love you right next to God.

Wuornos: You know what? I'm gonna tell you somethin'.

Moore: What?

Wuornos: When I die, my spirit's gonna follow you and I'm gonna keep you out of trouble and shit and if you get in an accident, I'll save your life and everything else. I'll be watchin' you.

Wuornos: I probably won't live long, but I don't care. Hey, by the way, I'm gonna go down in history.

Moore: What a way to go down in history.

Wuornos: No, I'm just sayin...if I ever write a book, I'm gonna have ...give you the money. I don't know. I just...let me tell you why I did it, alright?

Moore: Mmm.

Wuornos: Because I'm so...so fuckin' in love with you, that I was so worried about us not havin' an apartment and shit, I was scared that we were gonna lose our place, believin' that we wouldn't be together. I know it sounds crazy, but it's the truth.

Wuornos: ...I just hope you find somebody that loves you as much as I do. I don't want you to live alone all the rest of your life. You're a good person.

Moore: After you, I may live by myself for the rest of my life.

Wuornos: Ty, I don't want them messin' with you. You go first and then I'll tell 'em. Okay? I'd rather have you with your parents. Alrighty?

Wuornos: ...I just wish...I never went...met Toni. 'Cause Toni turned me into a lesbian....then I fucked up because I... see, when I love somebody I love 'em all the way and I love 'em with all my heart and all my soul and all my mind. And I'll do anything. I'll go nuts.

Moore: . . . You turned me against everybody. I won't trust a person for the rest of my life.

Wuornos: . . . I love you very much.

Moore: I know that.

Wuornos: Will you get over me?

Moore: Yeah. . . . I don't think it'll be any problem at all.

Wuornos: Okay. I'm sorry. I know this hurts. It is hurting you a lot. It hurts me because I don't have a family and I'm thinkin' about you. And you got a family and you're thinkin' about your family. I know. I wish I had you so I could hold you and hug you and kiss you and tell you how much I'm sorry. Here is a kiss.

Wuornos: Okay, I'm gonna eventually confess. What time do you check out? There's a tap on the phone.

Moore: Eleven . . . really?

Wuornos: Yep.

Moore: I didn't even hear it.

Wuornos: I heard a little tick.

Moore: Well, I'm getting ready to leave so if you wanna go ahead and get it over with, go for it.

"I was sure it was being taped," Lee said later. "The way she was talking. I felt it. The way she was able to come back to Florida so quickly. She was staying in a motel for fifty dollars a night. Where'd she get fifty dollars a night? But she kept crying, 'They're going to destroy me. I might as well kill myself. I need you to talk to the cops so they'll leave me alone.' So I went and told the police that she had nothing to do with the crimes. But I also told them thirty-seven times that it was in self-defense."

Marjorie Bertolani is a jail officer at the Volusia County Branch Jail who

befriended Lee Wuornos during that period. In her deposition, she recalled her conversations with Lee.

"What did she inform you?"

"I told my corporal, you know, that Ms. Wuornos wanted to speak to
me. She looked really upset. So, Corporal Cresta let me inside the block.
When I got into the sally port she had gone to the telephone. She signaled
for me to come in. I went over to a couple of the other girls that were by a
table. Ms. Wuornos was on the telephone. She was very upset...

"I was going to go ahead and leave again and Ms. Wuornos got off
the phone and signaled for me to come over to the table. And I sat down
with her at the day room table. She was sobbing. She was very, very upset. She asked me if I—she said she had done something terrible, and she
wanted to get something off her chest. She asked me if I was a Christian.
I told her, yes, I was....

"She proceeded to tell me that she had done some bad things. And
she was one of the people that was wanted on these murders. And I just
kind of—I really didn't know that much about the case. I knew she was
our mystery guest, you know. We just treat them like anybody else.

"She told me she had this lover named Tessie. She had nothing to do
with the murders. And they had gotten drunk one night, and she had
said something to this girl, and that she wanted to confess. And I asked
her if she had an attorney. She said, 'No.' I said, 'Well, I suggest you get
yourself one.' I told her, 'You know, anything that you said to me I have
to tell it to my supervisors.'

"She said, 'Well, I wanted to get it off my chest,' and she would speak
to anybody, investigators, police, anybody. She said she wanted to go to
heaven. She was afraid she wouldn't go to heaven. That's why she was
telling me. That's why she wanted to confess to someone.

"What shift were you working that day?"

"Eight to four shift."

"This occurred at what time?"

"This was about ten o'clock."

"In the morning?"

"Yes, sir."

"Had she, to your knowledge, up to that point been pulled from her
cell and taken to any other area of the jail?"

"You mean like to be questioned or something?"

"Yes."

"No, not at all. Nobody bothered her at all."

"Was she, to your knowledge, taken later that day?"

"Yes, she was."

"The block that she was in, they have a telephone inside that area?"

"Yes, they do."

"And they can make collect calls out of there?"

"Yes, sir. She was trying to get ahold of this Tessie. I don't believe she got ahold of her that day. She was really upset. I don't know who else she had called."

"You're saying that she was visibly upset. Was she crying?"

"Yes, she was sobbing."

"For longer than just a brief moment?"

"The whole time I was at the table she was. She asked me what I would do. I said, 'I'd ask for forgiveness, you know. I'd forgive myself.' Because she was really very, very upset. Of course, anybody that upset we really watch for suicidal tendencies."

"Her emotional state was enough to at least concern you?"

"Yes, it was. She told me she had killed six, not ten."

"Where did the figure ten come from?"

"I have no idea, sir. She said, 'I killed six. I did not kill ten.'"

"Did you at any point in time during that contact with her—you're familiar with Miranda warnings?"

"Yes, sir."

"Did you inform her of those warnings?"

"I just told her she had the right to counsel before she even, you know. After she had said—I said, 'Well, you should have an attorney. You should be telling this to an attorney.' She said she wanted to get it off her chest, and she would talk to anyone. She said, 'I'll talk to investigators, I'll talk to detectives. I want to get it off my chest. I want to go to heaven,' she kept saying."

"Did she describe any conversations she may have had recently with this Tessie?"

"Only that she loved her very much, and that she was a Christian and goes to church a lot, and had nothing to do with it, and really hated to see her go through any of this; and she'd probably never talk to me again. Her words."

"In talking about this situation, wanting to talk to someone, based on what she was telling you, why did she seem to want to get this off her chest?"

"Because she said she was a Christian. She said she had really studied the Bible before. She wanted to go to heaven. She was afraid she was not going to go to heaven. She said they're going to give me the electric chair."

"Did she mention anything about wanting to protect this Tessie?"

"No. She said she had nothing to do with it. She had told her about something in one of these episodes that she had had. She was drunk, in a drunken state, and she had confessed this. And Tessie really didn't know anything about it."

"Did it seem important to her to want to make sure people knew that Tessie didn't have anything to do with it?"

"Not really. It was more like she wanted to go to heaven. She was more worried about that."

Shortly after 10 a.m., on January 16, 1991, Lee arranged to talk to investigators Lawrence Horzepa of Volusia County and Bruce Munster of Marion County. Her conversation was both video and audio recorded. She had to tell them that Tyria Moore was innocent. And if she confessed, maybe she would go to heaven.

Advised by the two investigators that she had the right to counsel ("If you want an attorney to be present at this time or any time hereafter you are entitled to such counsel"), Lee requested an attorney, though it seemed of little importance to her. ("What's an attorney gonna do? I know what I did. I'm confessing what I did and go ahead and put the electric chair to me.") In the presence of Assistant Public Defender Michael O'Neill she confessed to the murders of Richard Mallory, David Spears, Charles Carskaddon, Peter Siems, Troy Burress, Walter Gino Antonio and Charles Humphreys.

The investigators seemed kind. ("I wish to go ahead and talk with you and get this over with and let you people know what really happened and let you know that Ty is not involved, at all.") They supplied her with cigarettes, coffee and a warm jacket in the chilly office and Lee's confession rushed out in a torrent. She had to protect Ty, and perhaps, if she explained what had happened to her in the woods, these people would understand why it had been necessary for her to kill and she could make her peace with God.

"I think this is the best thing for me to do and I don't want my girlfriend in trouble 'cause she didn't do anything. Even if she even knew, most of the times I would tell her shit off the wall when I'm drunk. I think when I'm drunk, I get crazy. And if I told her something I told her like...okay, 'cause remember the guy with the red car...carpet? The guy that was found under the red carpet on 90...uh, U.S. 1? That was me. Okay, I told her, I said, I came home and I said, 'I was ridin' my bicycle and I stopped in the woods and dropped it off and I found a guy under a carpet.' And I told her that. She said, 'What!' And I said I found a guy underneath a carpet. Then later on, when I was really drunk, and it's like truth serum or something, I told her I killed him. But I don't know if she could believe it or not. But she was pretty much like, 'No, you're kidding.' And I was, 'Yeah, I did.' But then I don't...can't say that I said that I really meant it 'cause I don't remember 'cause I'd be drunk but I'd be tellin' her stuff and she didn't...wouldn't want to believe it, see. Uh...so, what I'm saying is that even though I might have said somethin' to her, she really didn't know the truth. She's very innocent. Really. She's not...look at Casa Del Mar. Tyria Moore's her name, she worked there all the damn time, all the time all this stuff was happening and when I...the last person that got hurt, she was up in Ohio. She is innocent. It was me. I can tell ya...blow by blow, as much as I can, everything. I'm bein' as honest as I can be. And she's...I told her if anybody comes to talk to you, just be as honest as you can be. Tell 'em that I told you or anything, 'cause you are very innocent of this stuff and I don't want you to get in trouble for it 'cause you didn't do anything. I may have told you stuff when I was drunk and everything else, but you didn't know if you believed me or not because...and she said, 'But I...I remember you takin' a car and we were movin' our stuff.' I said, 'I know, but remember when I told you I was borrowin' it?' She said, 'No, I don't remember that.' I said, But...I...and...but...I don't know. It's...all I can say is I know that she did...she...she's innocent. That's what I'm saying. "She's not partake...she did not partake in ANY of this. And ...if...only thing that she would partake in anything, it would be knowing...it would be my lips saying to her something and she didn't know if she could believe me or not, is what I'm saying. See, she was... she was very innocent.

"She didn't do anything. All I know is...and when the car got wrecked...and they were looking for the two girls...that was me and her in that wreck. Now, she said she'll tell you that she was drivin'. She was drivin', but she did not know that this car belonged to a murdered victim. I told her I was borrowin' it from a friend. And then when we wrecked, after we wrecked, I told her, I said, 'Man, we gotta get outta here.' She said, 'Why?' you know. And I said, 'Because this is the car of a murdered guy.' And she said, 'What!' And that's why we hauled ass. She was scared shitless and I don't blame her. She was innocent. I mean she's a sweet, kind person. She didn't...and then she was scared shitless. And then she started hatin' my guts and wantin' to leave and everything. But, then again, she didn't know if she could believe it or not and then she heard about it on the news and then she still wondered what to do. She was my lover. And she loved me and I loved her. And she loved me a lot and she just didn't know how to part...with this...you know. We really were lovers. I loved her to the max. And the only reason I'm confessin', too, is because I loved her so much, I don't want to get her in trouble because she's not the one. I am the one. But I don't think that half the time she believed anything I said 'cause, if you knew me as a person straight, I'm a good person. And she knows me. I'm a very kind person, but when I get drunk, I do stupid things. And if you're a hooker, and you get somebody who starts messin' with you, then you get pissed off. And I'm sorry 'cause I been raped nine times in life. And I wasn't about to let somebody skip out on my money that I'm working for and I think is very...kinda clean, 'cause I used rubbers all the time. And I wasn't about to let somebody rape me either. So when they got really huffy with me, which I had gone through over 250,000 men, and they got (inaudible) I got six guys. That's because they got rough with me and I defended myself. So, that's...I just want to clear this...I want to get this all out in the open. I wanna clear it and I wanna clear my girlfriend because she's not involved. She is very innocent. She's not a witness. She didn't see anything happen. All I did was talk...to her, and she's willing to tell you what she knows. I just got done talkin' to her. What she knows what I said to her when I was drunk as shit all the time. Most of the time I was drunk. 'Cause I'll admit, I'm an alcoholic. I mean twenty-four hours a day I was drunk. I'd sleep a little, get up and drink some more. I just...I have to say it, that I killed 'em because they got violent with me and I decided to defend myself. I wasn't gonna let 'em beat the shit outta me or kill me, either. And I'm sure if they found out I had a weapon on me, which was very easy to find, 'cause I always had it in plain view where I could grab it quick, and if after the fightin' they found it, they would've shot me. So I just shot them. I really can't believe I'm in here tellin' you guys this. But I'm glad because I feel very guilty. Uh...I don't think I should live. I think I should die. I'm not gonna commit suicide. I'm gonna get right with the Lord and live a normal life until I'm to die or I die a normal death, but I don't think I'm...I should live, I think I should die because I killed all those people. Well, I think it was self defense, myself, but no one can judge that but God. 'Cause nobody was there but me."

For more than three hours, with no thought of the consequences, and against the continuing advice of her attorney, Lee told the three men over and over again why she had done what she did.

"I know what I did. I'm confessing what I did and go ahead and put the electric chair to me. I should never done it. See, most of the time I was drunk as hell and I was a professional hooker and these guys would take my offer. I'd give 'em a little shit sometimes, you know, and so when they started gettin' rough with me, I went...I just like opened up and fired at 'em. Then I thought to myself, why are you givin' me such hell for when I just...I'm just tryin' to make my money...and you're givin' me a hassle....

"I've dealt with a hundred thousand guys. But these guys are the only guys that gave me a problem and they started givin' me a problem just this year...the year that went by. So I, at the time I was stayin' with some guy and I noticed he had some guns and I ripped off his .22, a nine-shot deal...So when I'd get a hassle, if the person'd give me my money and I...I wouldn't do nothin' to 'em. But if the person ga...gave me my money and then started hasslin' me, that's when I started takin' retaliation....I just wish I never would've done this shit. I wish I never woulda got that gun. I wish to God, I never was a hooker. And I just wish I never woulda done what I did. I still have to say to myself, I still say that it was in self defense....

"Really inside, right inside me, I'm a good person. But when I get drunk, like I said, I'd be drinkin' with these guys and...and when they start messin' with me, I wouldn't tou...I would never hurt nobody. But if they messed with me, then I would. I'd just...I have to say I was...I'd get just as violent as they would get on me...to try to protect myself."

On the previous day, Tyria Moore had appeared before that same camera. Her testimony, along with Lee's, led police to the .22 handgun which was recovered from the brackish water of Rose Bay, a half mile from The Last Resort.

Corrections Officer Susan Hanson was on duty two days later, assigned to keep an eye on the jail's celebrity inmate, Lee Wuornos. Through a panel of glass, she watched Lee in her cell, where she sat on her cot with her foot propped on the toilet, thumbing through a pile of newspaper articles which grew larger each day.

"Listen to this," Lee said to Hanson. "They say here, 'This woman is a killer who robs, not a robber who kills.' That's...Sure, I shot them, but it was self-defense."

Hanson recalls that Lee said she had been raped many times "and I just got sick of it....If I didn't kill all those guys, I would have been raped a total of twenty times maybe. Or killed. You never know. But I got them first.

"...I figured that at least I was doing some good killing these guys. 'Cause if I didn't kill them, they would have hurt someone else," Lee told Hanson.

"I shouldn't be telling you any of this," she continued, "but...get this, I had these two guys say they were cops, or at least they flashed their badges at me. They picked me up and wanted sex but didn't want to pay. Said if I didn't they'd turn me in. One grabbed my hair and pushed me towards his (penis). We really started fighting then.

"So I killed them," she shrugged. "Afterwards I looked at their badges and one was a reservist cop or something and the other worked for like the IRS."

Walter Gino Antonio was a Brevard County Reserve Deputy. Charles Humphreys worked as a supervisor for the Florida Department of Health and Rehabilitative Services, referred to as HRS.

"I had lots of guys, maybe ten to twelve a day," Lee continued. "I could have killed all of them, but I didn't want to. I'm really just a nice person. I'm describing a normal day to you here, but a killing day would be just about the same. On a normal day we would just do it by the side of the road if they just wanted (oral sex) or behind a building or maybe just off the road in the woods if they wanted it all.

"On a killing day those guys always wanted to go way, way back in the woods. Now I know why they did it; they were gonna hurt me."

"She was laughing a lot when she talked to me," Officer Hanson says. "When she would talk about, specifically, how she shot the guy, the one guy with the .45, she just stood there. She was very—sometimes she would laugh, sometimes she was calm in explaining this. Other times she would just get very excited. She was never sad in any way. Never once did she say I'm upset about this. She just said if I hadn't killed him, he'd kill other people."

Officer Hanson had been told not to talk to the inmate, but to document everything she said.

"I figured if these guys lived, and I got fried for attempted murder," Lee told Hanson, "I thought fuck it, I might as well get fried for murder instead."

At one point, Hanson recalls, the prison medic came by to check on Lee, who had been given some medication for her nerves.

"I never really saw her down. She was always jovial," he recalled.

Before the doctor left, Lee revealed to him and to Officer Hanson that she had "done 250,000 men in the last nine years."

"We kind of looked at her a little strange for that," said Hanson. "He [the doctor] just kind of walked away after that. And she sat down and began reading the paper again."

Chapter Eight

L ee Wuornos was not the only one reading the papers.
Reporters across the nation were picking up on the story of a woman who killed men. This was better than the old Black Widow cliche. The crimes had nothing to do with passion. Lee Wuornos did not know the men she killed and the manner in which she operated earned her the title of "the first female serial killer."

Everyone had an opinion.

"She was a predator," said Sgt. Bruce Munster. "She sought strangers and killed them."

Not so, said Alexander Schauss, forensic researcher from Seattle, Washington. Lee Wuornos had sex with eight to ten men a day. If she were a true serial killer, she would have killed more men, he said. She could not have resisted the temptation.

"Because of the confusion in sexual identity," offered Dr. Kathy Morall, a Denver forensic psychiatrist, "you have a person making an effort to put herself in the place of a male, physically and mentally. She would not truly represent a female serial killer. She would be an aberrant female killer."

"Serial killers have a compulsion to seek out a certain kind of victim, and they kill for pleasure," said Lee's attorney, Tricia Jenkins. "I sense she's not that way."

"I don't buy it for a second," said Schauss of the serial label. "She's not like Ted Bundy, who thinks his crime out ahead of time, who has a specific place he goes to do the violence, then molests them, then disposes of them.

"This is different. There's a tremendous element of randomness in her behavior."

Captain Tom Cronin of the Chicago Police Department is one of twenty-eight FBI-trained profilers assigned to detect serial killers. There are two distinct types of serial killers, he said: organized offenders and disorganized offenders.

Cronin described the disorganized offender as an individual who doesn't fit in well with society and spends a great deal of time fantasizing. These fantasies will develop sexual aspects, although he or she is sexually ignorant.

This offender is a loner who operates at night, he said, and is characterized as nice, quiet, shy, polite. He or she does not plan ahead and is apt to kill on the spur of the moment.

The organized offender is a predator who, during formative years, will exhibit chronic behavior problems and truancy and suspensions from school, Cronin continued.

As an adult, he or she will be unable to sustain consistent work patterns and will fail consistently to meet financial obligations. This person is a chronic liar, does not experience guilt, and if there is a problem, will blame others for it. He or she copes with the daily stresses of life by abusing people, which increases feelings of importance.

The organized offender will take souvenirs in order to relive the violence of the act, and will carry a "murder kit" made up of tools for killing. Although Lee Wuornos exhibits some characteristics from both categories, she fits neither.

Former FBI agent Robert Ressler, author of *Sexual Homicide Patterns and Motives*, said: "What you have to look for in a true serial killer is a predator, one who for his own motives is hunting down people with murder in mind. . . . When there is violence involving women, it's usually in the home, with husbands and boyfriends. It's a close-in, personal crime.

"If Wuornos is said to be a serial killer," Ressler added, "we have to rewrite the rules. With women the base may be hatred, mental disorder, even monetary reasons—there could be a number of possibilities."

"I had no intentions of killing anybody," Lee had told the investigators. "I told you I had dealt with people, maybe five, eight maybe ten people in the same day, sexually or not sexually, see, maybe the guy was interested and he'd give me thirty bucks and I'd give him head, you know, and I'd get my money and then I'd go my way . . . merry way and then try to go to the next car. And then some cars would pick me up and they'd say, 'No, I'm not interested. Thanks anyway.' And I'd say, 'Okay, have a nice day.' And I'd go. So, no, there was no . . . it wasn't intentional killing. It wasn't just kill somebody. It was because they physically attacked me. Or tryin' to get free ass because they said they were a cop or something, which I didn't think they were."

Serial killer or not, the story of Lee Wuornos repulsed and enthralled the nation, and media people followed it to its source—Daytona Beach.

The frenzy began with the distribution of the composite sketches of the two women suspected of murdering seven men along Florida highways.

According to Sgt. Jarvis, producers, reporters and journalists of all kind began calling Capt. Steve A. Binegar, the Criminal Investigation Division commander for the Sheriff's Office in Ocala.

"What [Binegar] told me was, 'We can't all be talking about this. We need one person to take care of the media, and that's going to be me,'" Jarvis recalls.

Before long, Jarvis found himself removed from any visible areas of the case. Binegar, Henry and Munster seemed to have taken the helm.

By the time Lee was arrested, "fifty, maybe a hundred" calls from the media were coming into Binegar's office, according to Dan Henry. "They'd say, 'Would you be interested in a contract where I could work with you more closely?' I'd say, 'Look, if you're here from the media in the news standpoint, I'll give you what's current, and if it's something beyond that, then you can call Rob Bradshaw.'"

As it happened, D. Robert "Rob" Bradshaw, an Ocala personal injury lawyer, was legal adviser to the sheriff's office. He was also a close friend to Binegar, Henry and Munster.

Immediately after Wuornos was charged with the first-degree murder of Richard Mallory, Jarvis says Binegar removed him from the case, demoting him from major crimes to property crimes, and replacing him with Munster.

But media involvement in the story of Lee Wuornos started even before her arrest.

Conflicting stories attend the involvement of Jackie Giroux, glamorous blond Hollywood-starlet-turned producer, head of Twisted Productions in Studio City, California.

Twice married, once to actor Steve Railsback, Jackie had begun her production company in 1985. Since then, she had produced a handful of movies, some of which she had also written. She was particularly interested in women's stories and had recently discussed producing a low-budget film for Lone Star Studios.

The media reported that Jackie, during a visit to her parents' home in Ocala, learned that her mother, Alva Lusky, had spotted a blond woman who looked exactly like the widely-distributed composite in a supermarket prior to her arrest. Thinking of her daughter, Alva handed Jackie's card to the woman and explained that Jackie would be interested in her story.

"Mother told me she just took the card and smiled," Jackie reportedly told the press.

Alva then notified the police that she had seen one of the two women she felt they were looking for. By the time they followed the lead, she had disappeared.

In her deposition, Jackie's account differs.

"It was in December...around the ninth. I had driven from Orlando. I was doing some business in Orlando, Florida. I drove up to Ocala, Florida. And my mother, who resides in Silver Springs, Florida, said to me, 'You're not going to believe this story.'

"I said, 'What story is that?' And she said, 'I saw a female suspect in a Winn-Dixie store.' And I said, 'Well, what kind of female suspect?' And she said, 'Well, there are supposed to be two of them and they may be killing elderly men throughout the state of Florida.' And I said, 'Well, tell me about this.' And she said, 'I'll show you an article.'

"And she showed me one of the Florida newspapers and a composite drawing of two women.

"And I said, 'Well, I don't think women normally go out and kill without good cause.' And I said, 'I'd like to find out what their side of the story is.' And I said, 'I'd like to know how to do this.' My mother said, 'I don't know how to do this.'

"So I started driving around in December leaving cards with the Sportman's Lodge and gas station attendants and so forth asking if anyone saw these women to please have them contact me. Of course no one did.

"Then it came out in the newspaper in January that Miss Aileen Wuornos had been arrested and that she was in Volusia County. And I called the jail first. And they said I'd have to talk to Ray Cass, who wasn't there."

While Jackie was in the processing of faxing information to Cass, he called her.

After Lee's arrest, two Volusia County assistant public defenders, Raymond Cass and Donald Jacobsen, were assigned to represent her. After talking to Jackie, Cass contacted Russell Armstrong, who had represented Lee in 1981. Jackelyn Giroux, he told Armstrong, wanted the rights to tell Lee's story.

Armstrong recalled that he received a phone call from Cass asking if he would handle any media contacts. As Lee's criminal attorney, Cass was ethically unable to do so.

"I agreed to represent Lee in this respect," said Armstrong. "And so I became involved in the contract with Lee and Jackelyn Giroux. There is a German company interested in this production, but only if Lee gets the death penalty. I try not to think of it as blood money," he said, shifting uncomfortably in his chair.

Ten days after Lee's arrest, Armstrong brought her a contract for her life story initiated by Jackelyn Giroux. The contract required the signatures of Lee, Giroux and Armstrong. It offered no dates and no percentages, only a series of loosely strung promises hinging on money from investors.

Shortly after signing the contract, which Jackelyn refers to as a "deal memo," Armstrong received a scalding letter from the Florida Attorney General, Robert A. Butterworth:

"This office has been advised that your client, Ms. Aileen Wuornos, has been arrested and charged with at least two murders and that you represent her in these cases. It has come to our attention that Ms. Wuornos apparently has entered into a contract or contracts with a filmmaking enterprise to tell her story.

"Please be advised that in the event Ms. Wuornos is convicted of these felonies or any additional felonies, it would be the intention of the State of Florida to file a lien against all royalties, commissions or any other thing of value payable to her or her assigns from any literary, cinematic or other account of her life story or the crime for which she may be convicted.

"The State of Florida hereby gives notice that it is against public policy for someone to profit from her own crime and that this lien will be rigorously enforced pursuant to Section 944.512, Florida Statutes. You are further notified that any individual or corporation who holds monies or other items of value derived from any account of this story holds these assets in constructive trust for the State of Florida and will be held accountable to the State."

Said Armstrong: "I went to the state's attorney and explained to him that I was only serving as Ms. Wuornos' civil attorney and that I had nothing to do with the criminal charges against her. I know nothing about the murders."

Cass and Jackie received similar letters and Cass told the press: "I had nothing to do with any sort of contract because we're prohibited from doing anything like that. I tried to put as much distance between that and myself as I could."

Circuit Judge Gayle Graziano rebuked Cass from the bench during a subsequent hearing: "He should not have brought in another attorney. He should not have acted as broker for the attorney. There's the appearance of impropriety in that appearance of brokering."

In a lengthy letter to Judge Graziano, Arlene Pralle, the woman soon to become the most important person in Lee Wuornos' life, attempted to explain the unethical approach taken by Cass and Armstrong to the Wuornos contract.

"I telephoned your office this morning before you left for the Wuornos hearing, but you were unavailable," she wrote. "My husband and I are friends of Aileen Wuornos.

"In light of the hearings and the testimony presented, I feel compelled to let you know the information we have found out. Yesterday afternoon I had my first conversation with Jackelyn Giroux. She informed me that Russell Armstrong had contacted her in California telling her that he knew someone he felt she (Jackelyn) would be interested in. He mentioned the possibilities of a bestselling book and movie. He then told her about Aileen. She flew to Daytona Beach and remained here a week while Russell Armstrong and Raymond Cass tried to get her in to see Aileen. Finally Raymond Cass told her the best he could do was set up a telephone interview. She never knew either of these men before January of this year.

"On February 14, 1991, I and a friend of mine went in to see Russell Armstrong. He denied knowing anything about a book and movie deal and said he didn't know who Jackelyn Giroux was!!! When I asked him why he couldn't help me to get visitation privileges with Aileen he told me it was the job of Raymond Cass. When Raymond Cass finally returned my many phone calls (it took him three weeks) I asked him the same question. His answer   that job of getting you on the visiting list is up to Russell Armstrong. When Aileen questioned Cass and Jacobsen about visitation, they told her point blank they hadn't wanted her to see anyone. Yet they told me a totally different story. They truly have given Aileen a terrible time, and I am sure they care only about trying to make money off of her. They do not care about her case or her defense.

"As a contrast, her Public Defenders in Marion County set up an appointment with me here at the farm right after Aileen told them about me. They wanted to make sure I was really who I claimed and that I had no hidden motives in wanting to be her friend. They cared enough about Aileen and her case to spend an entire afternoon with me literally 'checking me out.' Yet neither Cass, Jacobsen or Armstrong would even return my phone calls. Even after Aileen told them about me, still nobody contacted me. I easily could have been a crazy person out to hurt their client, but they never took the time or initiative to follow through and find out.

"These are just some of the highlights concerning this whole mess. I have more to tell you, but it is hard to convey it in a letter.

"Would it be possible to set up an appointment in your Chambers and discuss this further? I have heard many good, positive remarks about you and your fairness in judging cases. I strongly feel the pertinent information I have will be beneficial to you now and down the road. I have physical evidence here right now that I will bring with me. Aileen Wuornos is telling you the total truth concerning Cass, Jacobsen and Armstrong. When you see the papers I have, you will realize it."

It was not the only impropriety pending as a result of media interest.

Simultaneously, Robert Bradshaw, attorney for the sheriff's office, was dealing with inquiries from the entertainment industry. The inquirers were interested in the investigators who had solved the case. They also wondered about Tyria Moore's involvement.

A memo was sent to Brad King, state attorney for the Fifth Judicial Circuit of Florida, from his assistants and Brian Jarvis.

"On January 29, there was a meeting between Bradshaw, Munster and Binegar concerning the offers being received. On January 30, Tyria Moore contacted Bradshaw and asked for him to represent her in negotiations with those interested in the movie version of the case. Moore stated to us that she had received a call from Munster suggesting that if she contacted Bradshaw he could put together a package deal for her and the three deputies that would be worth more money than each person acting alone. She stated that she had contacted Bradshaw the day Munster called, or possibly the next day. Munster acknowledged that he called Moore and gave her Bradshaw's name and explained to Moore what Bradshaw was doing for the deputies, but was uncertain as to the exact discussion, including how much money could be made."

Somewhere along the line Jarvis questioned Munster about the handling of Tyria Moore.

"Munster told me that Tyria was more important as a witness than as a suspect. I believed him," Jarvis added.

When Moore's involvement in the media contract was revealed, Jarvis realized what had happened.

"Isn't it more exciting to have the views of the associate of the killer, who was with the murderer after these murders, before these murders, maybe even during these murders?"

Suddenly Lee Wuornos, yesterday's nobody, was today's star. She basked in the limelight and glowed in its reflection.

"I'm gonna be a millionaire," she told Armstrong. "I'm gonna be more famous than Deidre Hunt."

"It was up to me to tell her that she could not profit from the story of her crimes," says Armstrong. "I told her that she would not even make cigarette money off this story."

Lee told Jackie that she would like her portion of the money to go to Ty.

"I told her she could not do that either," Armstrong recalls. "After all, Ty is a witness for the prosecution."

On January 28, 1991, Lee was indicted for the murder of Richard Mallory. The indictment read:

In that Aileen Carol Wuornos, a/k/a Susan Lynn Blahovec, a/k/a Lori Kristine Grody, a/k/a Cammie Marsh Greene, on or about the first day of December, 1989, within Volusia County, Florida, did then and there unlawfully, from a premeditated design to effect the death of one Richard Mallory, a human being, or while engaged in the perpetration of or attempt to perpetrate robbery, did kill and murder Richard Mallory by shooting him with a firearm, to wit: a handgun.

Counts two and three charged her with armed robbery and possession of a firearm.

By late February, Lee Wuornos had been charged with the murders of David Spears in Citrus County and Charles Humphreys and Troy Burress in Marion County.

And she had become increasingly dissatisfied with her attorneys, Cass and Jacobsen. Her main objection was that they were men. Lee Wuornos wanted a female attorney and would do anything to convince the court that she should be rid of the attorneys currently representing her.

In a hearing before Circuit Judge Graziano on February 28, 1991, Lee made her preference clear:

"I would like to have a new public defender and I would prefer a female if possible because my public defenders that I have, I feel and know for a fact, are not interested in my case at all whatsoever.

"I've also been informed that they are best friends and fishing trips, restaurants and lounges and all that with the state's attorney, John Tanner.

"Before I was indicted, Mr. Cass presented Russell Armstrong to me before—I was—the fifteenth I was—some deal happened where the detectives—and fifteenth, sixteenth, seventeenth—the seventeenth or the eighteenth, Cass—Mr. Cass came over with Russell Armstrong and asked me if I wanted to have a book written about me. The story of my life. And then he asked me if I wanted Armstrong to be my representative.

"And they had me all confused and they were telling me I could maybe even use the money for—when I go to prison, because I might spend life or something like this. 'You might be interested in some income.'

"Well, I didn't know. I found out the contract that Russell Armstrong wrote and signed and Jackelyn Giroux signed, which I signed which I shouldn't have signed—I didn't realize what I was doing—but the contract states that Russell Armstrong will receive all the money and so will Jackelyn Giroux. I will receive nothing. It was the story of my life. It wasn't about criminal—any crime whatsoever.

"And my girlfriend came in to Russell Armstrong with a witness, into Russell Armstrong's office, and Russell Armstrong sat there and said, 'I do not know why Ms. Aileen Wuornos even thinks I had anything to do with the contract. We have not talked to her about anything.'

"I have the contract that proves it.

"And Cass was always talking about books and movies before and after I got indicted, it still kept on going and I don't even want to have anything to do with his associate, because to me they're a clan of people that are just interested in making money. They're not interested in my case. ...Everybody in jail really respects me, likes me. These people do not care about my case."

Judge Graziano listened attentively as Lee explained to her that Cass and Jacobsen did not return her calls, did not communicate with her on a regular basis.

"I will find a way," she told the judge, "because I'm telling you, they're violating my civil rights and they are not caring about my case. They are friends with the state attorney, John Tanner. I am going to find a way. Somehow, some way, no matter how I do it, I'm going to find a new attorney. I know my civil rights. I demand an attorney and I am going to get them."

Judge Graziano addressed Lee: "Ms. Wuornos, this contract that you referred to, do you have that?"

"I was going to take it with me, darn it, and I didn't," Lee frowned. "It's in my room. And I also have Trish Jenkins, the attorney in Ocala, has a copy. My girlfriend has a copy. Her lawyer in Iowa has a copy."

"And you're representing to this court that Mr. Cass had something to do with that," the judge inquired.

"Mr. Cass says he had nothing to do with it. Mr. Cass handed me the piece of paper with Jackelyn Giroux and said, 'This is my personal friend that is in movie productions and if you'd like to have some kind of income to help you out in case you spend life in prison.' And he said, 'You don't want the electric chair. You want life, don't you?'

"And he handed me the piece of paper. I looked at it and then I gave it back to him and I said, 'Yeah, well, I guess if I did happen to get life, wouldn't that be nice to have money in prison to support myself.' Because I don't have no family. I don't have no mother, no father, no brother, no sister, nothing.

"So, he said, 'Well, do you want me to hand this piece of paper to Russell Armstrong and get him right on it and work on the contract, so we can get this book written?' I didn't know what was happening. I was too confused. And this was only a couple of days after I had talked to the detectives. My head was swimming and there's a lot of—yeah."

That afternoon, the day before her thirty-fifth birthday, Lee Wuornos received a gift from the court. Tricia Jenkins, public defender in Marion County, who was already defending Lee against the murder charges there and in Citrus County, was assigned to handle her case in Volusia County as well.

Tricia Jenkins had questions: "Is this movie deal the reason Moore was not charged? She certainly could have been charged as accessory after the fact, at the minimum. Was this deal Moore's motive for testifying against my client?"

Asked if he were glad to be off the case, Cass replied, "Indeed, I certainly am."

There were rumors that inside Volusia County Branch Jail, Lee Wuornos had encountered Virginia Larzelere, a mysterious seductress charged, along with her teenage son, with murdering her husband. Like Lee, Virginia was awaiting trial and the two were seen on several occasions talking together. Other rumors from "inside" centered on Lee's desire to reap more publicity than Virginia. She had no intention of relinquishing the limelight.

Within weeks, the fickle spotlight shifted from Lee. Not to another inmate, but, instead, to a tiny wisp of a woman named Arlene Pralle, who rapidly became Lee's friend, confidante, support and mentor. To the outside world, she was a groupie and probably a lesbian. To Lee, she was the love that had always eluded her.

II

Is This You, Lord?

I was a stranger, and ye took me in:
Naked and ye clothed me:
I was sick and ye visited me:
I was in prison and ye came unto me.

St. Matthew XXV:35

Chapter Nine

Arlene Pralle never read newspapers or watched television news. Her world was bordered by the wooden fences of her horse farm, and she was content to read the Bible, her source of inspiration and comfort. She became a born-again Christian in the late 1970s and saw life and those with whom she interacted as "God's plan."

On January 10, 1991, the day after Lee's arrest, Arlene and her husband, Robert, had spent long hours in the Gainesville hospital, attending to her eighty-year-old father, Palmer Monte, whose Christmas visit from New York had ended abruptly when he collapsed at the Pralle home. After several weeks in the hospital, it was determined that the only hope of saving his life lay in open heart surgery, and the day of surgery seemed endless to the Pralles.

Several months earlier, the diminutive Arlene, chestnut-haired and hazel-eyed, and Robert, a field video engineer, had moved their horse-farm from chilly Iowa to sunny Florida.

"Robert said he would never move to Florida," Arlene recalled, "but finally he told me to go and look around."

Robert's decision to move began during the previous midwest winter when Arlene, in order to nurse a dying filly, Chrissy, moved into the cold, drafty horse barn.

She spent days attending Chrissy, but, in spite of her diligence, the horse died and Arlene developed pneumonia.

"After that, I just could not stand the cold anymore," she said.

The very day that Arlene began to make the rounds of real estate agents, a thirty-five acre horse farm, which was to be dubbed Maranatha, Syriac for "The Lord Cometh", came on the market.

"I saw the farm on the realtor's computer before it was even published," Arlene said. "I knew that farm was meant for us, but I looked at a number of them because I didn't want to put God in a box."

Within a few weeks, Robert came to Florida, looked at the farm and, with financial help from Arlene's father, bought it. On October 3, 1990, the farm was theirs. In March of that year, Arlene's mother had died. In December, her father had travelled alone to Florida to spend Christmas with his only child.

It was pure coincidence that Arlene picked up the Gainesville paper in early January 1991, in the waiting room of the Gainesville Hospital. As Arlene would later describe it: "God had a path for my life.

"When I saw Lee's picture, something happened to me," she told reporters. "I knew we were destined to be together."

Arlene and Robert met during their teens in Long Island and dated steadily until Robert married someone else.

"He just wouldn't wait for me," Arlene said. "I was twenty or twenty-one and wasn't ready to get married and he wouldn't wait. I cared a lot. I was devastated. I thought my whole world had ended."

She paused a moment: "Isn't it amazing how people can grow apart?"

In her early twenties, Arlene made her first move to Florida. She and her father thought they could convince her mother to move to the warmer climate if Arlene went there first.

"I was in Largo by myself hoping it would be the catalyst to bring my mother there. I had a job as a real estate secretary and it was so boring, I hated it. The only good thing in my life was the collie I bought to keep me company. And mom refused to move. I lasted two months, but I didn't go home to New York, I went to Connecticut because my mother wouldn't let me keep the collie in the house."

A few years later, Robert's marriage was over and the two of them took up where they left off. They were married soon after and stayed in Connecticut until they decided to move to Vermont and start a horse farm.

"His first marriage had changed Robert a lot," she said. "He put walls up. He started to be more open when Lee first came into our lives, but then he began to depend too much on me and not enough on God. You can't do that.

"Robert likes boring. It's the lifestyle he prefers. I've always been one to like being on the razor's edge. It was through Robert that I became born-again. I thought it was neat to be on the front line combat instead of just a soldier. Sometimes God had to put a bit in my mouth to hold me back. But with Lee, it took me two and one-half weeks before I told God that I would become involved with her. Everyone thinks I just jumped in the water impulsively, but that's not so. At first I rebelled against the idea of becoming involved. I just said, 'For sure, I'm not doing this, God. This can't be from you.' I didn't even give him a chance to say, 'Yes, Arlene, it is.' I just dropped it. Then one day I was out in the tractor, just driving around, when the Holy Spirit came very quietly and it spoke just how I talk when I say things in threes. It said, 'Fine, fine, fine,' very quietly, very gently. 'Don't do this, but how are you going to feel when you read in the *Banner*, Aileen Wuornos committed suicide...found hung in cell.' And then there was a pause and it said, 'And her life I will require at your hand.'

"That was the end. I looked up and said, 'Fine! Fine! Fine! I'll do it!' and I wheeled the tractor around out of the pasture, came back, parked it in front of the little shed, turned it off and said, 'Okay, okay, are you happy?' and I went up to the house and started to compose the letter.

"Two weeks into our relationship, I told Lee this, and she started to cry. I asked her what was wrong and she said, 'When I was in solitary, the day before I got your letter, I already had it all planned out. When they let me out, I was going to hang myself.' "

There could be no children for the Pralles because several years after their marriage, Arlene had a hysterectomy. It did not matter because she had never cared about having children of her own.

"I was adopted, so I wanted to adopt," she said.

But Robert did not share her enthusiasm, so they made no efforts to bring children into their lives.

"We had the critters and they were everything to us," Arlene admitted.

In 1981, while she and Robert were still living in Connecticut, Arlene befriended a woman who told her that her husband was physically abusive to both her and her older son. Arlene offered them her home and for several months the woman and her children lived with the Pralles. At one point, the woman tried to kill herself. Eventually she reconciled with her husband and he moved in. The older boy was so distressed by this that he attempted suicide.

"It got completely out of control," Arlene recalled. "The people stayed on and on. The woman beat me up physically when she discov-

ered that I had hidden a letter written to her by her husband. I had
gotten so wrapped up in their lives that I didn't see how it was affect-
ing me. Eventually, Robert left. He didn't want anything more to do
with me. The marriage was over. I was devastated. I went to stay with
my father, but that didn't work out. I came back to my house for the
purpose of killing myself. And that was when I found out they'd left,
taking all our credit cards, jewelry, and some horse equipment. About
$12,000 in all.

"I was completely at wit's end," said Arlene.

In a suicide attempt, Arlene took pills and was placed in an institution. Robert refused to sign her out.

"It was his revenge for the financial debt we incurred. As a result, my
father had to leave my ailing mother in the middle of the night alone
and drive from New York to Connecticut to get me out of there," she admitted.

For three months after that, Robert and Arlene lived apart, and
"then one day, while I was having a party for some friends, he showed up
on the front porch, with two suitcases in his hands. He asked what I was
doing and I replied 'having a party'. He came in and stayed."

Several years later, the father of the family befriended by Arlene became "born again" and for a brief time they all lived together at the
Pralles' home. The older boy did not want to live with his father and preferred to stay with Arlene.

"I wanted to adopt him," Arlene said, "but my friend wouldn't sign
the necessary papers and he ended up in a foster home. He has never returned to his family."

Maranatha Meadows came to life in Vermont, then moved to Iowa
when Robert was transferred to the Midwest. Shortly before the move
from Iowa to Florida, Arlene's life hit another low. Both her mother and
her best friend died. The illness of her filly, Chrissy, was improperly diagnosed by the local veterinarian. Chrissy's death was followed quickly by
the death of one of her wolves, Rahab, who was killed by a drunken
teenager with a shotgun.

"When we first started the horse farm in Vermont, we didn't have
wolves," she says. "Then a client offered us a wolf pup in exchange for
stud service and I didn't want to lose his business, so I accepted.

"People have a hard time understanding how important the animals
are to Robert and me. They have been our life."

And there was something more. A good friend, for whom Arlene
and Robert mortgaged Maranatha in an effort to rid her of debt, turned
against her.

"Betty almost destroyed me," Arlene shuddered. "She threatened to kill me, and a mutual friend of ours, a psychiatrist, told me I should not take her threat lightly. She would think she was doing the world a favor.

"We had become friends through the horses. In fact, some of my horses are named after her, and I couldn't believe what happened. But, in a way, she prepared me to deal with Lee. She needed the 'poor me' syndrome just as Lee does."

Robert, who shares an apartment with a friend in Chicago, expected to be transferred to Florida. When the transfer didn't come through, he had no choice but to stay where he was. And Arlene had no choice but to run the farm alone.

"When the three moving vans came to Iowa to get me, I felt as though they were a space machine coming to whisk me away," remembered Arlene. "I had packed all by myself, wrapped up the legs of twenty-one horses, gotten them on the vans, the wolves, the chickens. Robert was in Florida with our dog, Kingman, and the three expensive horses. After he left Florida and returned to the Midwest I was all alone. I was warm. I didn't need a snowsuit. Just me and God. I walked these fields and I prayed. All the hell I had been through over the past three and a half years before coming here—God took me back in time and healed me and healed me. It was an unbelievable experience," Arlene said.

And then Aileen Carol "Lee" Wuornos entered their lives.

"I suppose it began right after we bought the farm," Arlene said.

"Robert and I were walking in the fields and he said to me 'Something is going to happen here that will change our lives.' I thought maybe at last I was going to become a jockey, but he said 'It has nothing to do with horses. All that you've been through has prepared you for this.'

"He felt that it was going to be God's will. That's one reason why he has never been able to argue with me about Lee." A broad smile lights her pixie face.

In early January, at the time of Lee's arrest, Arlene and Robert were making daily trips to the Gainesville hospital where Palmer Monte was recovering from bypass surgery. Upon release, he would convalesce with Arlene until he had the strength to return to New York.

"One night when I was driving home from the hospital," Arlene recalled, "a song came on the radio...one that I had heard before... about being wounded, but being a soldier, and I said to God, 'These three months have been glorious. Just you and me alone. But I know there's a hurting world out there and I think I am ready to go into full time combat duty for you again.'

"Two days later there was Lee. I don't think I'm the first person God called to help Lee. I am not special in His eyes. I just happened to be there. He got ticked off at all those other people who wouldn't listen and he needed someone to reach out to this woman. I was primed and ready.

"When I think that God moved an entire horse farm 1,500 miles for the sake of Aileen Wuornos, it just blows my mind."

Arlene had, for years, read scriptures. She spoke to Jesus in a diary and compared those scriptures to actual events.

"I was led by the scriptures," she said. "It is so obvious that God led me to Lee."

January 15, 1991

"But watch at all times, praying that you may have strength to escape all these things that will take place, and to stand before the Son of Man." Luke 21:36

Dear Lord, I feel Jesus is coming so very soon. Help me to be found ready and waiting. Is the situation in Saudi Arabia and the possibility of war the birth pangs that are to happen just near the end? It is like there is a stirring in my spirit and I don't understand what's going on. Are you preparing me for something? Or is it just my spirit is sensing the soon return of Jesus? Please Jesus, come quickly! There is so much evil in this world. So many suffering people.

January 18, 1991

I am exhausted over this whole ordeal with my Dad. It is so hard to see him in pain. All my life he was healthy and I never saw him even with a cold. Help me to deal with this. It really is hard. Also something odd happened today. I read in the paper a woman was arrested and they suspect her of being a serial killer. I got genuine butterflies in my stomach when I stared at her picture—why? She doesn't remind me of anyone I know, yet when I saw her picture on the front page, I felt butterflies deep inside.

January 19, 1991

Well, here I am again Lord. I don't understand my feelings or what is going on inside of me. That suspected serial killer was in the paper again. Her name is Aileen Carol Wuornos. They showed a different picture than in yesterday's paper and when I saw it, my heart just ached for her. The article itself is entitled "Serial Killings Suspect Has Led a Troubled Life." I read it and my heart just breaks for her. Deep inside I don't think she is guilty as a serial killer, but I can't imagine how she got into such a mess. And I don't understand why I feel so drawn to her.

Is this you, Lord?

The following week, Arlene brought her dad home to Maranatha to care for him.

January 23, 1991

Dear Jesus: Well I still remain confused about the feelings I have inside. They have not gone away—they have only increased. Despite my time being taken up so much with caring for my Dad and trying to run the farm alone, I find my thoughts dwelling on the case of Aileen Wuornos. They showed a closer, bigger picture in today's paper, and all I wanted to do was reach out and hug her and be her friend. Is it because of my own past that I feel such compassion for her? Please tell me what is going on?? I've never felt like this. Help!"

January 26, 1991

The scripture of that day read:

Dear one, silence comes from practice. It is a way of the heart. From a spirit that is calm and uncluttered. Stop all activity to free yourself from a fretful moment. . . until absolute calm returns. Do not be scared about what I am showing you and calling you to do. I am about to take you down a path you've never been on before. All you need to do is follow my promptings and follow me and trust me totally.

Dear God: Is this really from you?

January 29, 1991

Well Jesus: The way seems clear before me. I am going to the Volusia
County Branch Jail to attempt to reach out to Aileen Carol Wuornos.
Every person I've talked with has a real positive feeling about me doing
this. So today is the day. Please go before me and prepare her heart to re-
ceive me. I feel for sure you are behind this, but I'm still very nervous.
I've never done anything like this before.

At first Arlene was shy about communicating with Lee. But that day
she wrote her a letter:

Ever since the first day when I saw your picture, I felt such a compassion deep within me for you. I kept feeling, "there but by the grace of
God I would be." You and I have a lot in common. I too have had a very
"stormy" background. Until I turned my life over to Jesus, I was in rough
shape.

January 30, 1991

Dear Lord: Well, I have a great feeling inside though yesterday I
didn't get to see Aileen. I mailed the letter from Daytona and I feel sure
you are in this. I can't wait until I hear from her. I've done everything
you asked me to. The rest is up to you to work out. I'll be sensitive for the
promptings from the Holy Spirit to see what you want next. I feel good!!
I'm not scared anymore! Why did I feel so very sad though when I saw
the article in yesterday's paper. Barbara gave it to me today and I sat in
the car and cried my eyes out for someone I don't even know. What is
happening?

Unbeknownst to Arlene, immediately after her arrest Lee had
prayed, "God, if you are real, send a born-again woman into my life to
help me through this mess."

After receiving the letter, Lee called Arlene—collect.

January 31, 1991

Wow! You, dear Lord, really did prompt and inspire this whole endeavor. Aileen called tonight. She said she had prayed and asked you to
send her a Christian friend to help her through this mess. She sounds so
nice. I can't believe she is the same one the papers are writing about. She
is so very different from what they portray. Totally different. She has a

kind, soft voice and seems to have a great deal of compassion toward people. We did not discuss the case at all—told her I didn't care about it—I just wanted to be her friend. Jesus, I'm higher than a kite—so excited inside. I am in awe that you brought me into this mess and that you have placed such a caring compassion in me for Aileen. She said to call her Lee—her nickname. She is so neat. When we were getting off the phone (I asked her to call me tomorrow) she said "angels on your pillow." What a beautiful saying. It really touched me when she said that. What a nice, nice lady. Thank you for bringing me into this. I'll do whatever you prompt me to do. I prayed for you to surround Lee with a wall of fire of protection. I thank you that you are doing that.

"The first conversation that we had, she was not her real self," Arlene remembered. "She didn't know me from Adam or what my game was and she had built a thick, thick wall around herself...she was a person who had been hurt and was keeping everyone at arm's distance. Her real self was not coming across at all. She could answer questions intelligently, asked me about myself, but baring her soul—that didn't happen for a long time.

"And when I saw her for the person she really is, I saw a frightened little girl, wanting to come out, but scared to come out because every time she tried to, she was hurt.

"During the first ten days, we dealt with the possibility of death row, the situation she was in, her fears, my fears, and then right after that, after we had cried together over the situation that we found ourselves in, she began dwelling on the past—on her childhood. She had had it bottled up inside, and she wanted it to come out and she needed to talk about it. She would remember things as she went along. We both cried, but I think I was more on the tear end.

"About a month into our friendship, she told me that she had believed I was a member of one of the victims' families, a spokesperson. Sure I was fighting to get her released. She thought we were going to bring her to the farm and torture her beyond anything the state could do. Then she thought I was Jackie's spy, or with the mafia, or in conspiracy with the cops for the book and movie deal."

Within three months, the Pralles' phone bill topped $4,000 and Lee and Arlene had become soulmates. They did not, according to Arlene, discuss the crimes.

"The case itself is completely irrelevant because God does not want me involved with that," Arlene told reporters. "He brought me into Lee's life to be her friend. She is my friend regardless of how this turns out. She'll be my friend forever."

More than that, Arlene did not want to be called as a witness for the prosecution, inevitable if people knew she had discussed the murders with Lee.

February 4, 1991

Lee was moved to Marion for a few days and I panicked. She never called and I really worried big time. I've never had a friend in jail before, so this is all a new experience for me....But being separated for the last four days was good because it showed me how much I really care about her. I actually feel I love her. But how can one love somebody they haven't even met? I've never felt this way before. What on earth is going on??

February 5, 1991

Well today was good and bad. The good part is I met the Marion County Public Defenders. They are GREAT! I have a real good feeling about them helping Lee. A real good feeling. I pray you will supernaturally help them through this whole ordeal. Give them wisdom beyond their human capacity. For the first time Lee and I spoke of the electric chair. We both cried. Dear God, please bring about a miracle for Lee. Please. Don't let her die.

February 7, 1991

Dear Jesus: My dad is on the warpath. He is furious. It hurts so bad, but I know I'm doing the right thing. Please help bring harmony and peace to our home.

February 8, 1991

...I love her so much and can't imagine losing her. You are God. You know the end from the beginning. You were there when all this happened. You know the truth. Please help us. I am positive Lee is no serial killer. When I read the papers, it doesn't register in my brain. Give us a miracle, I pray. And always let my spirit be sensitive to your promptings so I can immediately obey. I really love Lee.

February 13, 1991

Please use me to help Lee. I love her so much. But I'm so scared for her. I know in my heart she is innocent. Please bring about a miracle.

February 20, 1991

I still remain nervous at times cause I've never done this before. I want to do only what you prompt..nothing of the flesh. And more than anything my desire is for Lee to be saved. She is so close, but she is scared to make a commitment. Draw her by your Spirit.

Arlene admitted she loved Lee more than she has ever loved anyone, even her husband.

People are going to try to make it into a "sexual perversion" but it's not like that at all. It's a soul binding. We're like Jonathan and David in the Bible. I wish we could show the world what true, unconditional love is all about.

The press loved it. "Country Housewife Falls for Lesbian Serial Killer" rang out the *Globe* headlines.

February 21, 1991

Wow...how scary! I was on TV...what is this all about? All I know is you sent me to Lee...I love her and want her to be saved. Why is everyone making such a big deal about this? We're just friends...that is all. I can't comprehend why everyone wants to talk to me. Put your Words in my mouth.

February 24, 1991

Well—more reporters. And I'm not scared anymore. Are you going to use Lee and I to show the world what real "Jesus Love" between friends is all about? If that's what this is all about, I'm really excited. Our relationship will be broadcast around the world (just like Ruth and Naomi) and you will get the credit. Praise your name—Wow!

February 25, 1991

Dear God: Please give me the assurance that you have brought Lee and I together for more than just to prepare her to die...I can't handle the thought of losing her. It truly will be my end too. I've lost too many loved ones already. Let Lee and I enjoy life together as two free people in planet earth before either one of us die. Please!

February 27, 1991

Wow! Awesome. People think I'm nuts, but I guess that's okay. As long as I'm doing what you want.

March 10, 1991

There is a fine line here and I want to stay within your boundaries. Besides the love I have for you, my Lord, I love Lee too much to screw things up. She is such a beautiful person and I thank you for bringing her into my life. I really love her. Lord, please let my love for Lee always remain pure and holy. I don't ever want to step beyond the boundaries you set as acceptable in a very close, tight friendship. I never want to do anything to cause you to take your Hands off of my relationship with Lee.

I love Lee as my own soul, the way David loved Jonathan. And I want to have her with me forever. A companion, a soulmate, a sister.

March 13, 1991

Well today sure was hard for me. I got to see Lee again through a glass (the third visit). She openly cried in front of me and I felt so totally helpless cause I couldn't hold her. The pain I felt is beyond anything I've ever felt before. How can all this be happening? I know she is no serial killer—she doesn't belong there. Her eyes are full of such pain. I wish there was a way to carry the pain for her. Oh Lord, I do love her so much.

March 17, 1991

This path you have me on is so different than any I've been on. The only reality is my family, the farm and my new beautiful Christian sister Lee. I've never felt this way before about anybody. For the last three nights I cried when she and I talked. I love her more than anything and I can't handle the thought of losing her. I try to concentrate on reality and it escapes me. I can't comprehend Lee is in jail as an accused serial killer. I know she is innocent, but why can't anyone else see this?

March 18, 1991

I feel so tired this morning. The last two days of interviews has me drained. Yet life goes on and I still have my responsibilities to tend to. Please fill up my cup as I meditate on you throughout this day. I have nothing to give out to anyone...I feel empty and tired.

In March, Lee Wuornos became a born-again Christian and Arlene provided her with a covenant promising life-long love and support:

"I, Arlene Pralle, do hereby vow before God and His Holy Angels, to stand by Aileen Carol Wuornos from this day forth and into eternity. I will love her, respect her, honor her and provide for her needs. All spiritual resources available to me will be given to her for her encouragement and edification. She will be bathed in prayer on a daily basis. Her financial needs will also be taken care of....I will make myself 100% available for her to lean on and draw strength from during the rough times in her life. I will never turn my back on her or walk out of this relationship which God has put together...

"Then Jonathan and David made a covenant because he loved him as his own soul." 1 Samuel 18:3

And Lee was writing messages and poems to her new friend.

A friend is one who'll stick like glue,
never leaving nor ending it too.

A friend is one who fights to the end,
To make things right, our pick as a friend.

Cheering you up, never bringing you down,
and making sure your life's safe and sound.

So this is what I feel for you,
Our friendship will my Dear never be untrue.

Arlene was having trouble obtaining visiting privileges to see Lee, and she went to Russ Armstrong at Lee's suggestion.

"Arlene Pralle came into my office," Armstrong remembered. "What she wanted, it turned out, was for me to help her get on Lee's visitors' list. I told her I couldn't do that and she left in a huff. I don't like that lady," Armstrong's eyes narrowed as he spoke. "I think she's got an angle. I don't know what it is yet, but it'll come out. She's after something."

Chapter Ten

O ne of the things that Arlene Pralle was after was a fair trial for her newfound soulmate. She disliked the fact that Lee had been encouraged to sign a contract for her life story and she shared Lee's belief that Ray Cass and Don Jacobsen were not representing her adequately.

"I know that they're not for my case," Lee had said. "They don't care about me. I can't get through on the phone to them. I can't get them to send me any letters explaining what's happening. They have not come over to tell me anything that's going on. I mean, they're just purely blase. Nothing. Nothing."

"We feel that Lee is being given a raw deal," Arlene told the press. "She really is a neat lady and is totally opposite of the way people have portrayed her."

Arlene and Robert were prepared to hire private counsel for Lee and, through friends, contacted Michael Hauptman, president of the Georgia branch of the American Civil Liberties Union and a board member of Georgia's Criminal Defense Attorneys Association.

"Aileen Wuornos called me and asked for my help," Hauptman said. "There is a possibility I may defend her; I think it's a fascinating case . . . . She doesn't have any money, but her friends are trying to raise it." He added that he might consider giving her a cut rate on his fees.

"She's a national figure now, so I guess she feels she needs a private lawyer," Ray Cass speculated.

In spite of their willingness to mortgage the farm to raise the money to help Lee, the Pralles did not hire Hauptman. Arlene and Robert flew Hauptman and his assistant to Ocala to consult with them and see their prospective client.

"When we first spoke to Hauptman, he gave us a tentative figure of $25,000. After spending $1,300 to fly them to Florida, they upped it to $50,000 to $75,000. And Lee didn't like them," says Arlene.

Finally Arlene and Lee decided that they wanted Tricia Jenkins to handle the Volusia County charges as well as those in Marion and Citrus counties.

"My lawyers in Ocala (Tricia Jenkins and Ed Bonnett) come to see me every nine days—every seven days to nine days from Ocala, just to let me know what's happening. And they always—I mean, when I call, they accept all my collect calls and they always come to see me and tell me what's going on. They are always talking to me," Lee told Judge Graziano.

Tricia Jenkins, chief assistant public defender for the Fifth Judicial Circuit, was no newcomer to the representation of people bearing the label "serial killer."

With her newest assignment, Jenkins, sporting frizzed blond hair and husky voice, was handling Lee's indictments in three separate counties. At the same time, she was also representing several men accused in serial killings.

"She believes in what she's doing," Bill Miller, another assistant public defender, told the press. "She cares about her clients and protecting her clients' rights."

"I respect Tricia a lot," said Assistant Public Defender Billy Nolas. "She's a very decent person and it isn't easy for a woman to do what she does. Women have a tough time. She has reached a level in this business when she knows she could do other things, but she is a public defender by choice."

Jenkins, who was widowed when she was very young, and fills her office with photos of movie stars and accessories from the 1930s and 1940s, is used to representing the underdog, the outcast. She describes herself as "cause-oriented" and "philosophically drawn" to criminal defense. This philosophy encouraged her to enter law school after the death of her husband.

"A lot of people ask me, 'How can you defend that person?'" Jenkins recently told the press. "Easily," she replied. "I wouldn't want to do anything else. Everybody has the right to a fair trial. The people we represent, many of them, can't communicate effectively. We're their voice."

Lee's voice, in the form of a confession, had already been heard and it put her defense team, which now consisted of Tricia Jenkins and Assistant Public Defenders Billy Nolas and William Miller, in a difficult position. Although it had not yet been ruled admissible at trial, the mere fact of its existence left no doubt in the public mind that Aileen Wuornos had killed seven men, although she had only been charged with five.

National reporters and newscasters proclaimed her the "first female serial killer" and her story was told in *People, Glamour, Vanity Fair* and *Premiere*, as well as in newspapers across the county. Arlene Pralle quickly became Lee's official spokeswoman and *Geraldo*, *Current Affair*, *Hard Copy* and *The Real Story* interviewed her for their shows.

"I had gone to a nearby town to run errands and called home to check in. The woman who helps me said, 'Please come home. The television station is here taking pictures.' And that's how it all began," said Arlene.

At Maranatha, business began to decline.

"We've had people stop bringing their horses for stud service since I befriended Aileen. And I began to receive death threats," Arlene said.

The Pralle farm sustains thirty-two show horses, three cats, four wolves and a 150-pound dog, half malamute, half timberdog, named Kingman. For Arlene it is a full-time job; when she leaves to attend a hearing or to visit Lee, she must bring in outside help to take care of the animals. The money set aside for the balloon payment on the farm is dwindling and she fears what will happen financially. Robert's job as a broadcasting engineer supports them, but expenses are mounting.

Inside the small modern farmhouse, pen and ink drawings by Lee and framed verses that she has written to Arlene are prominently displayed. On the back of the sofa sits a small, floppy teddy bear encumbered with the name Thurgood Brennan in honor of Arlene and Lee's favorite Supreme Court justices. The bear was purchased by Tricia at Lee's request.

The second bedroom has been decorated in wolf paintings, a special favorite of Lee's.

"Lee has the idea that when she is released and comes to live here, we will get rid of the horses and let the wolves roam free," Arlene said, aware that it is an impractical, if romantic, suggestion.

The kitchen is filled with liquids and powders designed to help Arlene gain weight. She has dropped from 100 pounds to 93 pounds, partly due to the stress of Lee's situation, and partly due to an almost fatal kick from the hoof of a breeding horse.

For two months, in spring 1991, she lay in the Gainesville hospital, her liver lacerated, her ribs broken. Five hours of hemorrahaging stopped just short of death when her doctor, a born-again Pentecostal Christian, like Arlene, "laid" his hands on her.

"They say that I kept calling out for Lee," Arlene remembered. "I kept saying that I couldn't leave her. The doctors think that's what kept me alive."

In preparation for Lee's life on the farm, Arlene had made her half owner of a filly named Arlee, the Only Soul-Binder.

It was all somehow reminiscent of Charles Dickens' Mrs.

Havisham. Lee and Arlene had their own "great expectations." "I feel God is going to perform a miracle and get her out of there," Arlene said.

When Arlene first came forth on Lee's behalf, she was willing and eager to tell the abusive incidents in Lee's childhood. One of the first reporters to cover her story quoted Pralle as saying Lee's grandfather beat Lee "not as a means of discipline, just sadistically, whenever he got drunk. The first time he caught her smoking he got so angry that instead of just beating her, he turned his belt around and held it in the middle and [hit her with] the two loose ends, one of them being the buckle. After that she was bleeding all over. . . . I wish he were alive today because I'd kill him."

In her attempt to write a screenplay, Jackie Giroux found that Lee continued to be inconsistent in her stories.

At one point, according to Giroux, Lee admitted that she had had a sadomasochistic relationship with at least one of her victims.

"Why do you have handcuffs?" Jackie had asked Lee.

"Because I used them," Lee replied.

"Were you a dominatrix?"

"Yes," Lee said.

"So you used to inflict pain?" Jackie continued.

"When they asked me to."

"What kind of pain?" she asked.

"The ultimate," said Lee. "A bullet here, a bullet there. . . first an arm, then a knee, then the other leg."

Like the story of sexual abuse by her grandfather, Lee now denies this conversation.

Jackie could do the screenplay, but Lee wanted to do the book.

"She has already begun to write it," said Arlene.

"I am under direct orders from Lee not to talk about her childhood anymore."

In April, Pasco County joined Marion, Citrus and Volusia counties by indicting Lee, this time for the murder of Charles Carskaddon, a rodeo worker on his way to Tampa Bay when he was murdered. This brought the number of murder charges against Lee to five.

Speculation continued as to whether or not Dixie County would join the ranks by indicting Lee for the murder of Walter Gino Antonio, to which she had also confessed.

The body of Peter Siems was still listed as missing and Lee's confes-

sion did nothing to aid in the location of the body — she could only remember it was somewhere in Georgia.

"He took me way out in the fuckin' wilderness, man, and way out in
the wilderness somewhere....It was I-75 in Georgia somewhere...we
were both naked."

In late June, Lee was moved to Citrus County Jail so that she could
be closer to her attorneys. She had favored the Citrus County Jail instead of the Marion County Jail because she could smoke there.

In reality, the guards at Citrus County Jail were kinder, she said, she
received better care and was allowed contact visits with Arlene.

"The first time I was with Lee," Arlene said, "she was surprised to see
how little I was and she was afraid to hug me. One of the guards said, 'Go
ahead, she won't break.' "

"We like to keep our clients happy when they go to trial," Public Defender Howard Babb was quoted.

Five trials were scheduled as a result of the indictments and, despite
Lee's desire to tell her own story, as many books and screenplays on the
case were already in various stages of preparation.

Pralle, in her slightly husky, little girl voice, did not hesitate to share
her desire to turn the prosecution "into toads."

From her jail cell, Lee Wuornos told the press: "I'm not a man hater.
I'm not a verbal or physical fighter. I like to be tranquil and at ease and
enjoy life. I've been through so many traumatic experiences that either
I'm walking in shock or I'm so used to being treated like dirt that I guess
it's become a way of life.

"I have lots of love in me, but I never got a chance to give it to somebody because every time I gave it to somebody, they took from me. I'm a
decent person."

Rumors that media contracts had interfered with the prosecution of Tyria Moore became an issue in August when Marion County prosecutors
investigated whether Munster, Binegar and Henry had compromised the
investigation by pursuing a movie deal, aided and abetted by Tyria
Moore. Their report, initiated by the accusation of Brian Jarvis, stated:

> Although there is no evidence to support Jarvis' suggestion of improper
> motive, Jarvis' opinion of weaknesses in the investigation, together with
> our own independent review of the files, identified several areas where
> the investigation needs to be supplemented.

By the time the report was released, Brian Jarvis had already re-signed, signed an agreement to sell his story, received $1 for the rights and paid an agent $500 to promote a book or movie of his "life story."

Addressing the circumstances of Tyria Moore's involvement with the three investigators, the report found that movie prospects impeded more information from Moore. And each deputy could make as much as $100,000 as a consultant for a movie.

Dan Henry retaliated. "I think the jury will forgive the police officers for being human beings and making human mistakes. I don't think they will forgive Aileen Wuornos for killing seven men."

But there were those who felt that Tyria Moore should have been sworn in as a sheriff's deputy before her taped telephone conversations with Lee Wuornos.

Several days later, in DeLand, Tricia Jenkins convinced Judge Graziano that CBS had obtained the videotape of Lee's confession and was attempting to peddle it for $10,000.

"I've got to pursue that," Jenkins told the Judge. "We feel there's a possibility of finding ourselves in federal court against CBS."

Tricia also expressed concern over the book or movie project being handled by Bradshaw for Binegar, Munster, Henry and Moore.

"If she [Tyria Moore] signed it, that's why she wasn't charged," Tricia contended.

Over the objections of Assistant State Attorney Sean Daly, Judge Graziano, who had originally scheduled Lee's trial for September, con-tinued it to January 13, 1992.

"Ms. Jenkins, you will be ready to proceed," she warned.

Lee was in particularly good spirits that day. Arlene Pralle was present and, in her honor, Lee had curled her hair and was wearing a smile.

"You look good," Arlene told her.

"Hangin' in there," Lee said. Extending her handcuffed wrists, she la-mented, "too bad we can't touch."

Chapter Eleven

Tall, dark-haired David Damore, of the flashing brown eyes and self-assured manner, was the assistant state attorney and chief prosecutor against Lee Wuornos. He had become a regular in Daytona Beach's high profile cases. One reporter described his tenacity.

"When he gets ahold of a case, he will not let go. Justice has nothing to do with it. As long as it's within the law, winning is everything."

Damore, his wife, Nona, and their two young children arrived in Volusia County shortly after John Tanner's ascension to the office of state attorney in 1989. It was a mysterious appearance. Damore had been a successful South Florida lawyer, a high-paid litigator handling big-time drug defenses. Why relocate to Volusia, people wondered. Why accept a state job?

Myths about Damore's past are rife in Volusia County: He was a fast-living Fort Lauderdale dope lawyer. He drove an Italian sports car and worked out of an opulent quarter-million dollar home. He hightailed it upstate to escape getting indicted or killed.

The record shows that Damore spent three years as a prosecutor in Fort Lauderdale, followed by nearly a decade as a defense lawyer. His actions in one case, a federal drug-racketeering prosecution, led to a reprimand by The Florida Bar. Damore was too closely involved financially with his client, the Bar said. A defense lawyer once pressed charges against Damore for shoving him. The case went nowhere.

Not long after joining Tanner's staff, Damore became the state attorney's strong right arm, professionally and politically. His courtroom successes in high-profile cases reflected favorably on Tanner. Damore is hot-headed, courteous or crafty, yet always righteous and always utterly merciless. On October 11, Damore appeared before Judge Graziano to complain that Tricia Jenkins had not told him when she was interviewing witnesses against Lee in other counties. When Judge Graziano refused to order Tricia to comply, Damore threatened:

"It will be the intention of the State Attorney's Office to file a motion to recuse [dismiss] the Public Defender's Office from the Fifth Judicial Circuit from this case."

Assistant State Attorney Sean Daly also complained about Judge

Graziano prohibiting witnesses from discussing the case among themselves, thus inhibiting his investigators.

It appeared that Damore's patience with the roster of females protecting Lee from him was diminishing. Graziano, Jenkins, Pralle—his colleagues speculated that he would like nothing more than to strip them away from the defendant and leave her in the clutches of male authority. If he could not rid himself of her female attorney, perhaps the judge was a better target. It was easy to switch judges. Just file a perfunctory motion. It could be a first step.

Even Damore was not prepared for the news that Arlene Pralle and her husband, Robert, had legally adopted Lee Wuornos.

Although the adoption had been in process since late summer, it was early October before the couple won approval from the court.

Lee initiated the action.

"I had only known Lee for about a month when she told me that she would love to become part of my family," Arlene said. "That was the closest relationship we could have and would I consider adopting her.

"I told her I thought it was premature and why didn't we wait a little while and see what happened. Then she suggested that maybe I could just be her legal guardian and I thought that didn't sound quite so scary.

"Tricia said absolutely not because they might want to put me on the witness stand and as her legal guardian or parent, I wouldn't have much credibility. When I found out they weren't planning to use me on the stand, I went to Steve Glazer, who used to be an assistant public defender, and he found out that there are no legal guardians in Florida, but Robert and I could adopt her.

"Arlene had asked me originally how to go about getting guardianship," recalled Glazer. Plump, curly-haired and soft-spoken, Glazer is an off-shoot of the "Woodstock generation," who has never forgotten the lessons he learned during those years. As a teenager, he lived in New York City, playing the guitar at folkhouses, waiting tables at night. A few years later, he decided to see the world. He bought a truck from North American Van Lines and traveled throughout forty-four states, playing the guitar at truck stops, earning room and board at college dorms.

"So there I was at twenty-three, a high school drop out truck driver," Glazer laughed, "and my brother talked me into going to college. The school kept trying to get my transcripts, but of course I hadn't finished high school. After a while, it wasn't important any more." Although he had planned to become a history teacher, "I always wanted to be a lawyer. I wanted to do something to change the world. I was shocked by the kids I went to school with. They were so right wing, so Republican."

During law school at the University of Florida, Glazer restored the National Lawyers' Guild ("It folded again after I left"), then joined the public defenders' office where he worked in the felony division under Tricia Jenkins.

"At first I was going to be a copyright lawyer and make an album with my first big paycheck, but my politics kept coming back to me. The public defender's office just chews people up. The state has resources. The public defenders have practically none."

When Arlene Pralle called Steve about the possibility of serving as Lee's legal guardian, he found that guardianship in Florida is only available to incompetents and minors. Lee was neither.

"Then I remembered old Professor McCoy at the University of Florida Law School who said, 'Anybody can adopt anybody,' and I told that to Arlene," Steve said. "She was immediately excited about it.

"Arlene believes she was commanded to help Lee in her search for God and must do everything possible to accomplish that. Lee feels she'll be saved through God and so it's necessary to get Arlene to Lee as often as possible and the only way for her to be part of Lee's life is by being her mother because otherwise she'd have no legal rights to visit her. On the county jail level, especially, only parental visitation was assured.

"Lee, on the other hand, was overwhelmed by the fact that somebody could care about her. Because the media's calling her a serial killer. The world is calling her a manhater, lesbian, coldblooded murderess. Yet Arlene Pralle comes forward with open arms to accept this person.... Lee has developed a family relationship with someone for the first time in her life."

Arlene remembered that, "The next time I talked to Lee, I said 'Guess what we're doing. I don't care who says what.' She was ecstatic and started calling me 'mom' immediately."

To the press, she said: "The reason we did it is we want her to know what it feels like to have a family that really cares about her. It makes no difference to myself or my husband whether she's guilty or innocent. She is still a human being and deserves to have a friend."

It was a close call. Florida law requires one year of residency before adoption is permitted. On October 3, when the court nodded its approval, Arlene and Robert had been in Florida one year to the day.

"Steve nearly collapsed when he realized how close the timing was," Arlene laughed.

News of the adoption rejuvenated media interest in the Wuornos case. Arlene was only nine years older than her daughter. The spotlight shifted from the confessed killer of seven men to the woman who believed in her.

"I've been called nuts and some other things," Arlene admitted. "But I'm getting used to it."

The press questioned Pralle's motives. Was she trying to make money off any media deals with Lee? Not so, said the born-again adoptive mother and her Jewish, but also born-again lawyer. It would be necessary for Arlene and Robert to show that they were dependents of Lee before they could receive any money from royalties.

The tabloid paper, *Star*, reported that Arlene and Robert were getting a divorce and she was marrying Lee.

"I didn't see that article, but I sure heard about it," Arlene laughed.

David Damore viewed the adoption with cynicism.

"I think she's being used, she's misguided," he said. "I feel terribly sorry for her because I really think that in her heart of hearts she's doing this because she's trying to be religious and trying to do something to help another human being."

"All I know is if I had adopted her when she was young, she wouldn't be in this mess right now," Arlene told the press.

Chapter Twelve

While the media focused on the adoptive mother and her new daughter, curiosity grew about the man who was now father to a woman who killed men.

Where was Robert Pralle and how did he feel about his role in this unfolding drama?

When Robert and Arlene bought the horse farm in Florida in October of 1990, Robert expected to be transferred from the midwest in a matter of months.

Robert had been scheduled for an interview for an opening with his company in Florida when he was called away from the convention he was attending in California because of Arlene's accident.

"After that politics took over and the job was given to someone else," Robert recalled. "When Arlene wanted to move to Florida, I said, 'Just so I don't get stranded in Chicago,' " he laughed. "And that's exactly what happened."

Robert's thatch of gray hair seems at odds with his boyish face. He is good-humored about the situation he finds himself in. Robert has been married to Arlene for almost twenty years, and considers this just the latest, if most publicized adventure.

"I guess if I had wanted to be married to a homemaker, I wouldn't have chosen Arlene," he chuckled.

For the time being, the Pralles live apart, but Robert does get to Florida for important occasions—like the adoption of Lee Wuornos into the Pralle family.

"The key here is that Arlene never read the newspapers, never looked at newspapers," Robert said. "When Arlene saw Lee's picture in the newspaper I didn't pay much attention. The most attention I took was that Arlene was reading the newspaper. A few days later I remember her saying that she felt she should write a letter. Bells and whistles should have been going on, but I thought this would pass. If I had thought about it, I would have realized it wouldn't just pass because none of the other things have passed either, no matter how much I wanted to ignore them."

Robert and Arlene first met just before Arlene's sixteenth birthday. Robert was seventeen. "She came up to me at high school and gave me permission to date one of her friends. I wondered why she was giving me permission. I didn't even know her. However, I ended up not going out with her friend. Instead I went out with Arlene.

"She has more spunk and more guts and more stick-to-it-iveness. I admire it, but I must admit sometimes I wish she wasn't so much that way.

"But in this case, I told her right after we bought the farm that 'We're down here to make the horses better, but, I don't know, I feel something else is going to happen. Something that we don't know about and never dreamed about. But something's going to happen. And it's going to be so different, we'd never, ever guess it.' My words. If it wasn't for the feeling that I had at that time, I would have freaked out a long time ago.

"I'm an ostrich. When she first told me about her plans for the adoption, I thought this will pass. There's no way we'll be able to do it. But I keep underestimating Arlene's ability. I get hit with things on a 'need to know' basis only.

"What Arlene did was see something in Lee's eyes that went deeper than what people ordinarily look for. There's a person under all this who needs to have someone who cares. And I think that's gotten Lee through everything that's happened since she went to jail."

The hardest part was learning that Lee would be sharing the Pralle family name.

"Arlene sneaked that one in. It had crossed my mind, but I thought she wouldn't do that. Until we got in the car on the way to the courthouse to finalize the adoption. She said she had something to tell me. I knew what it was. I just said, 'You've got me where you want me. There's nothing I can do about it. I have been had.' Trying to explain it to my mom—my whole family lives in Florida—she still doesn't comprehend."

It is obvious that marriage to Arlene has filled Robert's life with a series of ups and downs.

"She's outgoing and let's do this and let's do that and everything's okay, and I'm, 'whoa, let's slow down a little bit.' She likes to say I'm so laid back that I'm horizontal."

It was Robert's influence that caused Arlene to become born again, and he remembers the way she plunged into it.

"Her parents threw her out of the house. She became Billy Sunday and it drove them crazy. They couldn't take that much religion. They said, 'We can't deal with this. Either give up the church or give up us.' She never does anything half-heartedly," Robert said.

"What she started out to do was very good," Robert said. "I never anticipated it going this far. But when Arlene feels she is doing something that God wants her to do, nothing can stop her."

Robert enjoys his anonymity and has been thankful, in some ways, that he has not been in Florida during the media craze.

"I'm used to being on the technical end of the media. Behind the cameras. Many people wonder if I really do exist. At Volusia County Branch Jail, the police reports had us divorced. But I've definitely had to take some comments at work. My reply is, 'Well, you know, you bring them up and sometimes they go astray.' "

At one point Robert was at WTMJ television in Milwaukee. The trial of Jeffrey Dahmer was underway and Lee's case was also in the news.

"Two men were walking out of the newsroom and one of them said, 'That gal's going to fry.' I turned around and looked at them and said, 'You shouldn't talk about my daughter that way.' It went completely over their heads.

"When Arlene was on *Current Affair,* my boss brought me into the office and asked me 'How long has this been going on?' For the most part, they just all shake their heads."

The funny thing is, Robert reminisced, every time there was a crisis in Lee's life something else in the news preempted it in the midwest.

"When Arlene first got involved, along came the Gulf War, then there was the Dahmer trial which overshadowed the Wuornos news here in this area. And when Arlene went to New York to appear on CBS news, the president came home from Japan and her spot was not shown here."

Robert acknowledged that they are barely hanging on to the farm at this point.

"Two things happened. One was the expenses associated with Lee and the other was Arlene's accident. For a long time she had to pay people to do what she ordinarily did herself. I just can't believe that we would go through all this and lose the farm.

"The farm and Arlene are one and the same. Take her off the farm and she would not be the same person."

Robert feels that years from now, Arlene's part in the Wuornos story will still be recognized.

"It is just so incredible to have that much compassion for another human being. Just because that human being happens to be in trouble, what makes us so self righteous as to believe this person should just be forgotten and written off?"

Tyria Moore turned up missing in November, when the defense team attempted to bring her into court to question her about the confession of Lee Wuornos. The defense wanted to disqualify the confession by proving Moore's complicity in obtaining it.

Judge Graziano listened attentively as Billy Nolas, the young Greek spitfire of the defense team, explained that he and Tricia had been unable to locate Moore to subpoena her for court.

"For them to assert they can't get Miss Moore here is garbage," retorted Assistant State Attorney Sean Daly.

"Where is Miss Moore, Mr. Daly," inquired Judge Graziano.

"I don't know," he conceded. Investigator Larry Horzepa had been placed in charge of Tyria and he could be reached only through his beeper.

Tempers grew short as Jenkins and Nolas interrogated three investigators who had dealt with Tyria Moore. In the absence of Tyria, they hoped to unveil the truth through their testimony.

"This is an affront to this court's dignity," Damore interjected during protracted questioning by Nolas. Having received no satisfaction from the investigators, Nolas requested a continuance to subpoena Tyria. Damore and Daly asked once again that the defense be disqualified from the case.

The frustrated judge stalked from the bench, ignoring the still unanswered questions of the attorneys.

Attention of the audience, however, was not focused on the attorneys. Of greater interest was Arlene Pralle, blowing kisses to her newly-adopted daughter, Aileen Carol "Lee" Wuornos Pralle.

The legal tug of war continued. The prosecution attempted to have the confession declared admissible. Jon Kaney, representing the local *Daytona Beach News-Journal*, attempted to have it declared public.

"That knowledge [that Wuornos confessed] is a bell that has already rung," he said. "What could be more damning than saying, 'I did it'? That part's been said."

Billy Nolas argued that "the case has attracted sensationalized media coverage...of a shoddy variety. That type of information has a great detrimental effect on potential jurors."

"Volusia County is no stranger to high-profile murder cases," interjected Dale Evans, attorney for the *Orlando Sentinel* and WESH-TV. "It makes the general population a little more sanguine about these things."

Kaney agreed, adding that "Aileen Wuornos is no Ted Bundy in terms of pretrial publicity," yet Bundy was tried in Florida.

During the state's motion to continue the suppression hearing, the antics between the two camps became unbearable for Judge Graziano.

"Unless there is some outrageous conduct on behalf of the officials of the Public Defenders Office of the Fifth Circuit I don't want any more of these motions," she told the attorneys. Counsel has both tried to put the attorneys on trial. The attorneys are not on trial. Ms. Wuornos is on trial. . . .

"As to the conduct of the attorneys during the proceedings, I've noted attempts to go over this court into error. I've noted dilatory tactics and unnecessary theatrics. Whether you classify it as cute, obnoxious or abusive behavior, it has no place in this courtroom. I'm not going to allow this legal event to become a media event for counsel. Ms. Wuornos will have a fair trial. And I will not hesitate at the proper time to deal severely with inappropriate conduct by anyone in this case.

"Except for the media interest, counsel, this case is no different than any other first degree murder trial. . . . I didn't ask for this case. And unlike some people involved, I do not particularly relish the necessary difficulties of such a case. And I certainly object to the unnecessary difficulties being caused by counsel and the media."

On December 5, interrogation of the investigators who had dealt with Tyria Moore continued. Bruce Munster took the stand and, under questioning by Billy Nolas, quoted Tyria Moore as saying "I wish I had come forward earlier. Maybe all those men would have lived."

It was the beginning of a particularly bleak period for Lee Wuornos. Hands over mouth, she broke into tears during the replay of the telephone conversations between herself and Tyria Moore.

In addition, she announced to the judge that she was being mistreated in Volusia County Branch Jail, where she had been brought from Citrus County. Not only was she being deprived of proper medical care, but she had spent Thanksgiving Day in isolation, dressed in paper clothes, on suicide watch. She had been scheduled to return to Citrus County, but had, instead, been kept in Volusia.

To add to her grief, she was being given massive doses of Vistaril in order to keep her quiet, she told Arlene.

And she accused Warden Wayne McCracken of saying: "By the time we get through with you, you will want to hide in the corner and rot."

On the following day, Judge Graziano denied a defense motion to suppress the three-hour confession tape, ruling that "Her statement was voluntarily and freely given. The motion to suppress is denied."

The judge also released the tapes to the public.

The order entered that day stated:

1. This case has been the subject of widespread publicity in news media circulated within Volusia County, Florida; and

2. The essential contents of the videotaped statement already have been publicized, including the fact that Defendant purportedly confessed to the murders with which she is charged.

3. Sealing the videotaped statement will not prevent or lessen this adverse publicity, and opening it to the public will not aggravate the adverse publicity to such extent as that it will pose a serious and imminent threat to the fair trial interest in view of what has already been published.

To soften the ruling, Judge Graziano agreed to give the defense several days to file an appeal.

Assistant State Attorney Sean Daly, brash and baby-faced, whose mere presence in the courtroom was known to aggravate Judge Graziano, approved the decision.

"Her [Lee's] decision to confess was her own. Now she has to live with it," he told the court.

In the courtroom, Arlene Pralle burst into tears. She knew what the release of her daughter's confession could mean to her case. Tricia Jenkins turned to her and confided: "It's not over."

This time Tyria Moore was available to take the stand. All eyes followed the plump, brightly-clad figure as she approached the witness stand, while Lee tried unsuccessfully to catch her eye. Placed under oath, Ty continued to avoid Lee's gaze. Lee stared at her ex-roommate, ex-lover, ex-friend for a few moments, then placed her hands over her face and cried.

Obviously tense, Tyria told the defense team that she had cooperated with the investigators in order to clear her name. She was remorseful over not having saved the lives of many of the men by turning Lee in to the authorities.

Arlene Pralle and Jackie Giroux were asked to leave the courtroom. They had been subpoenaed by the state for depositions and, therefore, could not be permitted to listen to Tyria Moore's testimony. Arlene was furious. David Damore had promised to allow her in the courtroom at all times.

"Hypocrite!" she screamed at him as she was escorted out.

In the small hallway of Volusia County Jail, where the present hearing was taking place, Arlene paced the floor, asking reporters to take a statement about the actions of David Damore.

"You're from the hometown newspaper," she approached a reporter. "I want you to print his spiteful remarks. If you put all this in the paper, I will talk to you forever. The prosecutor is evil."

It was the first of many statements Arlene would make during the next few months, chastising the authorities and their treatment of both her and the defendant.

Bruce Munster, also in the hall, carefully observed the happenings.

"This is not a good idea," Damore said to Arlene during recess. Damore had lunched with Munster and heard about Arlene's actions.

According to both Jackie and Arlene, Assistant State Attorney Sean Daly approached them as they sat in the hallway.

"Do you know that Trish Jenkins has a potential movie or book deal?" he asked.

The two women looked at him incredulously.

"I don't know about any kind of movie or book deal Miss Jenkins has," responded Jackie.

"Well, we've heard about that," Daly continued.

"At the time," Arlene said, "I didn't believe it. But then I kept noticing the way she spent so much time with Mike Reynolds, who was under contract with Warner books, but would never talk to any of the other authors there."

Although the prosecution had won on many points, including the release of the confession, Damore had not lost his desire to rid himself of the female judge. He and Daly filed a motion requesting that Judge Graziano disqualify herself. As grounds, they cited the appointment of public defenders from outside the circuit to represent Lee Wuornos. They also felt that the judge favored the defense in rulings and scheduling. Declaring the request "insufficient", Judge Graziano asked the prosecutors to act swiftly if they intended to refile the motion. The trial date of January 13 must be met, she said.

In the hallway, Arlene apologized to Damore for her outburst and he said she was free to reenter the courtroom. Having heard Jackie smart off about "small town justice," he replied that "Well, this is the way we do things here in Podunk," but made no effort to stop her from returning to the hearing.

As he stepped into the courtroom, he turned to a reporter and vented his disgust: "I can't stand these blonde bimbos."

Chapter Thirteen

Jackie Giroux was relieved to leave Florida.

Her techniques had angered many of the investigators, particularly Binegar, Munster and Henry, on whom she had blown the whistle concerning their movie contract by revealing the scheme to Phil Long, a reporter for the *Miami Herald*. Jackie had first learned about the agreement, which included Tyria Moore, from a "source", and had immediately taken the information to the press.

"If you ever tell anyone where you heard this, I'll kill you," the informant had told her. It was a threat she did not take lightly.

Linda Sawyer, producer of Geraldo's show *Now It Can Be Told*, following through on information given to her, flew to Ocala to look into the allegations.

"I realized something wasn't clear," she said. "Was Tyria Moore an innocent victim? She didn't have an opportunity to get to the police and now she's in a package with the police? Holy Jesus."

On-camera, she spoke with Dan Henry.

"Oh, I just believe Hollywood is doing their job," he told her. "People's appetites need more than just the blips on the evening news. That's the way it goes."

Jackie had been diligent and aggressive in her investigation of the case of Lee Wuornos. Not only did she have a contract with Wuornos and Armstrong, but she had also executed side contracts with a number of key witnesses in Michigan who remembered Lee's childhood, the most important of which was Lori Grody, Lee's aunt/sister. When Jackie first interviewed Lori, soon after Lee's arrest, Lori admitted the abuse Lee had endured at the hands of Lauri Wuornos.

"It took me three days, but I finally got her to talk about it," Jackie told Arlene.

"She said that being hit with a belt was not abusive, she didn't think. And she didn't feel that her father screaming obscenities and using abusive remarks was abusive. And when we got into reading descriptions from dictionaries and other child abuse cases, then she began to see that that could be considered abuse."

The contracts initiated by Jackie were important to her. She could not take the risk that information about the early life of Lee Wuornos would be given to anyone besides herself.

"I told Lori," Jackie said, "eventually this will come out in a courtroom. This is going to become public domain. People will be having access to it and doing other stories. And I advised her it was for her better interest to read and control what was being written."

"And she then agreed to do that?" Tricia Jenkins had asked at the deposition.

"She then agreed to do it," Jackie replied.

"Did you ever advise her that, as a result of that contract that she has signed with you, that she could not speak to anybody else or give any specific facts as to Lee's background, incidents of abuse, anything of that nature?"

"I have said to her, and to, you know, everybody...it would be very wise not to speak with anyone else when it comes to reporters and anyone else that you feel the information could be coming out in the newspaper, which, therefore, makes it public domain. I did advise her of that right."

Jackie wanted her screenplay to be the first to hit the market. And rumors had it that the cops already had a deal with CBS.

During Jackie's deposition, David Damore had hammered at her. He questioned her again and again about the source of her information on the "cop script." Who had told her and who was she protecting?

Jackie had communicated with Republic Pictures on the advice of a friend in the business. In response, she received a phone call.

"I cannot tell you this guy's name because he threatened me," she told the attorneys. "He said, 'This is a courtesy call. We're not going to do your story, because we already have a story on Aileen Wuornos.' And he said, 'I'll kill you if you ever tell anybody I told you, if you use my name.' He was pretty adamant.

"I said, 'What kind of story are you doing?'

"We have the story of three police, cops, from Marion County and a female informant."

"And I said, 'What?'

"He said, 'Yes, we do.'

"I said, 'Wait a minute. What do you mean you've got it?'

"He said, 'We have a contract. There's four of them and they are each getting $50,000.'

"I said, 'Well, God, I've been getting all these letters from Butterworth telling me, get away from this story. You cannot profit from this story. You cannot write on a killer'....Then I got a call from Phil Long of the *Miami Herald* and I told him."

Later, Jackie said, she saw the cop screenplay in the hands of Linda Sawyer when she appeared on the *Geraldo Show*.

"The screenplay was written by Fred Mills," Jackie revealed, "and the cover read CM TWO Productions."

"Who owns CM TWO Productions?" Damore asked.

"Chuck McLain...Chuck McLain is a producer for Republic Pictures."

Later in the deposition, David Eddy, prosecutor from Marion County, had returned to the name of the informant. It was of particular interest to him because Marion County investigators were involved in the cop script.

"One thing, the person whose name she doesn't want to disclose, because she would rather die," he said.

"She said she no longer recalls it," Tricia Jenkins interrupted.

"Is it that you no longer recall the name of the person that threatened to kill you or that you don't want to reveal it?" Eddy continued.

"I cannot remember at this moment," Jackie said, haltingly.

"Let me remind you, ma'am, you are under oath."

"I can't remember. At this moment I'm very nervous and upset. I cannot remember it."

Later, Jackie said, she received a message from the investigators' attorney, Rob Bradshaw, to keep her mouth shut.

Damore had forced her to talk about Lee's abusive background. If this deposition was filed, much of the information she had so carefully protected would be public domain. She had left the deposition in tears.

"She was unable to corroborate, or sustain, substantiate, any of the claims that she made....most of this stuff is a figment of her imagination," commented Damore.

At first, Jackie said, Lee was excited over the idea of the screenplay.

"She said to me, 'Have I got a story to tell you. I've slept with 9,000 men.' I said, 'Yes, I'd like to hear that story. How did you get started with 9,000 men?'

"She said to me, 'It was my father made me do it.' And she wanted to talk about all the things that she was made to do in her house. She said, 'I want to write a book.'

"I said, 'I'm not a book writer.' [She said] 'I want a book written about me. You have to understand I had this man was going to write a book about me, but was going to charge me $8,000. I didn't have the money.'

"I said, 'Well, we'll talk about that. . . . I want to do a movie.'

"She said, 'Great, I've got the story. I've been abused. I've slept with 9,000 men. They have stolen money from me, raped me.' She was just going on and on."

Shortly after signing the contract with Jackie, Lee had thought better of it. Undoubtedly she reconsidered it after learning from Armstrong that the Son of Sam law would prohibit any profit on her part. The next day, she wrote a letter to Jackie backing out of the contract and gave it to Tricia to mail for her. Jackie says she never received the letter.

Lee's distrust of Jackie caused long, verbal telephone battles with Arlene. She now wanted whatever money was available from her story to go to Arlene and accused Arlene and Jackie of conspiring against her. She ordered Arlene not to give out any more information about her childhood because she was determined to write her own book, to tell her own story.

Meanwhile, Arlene had met with Jackie and felt she was trustworthy. Arlene and Lee requested a revised contract, eliminating Russell Armstrong, fronting Arlene $5,000 for expenses, and funnelling Lee's share of the income to her. Jackie agreed to the contract, but failed to produce it. In spite of this, Arlene continued to pass on to Jackie everything she knew about the horrors of Lee's childhood. She had endured them all during the long hours of conversation following Lee's arrest.

"I had Jackie on one hand, who seemed to be wanting to help Lee, and Lee on the other hand cursing me for associating with Jackie. It was a position that I found impossible," said Arlene.

To add to the confusion, Jackie was advertising that she had interviewed Lee extensively, which she had not. Little of the information on Lee's childhood came directly from Lee. It had been filtered through Arlene and obtained from interviews with relatives, friends and neighbors of the young Lee in Michigan.

Within a few months, Jackie sent Arlene the first draft of the screenplay so that she could see for herself that her intentions were honorable. Entitled *Angel of Death*, the 235-page manuscript was "beautiful," says Arlene. "It dealt only with Lee's childhood, and was not an accurate portrayal, but a beautiful script."

Lee hated it. It was not honest, she told Arlene. It was nothing at all like the child, Aileen Wuornos. There was only one person who could tell the story and that was Lee herself. She pleaded with Arlene to write the book for her. And Arlene made Jackie promise that she would only write a screenplay and not a book.

"All I wanted was to make peace between them," Arlene says.

Arlene began to have dreams. In them she saw the young Lee and felt her pain. In the morning, she was unable to shake the dreams and they became more vivid to her than the reality of the day. She returned to her diary.

October 9, 1991

Why am I in this "time warp" like I'm in Michigan in the 60's and 70's? I can see Lee before me as a little girl. She seems so little, so innocent, so fragile, so scared. I don't understand this at all. Why am I seeing these things? Is it from you? This is weird. . .

"I saw things happening to Lee as a child," says Arlene. "Things that we had not talked about. When I told her about it, she said what I was seeing was accurate. It was just the way it had been.

"Most frightening of all was the vision of her grandfather, Lauri. I had never seen a picture of him, yet I envisioned him as looking like Jackie Gleason. Later Jackie Giroux, who has a picture of him, said, yes, that's exactly who he looked like."

Meanwhile, the German production company which had expressed interest in a 10 million dollar deal was not satisfied with a delicate handling of Lee's story. It was not sensational and they would back out of the deal unless some murders were introduced. Jackie began to rewrite the screenplay, and decided not to return to Florida for the murder trial of Richard Mallory.

Despite her assurance to Arlene that she was not planning a book, she had contacted one of her best friends, an attractive, London-born, California-based journalist named Sue Russell. Jackie shared the childhood of Lee Wuornos with Sue, and often took her along on interviews. When that was not possible, she gave Sue the names and phone numbers of people she should interview. Sue would attend the trial and share it with Jackie. Jackie would write the screenplay. Sue would write the book. It was an irresistible offer. After several rejections, Sue received a contract from Delacorte Publishing Company. Jackie did not need to go back to the hotbed she had created in Florida. Sue would do it for her.

The videotaped confession was released to the public on December 11. The media was elated. All local papers carried excerpts from the three-hour interview and any opportunity for an untainted jury was eliminated.

Billy Nolas told the press: "The fair trial right is the one that should be more seriously considered by the court."

In spite of Judge Graziano's ruling on admissibility of the tapes, David Damore and Sean Daley wanted her dismissed from the case.

If the first motion to recuse trial judge was insufficient, the second one was not. This time, Damore and Daly accused Judge Graziano of granting special favors to the Fifth Circuit Public Defender's Office. They should not have replaced assistant public defenders from the Seventh Circuit.

The original dismissal was brought on because of the defendant's desire for a female attorney, they charged, and since that time it was apparent that: "the Court, in its *ex parte* communication with that office (Fifth Circuit), apparently *granted a number of concessions and made various promises* guaranteeing the Fifth Circuit Public Defender's Office certain rights and privileges beyond those normally afforded to any other defense counsel in this circuit."

Judge Graziano had no choice but to recuse herself. In her order, she stressed that the truth or falsity of the prosecution's claims had no bearing on her recusal. Florida law requires that: "Every litigant, including the state in criminal cases, is entitled to nothing less than the cold neutrality of an impartial judge.

"The state has attached affidavits whereby it feels this cold neutrality does not exist. The court cannot consider, nor will it, the validity of these feelings. In its totality, the affidavits and motions are legally sufficient."

Gayle Graziano was embarrassed and furious at what had taken place. After leaving the courtroom, she secreted herself in an office to cry and scream her rage at the prosecution. Besides the humiliation, how would this look in an election year, she wondered.

The prosecution had its own agenda.

They wanted Judge R. Michael Hutcheson, tractable, malleable, to sit on the bench during the Wuornos case. Without Judge Graziano, they felt certain he would be appointed and asked his secretary about his upcoming schedule. They had objected strenuously to the location of the hearings. They should be held in Daytona Beach, not DeLand, they said.

The prosecution did not anticipate the reaction of Chief Judge McFerrin Smith. Aware that the prosecution was "judge shopping", he approached Uriel Blount, Jr., retired after twenty-four years with the Seventh Circuit. Judge Blount would accept, he said, but only if his two conditions were met. He wanted to try the case in his old courtroom in Volusia County Jail in DeLand and he wanted his old bailiff at his side.

The chief judge was aware of the limitations of the seventy-seat courtroom at Volusia County Jail, especially for a case that had attracted national publicity. He offered to put up the judge and his wife at the Marriott Hotel in Daytona Beach. Judge Blount refused, citing his wife's illness, and remained steadfast in his demand for his old courtroom.

Thus, the court room in the new courthouse in Daytona Beach sat empty. Although it is capable of seating 180 people, equipped with a small room especially designed for media cameras present during high profile cases, it was ignored. Meanwhile, preparations were made to install security equipment in the small, cramped courtroom in which the judge had spent much of his career on the bench.

This meant that the prosecution, with offices in Daytona Beach, must travel to DeLand on a daily basis. It was not what they had envisioned for themselves.

More unnerving to defense counsel than the admissibility and release of the video confession tape was the possibility that the judge would allow Florida's Williams Rule into court proceedings. Based on 1959 case law, *Williams vs. State*, the Williams Rule allows the prosecution to show that a defendant has committed a number of crimes of similar nature. It establishes a pattern. In the case of Aileen Wuornos, it would lend credence to the title "serial killer."

The first step to implementation of the Williams Rule is the filing of a Notice of Similar Fact Evidence. On August 5, State Attorney John Tanner and Assistant State Attorney David Damore had filed a Notice, stating their desire to introduce evidence from the other six murders to which Lee Wuornos had confessed into the trial of Richard Mallory. They would also introduce the testimony of Robert Copus, who had been solicited by Lee Wuornos.

Defense counsel knew how damaging this would be to their case. They had hoped to keep the focus on Richard Mallory alone, but had felt for months that this would probably not be possible.

Judge Graziano had failed to rule on the Notice and it would now be necessary for Judge Blount to make the decision.

The Notice included all three counts on which Lee had been charged: premeditated murder, murder while engaged in the perpetration of or attempt to perpetrate robbery, and in the course of committing the robbery, carried a firearm.

The defense fought back. During a hearing on January 3, they filed a Motion in Limine, excluding the Williams Rule from trial.

Introduction of the evidence sought will force her to:

Forego 5th Amendment privileges as to other pending charges or assert that right before the jury. This would gravely prejudice Defendant in the eyes of the jury.

At the same time, they asked for additional preemptory challenges to the prospective jurors, meaning simply that they could disqualify more than the usual number of jurors if they did not find them acceptable.

Chapter Fourteen

Palmer Monte agreed, reluctantly, to stay at Maranatha Meadows and oversee the farm while Arlene was attending the trial in De-Land.

"I don't want to be part of this. I just don't see why this is necessary," he told her.

"Please, poppy," she replied. "I need you."

Since his heart surgery, Palmer had been in New York, in the same house where he had lived with his wife for more than forty years. He had two woman friends now, one in New York and one in Florida, and was thinking about marriage.

Palmer and Carol Monte had adopted Arlene when she was only a few days old. They had wanted children, but Carol's poor health had prevented that.

An administrator for an oil company, Palmer provided his family with a lovely home on Long Island and regular vacations. Unlike Lee, Arlene was pampered and adored.

"My first mistake was putting her on a horse when she was five years old. She's never gotten off," Monte says.

Carol Palmer's health continued to deteriorate as the years went by. For a long period before her death, Palmer could not leave her alone. Whenever he left, he had to have someone stay with his wife.

They were both proud of their headstrong young daughter.

"I always raised Arlene to speak her mind and to realize that she was no better than anyone else, but she was just as good," he said.

"Arlene's always been into causes."

But nothing prepared him for her relationship with Lee Wuornos.

"You're a grandfather now," Arlene teases him.

More than a month before trial was scheduled to begin, David Damore and Tricia Jenkins discussed the possibility of a plea bargain. If Lee would agree to plead guilty to all seven murders, including the two for which there were no indictments, Damore would speak with the state attorneys and the victims' families in Marion, Citrus, Pasco and Dixie counties to see if they would agree not to seek the death penalty. Instead, Lee would receive seven life sentences with no parole consideration for twenty-five years for the murders, and seven life without parole sentences for the robberies.

"It would ensure that she would die in prison," Damore said.

"Under the Code of Ethics," he continued, "if the defense attorney is interested in a plea resolution, the state must discuss it openly." But the first step was the cooperation of the defendant.

"I was not going to discuss this with the other counties, or put the victims' families through any more unless Miss Wuornos would agree to it," he said.

Tricia Jenkins acknowledged that "We'll have to get Arlene to do this. There's no way that we'll be able to talk Lee into it."

Damore arranged for a meeting of Tricia, Billy, Arlene and Lee.

Over a period of four days, Arlene talked to Lee about the plea bargain. Finally she agreed to accept it.

"Then we go outside," said Arlene, "and we're not outside five minutes and Damore came up to Tricia and said 'I'm sorry, I made a mistake.' "

Damore said that at that point Dixie County was amenable to the plea bargain, Marion and Volusia counties had made no decisions, but Jimmy Russell, state attorney for Pasco County, would not agree. He wanted the death penalty for Lee Wuornos.

"There was no reason to further consider it because it was obviously not going to bear fruit," Damore said.

"I still wanted her to do it, plea for life with the other counties, then we would just fight it out with Pasco," said Arlene. "Don't forget, the guy in Pasco had a weapon. But the attorneys disagreed with me totally, said no, we'd fight all of them.

"We did everything we could to convince Pasco to go along with the plea bargain," said Billy Nolas. "Skip (Howard Babb) talked to Russell, the public defender in Pasco County talked to him, but he just wouldn't listen. We really didn't have any choice except to go to trial."

A final attempt by defense counsel to have their client's case removed from Volusia County took place on the Friday before the trial was scheduled to begin.

"It's a classic example where coverage has permeated the community from which the jury will be drawn," Billy Nolas told Judge Blount.

John Tanner disagreed.

"By and large the public doesn't pay a whole lot of attention to it beyond the headlines," he said.

Judge Blount delayed ruling on the request for change of venue until questioning of prospective jurors. If it became apparent that they could not seat an impartial jury, he would have the trial moved elsewhere.

Tanner had suggested St. Johns County as a possible alternative for the location of the trial.

The state requested the appointment of Dr. George Barnard as an independent psychiatrist to review the testing done by defense psychologists. Dr. Barnard had issued a psychiatric report on Lee in 1981 when she was arrested for armed robbery and was familiar with her background.

The possibility of introducing into the trial evidence of the six other murders to which Lee had confessed via the Williams Rule was again discussed in open court. Judge Blount refused to make a decision, preferring a "wait and see" tactic.

Throughout it all, Lee Wuornos sat patiently at the defense table. She hated being back at Volusia County and she had asked her defense counsel repeatedly to return her to Citrus County until the trial started. They would prefer that, too, they said, because it was closer to their Ocala based operation.

Judge Blount denied the request and the hearing ended. As she was being led back to her holding cell, Lee exploded.

"I'm in fear of my life in the Volusia County Branch Jail and I'm tired of them threatening me and trying to kill me there!"

On the night before trial, Arlene packed her bags. She had no idea whether the trial would remain in DeLand or be sent to another part of the state. She hoped that she could room with Lee's lawyers, but was not assured of that. Money was scarce, the breeding business on the farm had ceased, she had to hire extra help during her absence and she didn't know how she could survive if she had to stay in a motel room.

And she hated leaving the farm. Kingman sensed her imminent departure and kept her in his sight.

"Sometimes I wish that 'poof,' Lee and I could just disappear from this earth," she told guests who had come for dinner that night.

Palmer Monte disliked this kind of conversation. He does not share his daughter's particular brand of Christianity and grows irritable when she makes comments which he considers self-destructive.

The private phone line Arlene had installed shortly after she had begun talking daily with Lee was silent that night. Lee was being held in solitary confinement, without phone privileges. It was a continuation of punishment inflicted on her during a previous stay in Volusia County Branch Jail.

But Arlene was receiving letters regularly. Lee's flowing script, punctuated with tiny drawings, assured her:

"I want to thank you for being so brave again and sticking up for me on TV. All this filth in the law enforcement system needs to be revealed so imperatively to the public. You're the greatest. I don't believe my real grandmother, I mean, momma, would 'ever' of done what your doing. Not very many would. Proof positive, your the only one at first that showed the real reality of Godly love. Out of the whole wide world. That's what makes you so special to me. Cause I know your very special to God. Your at the very top in his realm. I haven't any doubts. That's why I feel 'so special' to know you. . . . Even though it's here, true it's sad, but at least in my deepest hour of darkness, he has proven to me. Like pointing a finger and singling me out, out of all the millions of people and said, 'I know you. I will help you. I send you my most precious and dearly beloved earthly daughter to pull you through. . . And, of course, being a spring chicken from a new enlightenment of reality, I will admit before with Tyria I wouldn't have 'Done His Will.' I was too lost in love with my own sex. Going down the wrong road just like everyone else. I was lost, but now I'm found.

"I look at you as a friend that we became. A sister that developed from the friendship and now the greatest closeness of all 'in writing' that can't separate us now. Your being my precious friend in being my adoptive mother. This is such a great joy inside of me."

Despite a large dosage of the medication her doctor had recommended for sleep, Arlene tossed fitfully, wishing that it were all behind her.

Predator? or Prey?

I believe that this neglected, wounded inner child of the
past is the major souce of human misery.

John Bradshaw
Homecoming

Chapter Fifteen

D eLand, Florida, a small community twenty miles west of Daytona Beach, was once known as an important steamboat stop on the St. Johns River, which runs through central Florida, and today retains much of its original charm. Unlike Daytona Beach, all hustle and bustle, there is a quiet dignity to DeLand which makes it an appropriate home to Florida's oldest private university, Stetson University, named for the cowboy hat that funded it. It also makes it an odd setting for a murder trial.

The first day of the Wuornos trial had all the sufficiency of a Broadway opening crammed into a high school auditorium.

The tiny courtroom at Volusia County Jail which Judge Blount had insisted on occupying had no special accommodations for television personnel.

During jury selection, prospective jurors were scheduled to be seated on one side of the courtroom, leaving only thirty-five seats for media and spectators. While directly across the street stood the DeLand courthouse, with empty courtrooms capable of handling more than twice as many people.

Reporters and cameramen from NBC, CBS, CNN, *Tampa Tribune*, *Miami Herald*, *Ocala Star Banner*, *Daytona Beach News-Journal*, the *Sun News*, *Orlando Sentinel*, AP, UPI, and three book authors crowded into the equivalent of twenty-two seats. Setting up cameras between the cramped benches jammed the traffic pattern. People quickly learned to know each other out of sheer proximity. *Court TV* personnel did not arrive until the second day and were almost refused admittance.

Security measures were nonexistent for this little-used courtroom and guards worked frantically to install the magna scanner security door.

Spectators hoping for admission sat patiently on the long row of benches along one side of the corridor as the cast of characters, the people whose names they saw so often in the newspaper, passed by them on their way into the courtroom. The restrooms, located on the other side of the narrow hallway, opened and closed regularly, often knocking into those who waited to be ushered to seats in the courtroom.

Arlene had driven in from Williston during the early hours of the morning. She had brought enough clothes for the week, bade her father and her "critters" good-bye and climbed into the farm truck she preferred to drive.

"If anyone tries to get at me, I feel protected in this," she told friends. "I can also outrun them."

Realizing that it would be a major media event, Arlene needed to be assured of a seat. Defense counsel felt that her presence in the courtroom would have a calming influence on their difficult client.

When, prior to 9:30 a.m., the defense attorneys arrived, she accosted them with questions concerning Lee's clothing for the day.

"Could you give her the jewelry and cosmetics?" she asked Tricia.

"Will the guards let her wear what we picked out for her?"

The clothes selected for Lee to wear at trial were a combination of items Arlene had purchased and donations from a friend. For the first day, Arlene had decided on a white blouse, black pants and jacket. Simple and tailored. Small pearl earrings would complete the effect she hoped to achieve.

Metal detector in place, the guards called for the media to go into the courtroom.

"This is the worst courtroom in the county," one of the reporters commented as he passed through the metal detector.

The room itself was austere, brightened only by an American flag placed behind the witness chair. The prosecution table was placed on the left side of the courtroom, the defense table on the right, directly in front of the spectators. Behind the defense area, a doorway led to the holding cell where Lee Wuornos would wait when she was not in the courtroom. She would never be without armed guards at her side, and they sat directly behind her during the proceedings.

Arlene paced nervously in the hallway.

"It stinks when the press takes priority over family," she complained to the person next to her.

That morning, her scriptures had prepared her:

God will rescue the righteous out of the grasp of the wicked, although they are now waging war against your life.

By 9:30 a.m., the media had settled into place and the prospective jurors waited anxiously for proceedings to begin. A few spectators filled the last row behind the media, including Arlene Pralle.

At the prosecution table, David Damore and Sean Daly had been joined by State Attorney John Tanner. It was no surprise that the State Attorney would serve as lead attorney for the most visible trial DeLand had ever known. Especially on election year.

Tanner, his figure as lean and rigid as his views, his smile tight, his hair sculpted, was best known for his assault on pornography shops immediately after he was elected to office. His insistence on being involved in the raids themselves had resulted in at least one carefully guarded photo of the State Attorney, standing before a table heaped with pornography objects, holding an enormous dildo in one hand.

The raids were not popular with many factions of the public and they felt his method of closing down "mom and pop" shops and putting people out of business was heartless.

It was typical of Tanner's approach to his career and life.

An active member of the Assembly of God in Ormond Beach, he and his family had for some years lived in a house in the woods at Flagler Beach. He had been running three miles a day for years and was well known as an avid hunter, an occupation which earned him the huge elk head adorning the wall of his office at home.

Tanner's porn campaign had resulted in a number of rallies, often pulling as many as 3000 citizens to the steps of the Daytona Beach Courthouse. Photos of him sporting Hitler's toothbrush mustache circulated. Undaunted, Tanner countered with a pro-Tanner rally.

A native of Daytona Beach, Tanner typified the 1950s beachtown teenager, the popular roustabout. As a lifeguard captain, he developed the athlete's mind-set that he would later carry into every endeavor.

But it was as a lifeguard in 1963 that he experienced a brutal coming of age. Tanner and two others were charged with the death of an initiate during a lifeguard hazing. A grand jury indicted all three for manslaughter, accusing Tanner and the others of holding George Beers under the surf until he drowned. The death occurred during a raucous lifeguard drill called the "water cure."

Tanner, a twenty-five-year-old college student at the time, later said he was on a surfboard twelve feet away during Beers' submersion and was only charged under his command responsibility as team captain. Beers, he said, died not so much from the water...he was alive when brought up...as from a pre-existing condition.

The charge was ultimately dismissed, but it surely had consequences whose effect on Tanner's life can only be a matter of conjecture.

Decades later, Tanner hinted at a personal redemption. He privately recalled rescuing a soldier from a raging stream during a Green Beret exercise. This time the man he plucked from the water was alive, and, he said, the soldier bore the face of George Beers.

The incongruity of Tanner's fundamentalism is the root of the man's enigma. As a Christian, he is expected to esteem all life. Yet he's a gun freak who goes to great lengths to hunt and kill magnificent beasts. He sends murderers to "Old Sparky," Florida's electric chair, while preaching the gospel on Death Row. He attacks obscenity, yet seems to enjoy uttering "fuck" in court. He once flipped his middle finger at an ACLU director, a woman.

For seventeen years he had worked as a defense attorney, yet when he campaigned for the office of state attorney, he ran ads in favor of the death penalty.

When his sensitivity was questioned, he could always point to the fifty odd conferences he had held with Ted Bundy, during which he had tried to save his soul. It was rumored that he still sent the Bundy daughter money from time to time.

Defense counsel and prosecution moved to their tables, and the door near the defense table opened to admit Aileen Wuornos, escorted by several guards. Dressed in a sheer white blouse and baggy black pants, she was agitated because they had not given her the jacket intended for the outfit, her bra showed through the filmy blouse material, and the pants were too big. Forced to give up beer, she had lost forty pounds since she was arrested.

"I gotta tell you, they messed with me real bad. I look terrible—my hair is stringy," she mouthed to Arlene, as she slouched into her seat. "And I want a skirt."

"They aren't allowing her a comb, toothbrush or deodorant," Arlene said to those around her. "They can't get away with this."

A few moments later, Judge Blount entered the courtroom.

Uriel "Bunky" Blount, Jr., of the crew cut, bow tie, white polo shirt and folksy manner, is a no-nonsense judge. Although both camps of attorneys had predicted that the Wuornos trial would be "long and protracted," Blount stated that he would have it done within a month. He made no apologies for the size of the courtroom. This was, he said, not going to turn into the circus which attended the recent Smith-Kennedy trial in Palm Beach.

Earlier in the morning, Judge Blount had refused to hear a defense motion asking for a continuance of the trial so that they could interview Jackie Davis. Larry Horzepa's interview with Davis had not been made available to defense until late Friday, Billy Nolas argued, and they needed to depose her to learn more about the abusive tendencies of Richard Mallory—"All sorts of stuff that it would be nice for the defense to know," stated Nolas. Lee's plea of self defense could be substantially enhanced by further proof that Mallory had a history of violence.

Judge Blount was seated and anxious to begin. He addressed the defendant, who advised him that her name was pronounced "Warn-us", producing a snicker throughout the audience.

"That's okay, you should hear what they can do with Uriel," the judge countered.

After the first twelve prospective jurors were called to the jury box, Blount explained what their duties would be, and advised them that people convicted of first degree murder receive either the death penalty or life in prison with no chance of parole for twenty-five years.

If a conviction takes place, jurors recommend a sentence to the judge after a hearing, and prosecutors and defense attorneys are entitled to jurors who are open to both penalties.

The attorneys advised the jurors: "Listen to evidence, apply common sense, and be fair. The defendant does not carry any burden. She does not have to prove herself not guilty. The burden of the proof is on the state. Your verdict of guilt or innocence must be beyond a reasonable doubt. Not any doubt is not necessary—only reasonable doubt."

And the weightiest consideration: "If you vote Lee Wuornos guilty, you must be prepared to address the death penalty."

And then the questioning began. "Have you served on prior juries? News programs have presented evidence of guilt. Have you formed an impression? Can prostitutes be victims of crime? Will you follow the law given by the judge even if you don't agree? How many people own a firearm? Would a victim of a crime be justified in arming himself? If the defendant makes the decision not to take the stand, would you hold that against her? If the trial ended right now, would you vote guilty or innocent?

And the most thought-provoking: "If you were on trial, would you want yourself on the jury?"

By the end of the day, which had dragged on to 7:30 p.m., ten jurors had been selected from a pool of fifty. The defense had exercised twelve out of sixteen allotted preemptory challenges, the state, five, and Judge Blount had excused about fifteen people because they admitted to prejudice or an inability to vote for the death penalty.

Everyone realized that if jury selection was not completed by the next day, Blount was bound to consider a change of venue.

As David Damore left the courtroom, Arlene grabbed his arm: "Will you please arrange for me to have five minutes with Lee to pray?" she asked.

"I can't make that decision," he said, withdrawing from her. "I'll have to ask Tanner."

A guard returned to Arlene to say that Tanner declined. Later in the day, Tanner said he knew nothing about the request.

Terry Moore, who ran the Volusia County Department of Corrections from his office just inside the front door at Volusia County Jail, told the press that all complaints by Lee Wuornos and Arlene Pralle were "totally without foundation." He added that he had previously been asked by Judge Graziano to look into Lee's complaints, but that he had received no formal complaint from the defense attorneys and they had not returned his calls seeking specific allegations.

Author Phyllis Chesler, who had spoken to Arlene on several occasions, wrote an article for the *New York Times* chastising the treatment of Lee Wuornos in Volusia County.

"Ms. Wuornos told her adoptive mother and me that she has spent long periods of time in solitary confinement, freezing and naked. . . .she has been deprived of daylight and exercise and is often forbidden to phone her lawyer. Ms. Wuornos cannot hear or see very well, but her frequent requests for a hearing aid and glasses have all been denied, as has permission for her to see a gynecologist for her almost continual heavy bleeding. She has lost forty pounds."

"I was angry about the way Lee was being treated, but we did not tell her that Lee was naked in her cell," Arlene remarked after reading the article. "And Lee has lost weight, but it looks good!"

She did, however, object to the lack of medical attention and the moratorium on phone calls and visits.

David Damore was angered by Chesler's article.

"Anybody that knows the jail system here in Volusia County would say this article is obscene. It's a lie. Why would a responsible newspaper print something without facts that are in evidence?" he asked.

Nevertheless, rumors circulated that Volusia County Jail would be picketed if Lee's treatment did not improve.

Deanie Stewart arrived at Volusia County Jail on the second day of jury selection. Her purpose was two-fold. She wanted to see the face of the woman who she believed had killed her brother. And she wanted to meet the woman who had adopted her.

Deanie's blue eyes were filled with tears when she approached Arlene Pralle in the courtroom.

"I am Curtis Reid's sister," she said, "and I think your daughter killed my brother."

It was said without malice. It was said with sorrow, and her pain was obvious, and Arlene greeted her and asked her to sit beside her. Together they watched the selection of the people who would ultimately determine Lee's destiny, and Deanie began to tell Arlene about her life, and her brother, Curtis, and the investigators at Marion County.

Curtis "Corky" Reid, Deanie's only brother, had been a senior engineer at Cape Canaveral. Twenty years earlier, he had fallen six stories from the roof of one of the buildings and survived. Other men had made similar falls, but none had lived.

For months, Deanie and her husband, Jim, who is in a wheelchair as a result of an accident in the early 1970s, cared for "Corky." In time he returned to work, but, by then, his marriage had ended and he was alone.

On September 6, 1990, Corky Reid stopped to see his sister at the car dealership which she and her husband owned. He offered to take their mother to the doctor, and Deanie thanked him. He was leaving that day for a long weekend during which he would meet his best friend, Ray, in Cocoa Beach and then continue on to Orlando to see his doctor. He had experienced a slight stroke several months ago and needed to have a check-up. He planned to leave after Mrs. Reid's doctor's appointment.

"I'm glad you're going to a specialist," Deanie said to him that day as they stood in the car lot.

Corky Reid was a family man who had lost his marital family, and he leaned heavily on his sister and his mother. Every Sunday, without fail, he spent the afternoon with his mom at her house, watching television, talking, sharing what was new in his life. Mrs. Reid's regular trips to the doctor and all other needs were shared between Corky and Deanie.

On that Thursday, Corky said good-bye to his sister.

"I had walked him to his car," Deanie remembers, "and I took his hand and said 'God, honey, you know how much I love you? More than anyone in this world. And don't you forget that.'

"I love you, too," he said, and kissed the sister who had seen him through so much.

It was the last time Deanie Stewart saw her brother.

On Sunday, Mrs. Reid called Deanie to tell her that Corky had not come by for his regular visit, but Deanie was not alarmed until Corky's secretary at the Cape called on Monday to tell her that he had not shown up for work.

Shielding her mother from her escalating fears, Deanie went to Corky's home to see if he had collapsed inside. He was not there, nor was his automobile. Inside, everything was in order, just as he would have left it before his trip.

"His badge was there, his work clothes—just as though he were coming back," she said.

Jim and Deanie contacted the Titusville Police Department and were told that Corky had no doubt gone off on a "toot." Deanie knew better.

"He would not have done that. If he had wanted time off from work all he had to do was ask. And he would never have left without telling us where he was going. Mom was sick and our sister, in Ohio, was dying of cancer. He had made arrangements to visit his son by his first marriage in Texas and then go on to our sister's in Ohio in a few months. He was looking forward to the trip."

At the Titusville Police Department, Deanie was advised to wait for seventy-two hours before filing a missing person report. She knew her brother and it did not take seventy-two hours for her to realize that something had happened to him.

"Within forty-eight hours, we had 2000 flyers made, and a search party of 500 people looking for Corky in Brevard and Volusia counties. There were no responses," she says.

And Dan Carter of the Titusville Police Department, while working on Corky's case, was coming across other similar cases. He joined the task force which had originated in Marion County. The group had one goal—to find the killer or killers of the men found near the highways in Central Florida.

On November 11, 1990, at 1:00 a.m., Deanie was notified that her brother's car had been located in a parking lot near I-95 in Orlando. Assured that the Orlando Police Department would meet her at the location, she and her daughter, Tina, drove to the lot. No one was there except the security guard for the parking lot who had called the car in after it sat empty for several days.

Deanie and Tina, attempting to maintain whatever fingerprints might be present, drove the car home to the family car lot. Keys to the car and NASA were on the floor, along with a torn prophylactic package and packages of Marlboro and Camel cigarettes.

The car, which Corky had always taken good care of, had no oil, no gas, and the brakes had been ground down to the drum. The glove compartment had been emptied out except for registration papers and Corky's tool box had been taken from the trunk. And the car seat was pulled forward.

Dan Carter continued to investigate the disappearance of Curtis Reid. He also became the friend of the Reid and Stewart families.

"It was funny," Deanie says, "but before Curtis disappeared, I heard from various sources that the investigators in Marion County were planning to write a book about the murders of these men. I couldn't believe it. They were talking about writing a book and they hadn't even found who was responsible."

Bruce Munster had elected to head the task force so that he could orchestrate the arrest of the killer or killers whenever it happened. It would mean more money and glory for the Marion County Sheriff's Department and assure him of the opportunity to be present. If he wanted a media contract out of this case, he had to participate in it.

After her brother's car was found in Marion County, Deanie Stewart began to call the Marion County Sheriff's Department to see what action was being taken on her brother's behalf.

"No one returned my calls," she said. "No one. They were always 'out in the field.' "

Out of frustration, Deanie called the attorney general and reported the non-action of the Marion County investigators. Shortly thereafter, Bruce Munster called her.

"Does this call have anything to do with my phone call to the attorney general?" she asked.

"Yes, ma'am," he admitted reluctantly.

When Lee Wuornos was arrested and Tyria Moore was brought back to Florida from Pennsylvania, Deanie asked Bruce Munster to show the women a picture of her brother to see if they could identify him as a victim.

"Bruce Munster kept telling me that my brother was not involved, and he kept saying over and over again, when I asked him why Tyria was not being prosecuted, that she 'was so dumb and stupid and ignorant and completely petrified of Aileen, she would have done anything to get away from her, and besides Ty was at work when the men were missing.'

"I didn't buy it then and I don't buy it now. Something is very wrong here. According to the law, Tyria Moore was an accessory. All Marion County cared about was their book and movie," Deanie says.

One of Corky's friends at Cape Canaveral learned that the Marion County investigators had not been cooperating with other members of the task force.

"They told me that Dan Carter's name was not even on the task force list," Deanie says.

Petitions began to circulate to try to force Munster to include Carter in the questioning of Aileen Wuornos.

> We the family of Curtis L. (Corky) Reid, ask for your help to sign this petition, so that Det. Dan Carter of the Titusville Police Department, can question one Aileen Carol Wuornos now in custody, about the disappearance and possible death of Curtis L. (Corky) Reid. Mr. Reid disappeared Sept. 6, 1990 from Titusville, Fl. where he has lived for the last 30 years.

"Within two days, I had received a phone call from Dan Carter asking me to pull the petitions in or Marion County would not cooperate," Deanie remembers.

Shortly before Lee Wuornos was tried for the murder of Richard Mallory, Deanie and Jim were called into the Sheriff's Department at Marion County to look at some property that had been held in custody. They were items that Tyria Moore had in her possession when she was brought back to Florida. These were among the things that Lee had given her, she said.

"My father's suitcase, which Corky had borrowed, was there. His Levi jacket and Members Only jacket were there. Sweatshirts like those my brother wore. I recognized all of them, but I couldn't prove they were his.

"Bruce Munster asked Dan Carter, who was with me, if I could positively identify these items beyond a reasonable doubt and I had to say no. There were no identifying marks, but I knew they belonged to my brother.

"None of these items had been sent in to Florida Department of Law Enforcement to be checked as they were supposed to be."

During the past year, Deanie and Jim have taken part in eight body searches. None of the bodies were Curtis Reid.

"My brother went to his death still in love with his ex-wife," says Deanie. "He was a lonely man. He would have picked up a hitchhiker.

"I think Lee Wuornos killed my brother. I don't want to know the details. I don't need to know what happened. I just want to bring him home."

Chapter Sixteen

During the second day of jury selection, the attractive red-haired woman who had described herself as a Christian on the previous day asked to be excused. She had been up all night praying for guidance and concluded that: "I could not sentence this woman to death."

As she left the courtroom, she touched the arm of Billy Nolas and said, "Good luck." Arlene Pralle slipped her a note which said, simply, "Thank you."

More than a dozen people during the two-day selection process had asked to be excused because they did not believe in capital punishment and could not, would not consider it even under directions from the judge.

Blount, short and chubby with protruding ears, handled his courtroom with a firm hand, but a light touch.

He had a wide range of Blountisms, including "the jury is getting hairy eyeballs " and "I'm sometimes in error, but I'm never in doubt." He enjoyed occasional humor, as long as it didn't interfere with business, and laughed with the rest of the courtroom when a potential juror was asked whether or not he was prejudiced against prostitutes. "Some of my best friends are prostitutes," he had responded. And a female prospect was questioned if pre-trial publicity had left an impression on her. "The only impression I have is the one on my flat rear end." It had been a long, tiring day in the courtroom.

By 3:10 p.m., the parade of prospective jurors had ended, and seven women and five men, including an equestrienne, schoolteacher, pharmacist, jewelry store owner, cheese salesman had been selected. Two alternates, one man and one woman, were also chosen to sit in on the trial. They would not be allowed to vote on the verdict unless they replaced one of the regulars, they were told. Those in the courtroom who were familiar with the oft-published picture of Richard Mallory noted that juror number nine looked very much like the victim, and wasn't it as though Richard Mallory was sitting in judgment at his own trial.

Tanner's teen-aged daughter, Carmel, sat briefly next to Arlene in the back row behind the media. Not recognizing Arlene at first, she mentioned that she hoped the defendant got the chair. Her face reddened when Arlene introduced herself, but she expressed surprise when Arlene told her that her father would not permit her to see Lee.

"Would you see if you can convince him to let us be together?" Arlene implored.

"Yes, of course," Carmel Tanner said as she left the courtroom.

Tanner followed his daughter out.

"I have no jurisdiction over that," he responded crustily to Arlene's request. "Ask the Department of Corrections."

The news media had already approached Terry Moore. "Tanner must give approval," he told the press.

"Of course Miss Wuornos and Mrs. Pralle can talk at any time," Tanner smiled for the press.

"I hope they all turn into toads," Arlene fumed.

Word circulated at the jailhouse that the sister of Curtis Reid was in the gallery. Outside, reporters asked her how she felt about the case.

Deanie Stewart told the press that she felt the Marion County investigators were interested in one thing. The book and movie deals that they had coveted long before the arrest of Lee Wuornos. They had protected Tyria Moore, she said, because they wanted her to be part of their deal.

"Lee Wuornos should not be taking this rap alone," she said.

As Arlene left the jailhouse, the press descended on her. She was furious with the treatment Lee had been receiving, she spat into the microphones. She was convinced that the Department of Corrections was trying to kill Lee by overdosing her on Vistaril. Lee was not given any of the toiletry items she had requested, and they kept her in solitary where she was unable to even place a phone call to Arlene. Despite numerous requests, they were not allowed visits, and Arlene's patience was wearing thin.

"I want you to know what kind of men are running the operation in Volusia County. They're evil. They're all evil."

In the courtroom, the judge spoke with the defense team. If they didn't keep Lee's adoptive mother quiet, he would find her in contempt of court. And he had just learned about certain accusations made by Lee Wuornos that needed to be resolved.

Lee had told her defense counsel that on a recent trip to Gainesville, where she was to be interviewed by the state's psychiatrist, Dr. George Barnard, the deputies transporting her had raped her.

Roy H. Shaffer, Jr., deputy sheriff of Volusia County, was called to the

Office of the Public Defender for questioning. He had nothing to hide, he told himself, and there was no reason to be nervous. Deputy Jim Albert had been with him when they picked Aileen Wuornos up at Volusia County Branch Jail at 6:00 a.m. last Wednesday.

"Ms. Wuornos appeared at first to be in a real good mood, and then when I put the waist restraint on her, she jerked away from me and told me she was tired of being treated like a criminal and she wasn't going with us," he told the attorneys.

"I advised her she was going. She had to go. I had a court order and she was going in a waist restraint just like we transport all the other prisoners.

"So she agreed to go. And when we was leaving the jail, we went out of the jail, on our way to our patrol car, she said something. I didn't catch what it was and when she got in the patrol car, before we got out of the sally port, she said something to the effect, and I don't know the exact words, I'm going to say you guys stopped along the way and raped me and I'm—I'm not worried about a lie detector because I can pass that too. Something to that effect."

When they reached Dr. Barnard's office, Lee told Shaffer that she needed to talk to her attorneys. She had some complaints to make about Deputy Shaffer and Deputy Albert.

"I asked her if she wanted us to contact the Gainesville Police Department, have a report filed and request a rape test. She refused it.

"Later in the transport," Shaffer continued, "we took her to the restroom. She made a threat toward me when we were coming back from the restroom. She pointed her finger at me like a gun and said 'bang—and I would if I could.'

"She said something to the effect, and I don't know the exact quote, that she would like to see us—excuse me—butt fucked by at least three guys and left on the side of the road for dead with blood running out of our ass."

Shaffer leaned back in his chair.

The defense team had listened quietly.

"Mostly she complained that the waist restraint was too tight. It wasn't too tight. You could stick your hand behind it and turn it sideways as we showed you," Shaffer concluded.

That night Arlene and Lee were allowed their first phone conversation since Lee had been brought back to Volusia County. Arlene had heard that Lee went to Gainesville to see Dr. Barnard, but knew nothing about the allegations.

"Just by way of conversation, I asked Lee about her trip to Gainesville," Arlene said the next morning to Tricia when they met in the ladies room before trial. "And she got very angry with me and began screaming what was I talking about, she had never gone to Gainesville. Did I misunderstand?"

Tricia stared unbelievingly at Arlene. "We're dead," she said, shaking her head.

Accusations from both Lee and Arlene that the guards at Volusia County Branch Jail were forcing lethal doses of Vistaril on Lee demanded the attention of defense counsel.

Ismael Lancaster Lopez, mental health counselor for the Volusia County Department of Corrections, was subpoenaed for deposition in order to clarify the issue.

"I believe the medication she was on was Vistaril and that was several months ago," testified Lopez. "I think it was shortly after she came in and was only on it for a short period of time."

"Why was she put on Vistaril?" Billy Nolas asked.

"She complained of, I believe, anxiety, and Vistaril is a mild...has a mild tranquilizing effect."

Lopez produced a medical request form from Lee.

"I would like to see a psychologist...emergency, please," it read.

"They took me to Ocala over the weekend and yanked my medication from under me when I got back. Please get in touch with me as soon as possible. I am in dire need of something to help my nerves. I was taking Vistaril—100 milligrams. But I know that I need Librium or Mellaril instead because I got weird head reactions and it is my nerves, *not* my head."

Nolas continued his questioning.

"In this report you indicated that Miss Wuornos said that she was still having...she was sleeping sporadically and having a difficult time coping with all the pressure she's under. You also indicate poor insight and poor judgment in this report.

"Did you see that in her?"

"Yeah," replied Lopez. "She presented herself as being very manipulative and overt."

"Do you know how her medication was terminated?"

"I believe...if I'm not mistaken...I believe that she ultimately refused the medication. She decided that she didn't want it anymore."

"What about the matter of poor judgment," Nolas asked. "Do you have examples?"

Lopez thought for a moment and then proceeded.

"I recall her getting in trouble in the cell block area and when I called her...when I spoke to her, her complaint was regarding a black inmate. She said that the black inmate threatened her. I asked her, I said, 'Well, what do you think might have provoked that?' She says, 'Well, nothing...' 'There's no way in the world somebody is going to approach you,' I told her. I mean Aileen is a very...she's in the spotlight...I can't remember who the girl was, but she was a small framed girl and Aileen is about five foot six inches and 140 pounds or so.

"Then she was let out of confinement and once again boom again her complaint was, you know, she was involved in a verbal dispute with another inmate again. Once again it was a black female again and once again of small stature. And it was the exact same complaint. 'Well, she approached me and she said that she was going to kill me and da, da, da.' And you know I said, 'Well, Aileen, what did you say to her? Did you say anything to provoke her?' 'Well, no, I didn't do anything.'

"Those are the kind of things I was talking about with regards to the judgment things."

Arlene was notified that the prison was not administering lethal doses of Vistaril to Lee. In fact she was no longer receiving medication of any kind.

"Let's get the jury out here and go to work," Judge Blount admonished the attorneys. For the better part of an hour, the fourteen men and women had waited while the attorneys cleared up last minute pre-trial matters.

When the jury was seated, State Attorney John Tanner moved the lectern closer and, in his usual friendly, homespun manner, he addressed them:

"Aileen Carol Wuornos is charged with the murder in the first degree, by premeditation, and the robbery itself, we'll ask armed robbery. The evidence that we believe will be revealed at the trial during the next several days will show that on November 30, 1989, a little over two years ago, Richard Mallory, age 51, who turned east on I-4, the state highway near Tampa, didn't know this would be the last day of his life. He didn't know that in less than ten hours he would be robbed, murdered, his body left to rot in the woods. Of course he didn't know that he was about to pick up a predatory prostitute who had had sex with over 250,000 men, by her own admission. He didn't know he was about to admit into his car, Aileen Carol Wuornos. At the time her lust for control

Aileen ''Lee'' Wuornos after her arrest. *(Courtesy Daytona Beach News-Journal)*

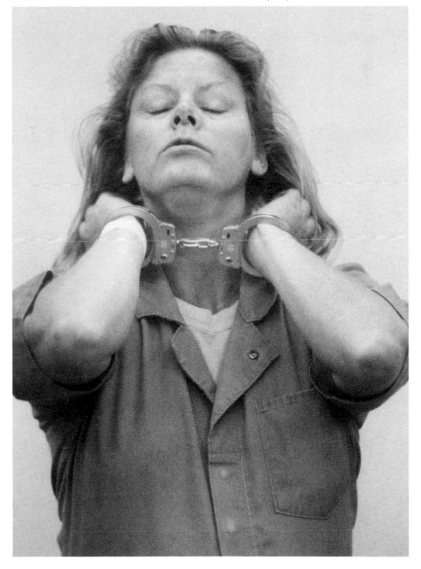

The Last Resort. *(Courtesy Daytona Beach News-Journal)*

Manager of The Last Resort, Cannonball. *(Courtesy Angela DiMaso)*

Pattern of killings.

VICTIM	RICHARD MALLORY	DAVID SPEARS	CHARLES CARSKADDON	PETER SIEMS	TROY BURRESS	DICK HUMPHREYS	WALTER ANTONIO
DATE BODY FOUND	DECEMBER 13 1989	JUNE 1 1990	JUNE 6 1990	REPORTED MISSING JUNE 22, 1990	AUGUST 4th 1990	SEPTEMBER 12th 1990	NOVEMBER 19th 1990
WHITE MALE	✔	✔	✔	✔	✔	✔	✔
AGE	51	43	39	65	46	56	60
TRAVELING INTERSTATE HIGWAY	✔	✔	✔	✔	✔	✔	✔
TRAVELING ALONE	✔	✔	✔	✔	✔	✔	✔
PICKED-UP WUORNOS HITCHHKING	✔	✔	✔	✔	✔	✔	✔
GUN-SHOT WOUNDS TO TORSO	✔	✔	✔	✔	✔	✔	✔

① Body of Richard Mallory, 51, found in Volusia County on Dec. 13, 1989

② Body of David Spears, 43, found in Citrus County on June 1, 1990

③ Body of Charles Carskaddon, 40, found in Pasco County on June 6, 1990

④ Car of Peter Siems, 65, found deserted in Marion County on July 4, 1990. No body found

⑤ Body of Troy Burress, 50, found in Marion County on Aug. 4, 1990

⑥ Body of Dick Humphreys, 56, found in Marion County on Sept. 12, 1990

⑦ Body of Walter Gino Antonio, 60, found in Dixie County on Nov. 19, 1990

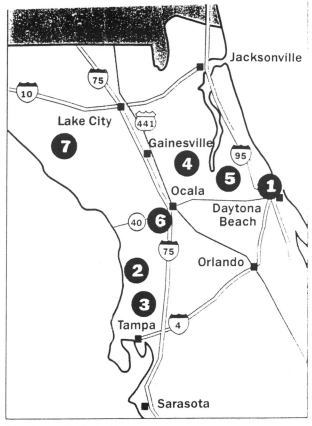

Murder trail of victims.

The first of Lee's seven victims—Richard Mallory.
(Courtesy Daytona Beach News-Journal)

Richard Mallory's girlfriend, Jackie Davis, testifies. *(Courtesy Daytona Beach News-Journal)*

Lee Wuornos with
Russ Armstrong
and Raymond Cass.
*(Courtesy Daytona Beach
News-Journal)*

Chief Investigator Lawrence Horzepa,
of Volusia County Sheriff's
Department; Lee gave her confession
to him. *(Courtesy Daytona Beach
News-Journal)*

Dawn Botkins waited to be called
as a character witness for her
friend Aileen.

MISSING PERSON

CURTIS L. (CORKY) REID

AGE 50, HEIGHT 5'7" - 5'8" TALL,
170 - 180 LBS, GRAY/BALDING HAIR, AND
HAZEL/GREEN EYES. LAST SEEN 9/6/90.
HAS TATOO ON LEFT FOREARM "82ND AIRBORNE..DO OR DIE"
AND TRAKE SCAR AT THROAT.

ALSO MISSING, 1986 WHITE 4-DOOR OLDS CUTLASS SIERRA
WITH BLUE INTERIOR. TAG # FL GVK-46H

IF YOU HAVE ANY INFORMATION, PLEASE CONTACT:

BREVARD SHERIFFS OFFICE OR FAMILY MEMBERS AT:
TITUSVILLE 268-5995 OR 269-5995.

T.P.D. 269-7500 ATTEN: DECT. WARREN

SHERIFF DEPT: ATTEN: -INV. NELL GEHRKE 267-2511

Missing person flyer for Corky Reid.

Arlene Pralle on the horsefarm. *(Courtesy Angela DiMaso)*

Tyria Moore—ex-roommate, ex-lover, ex-friend. *(Courtesy Daytona Beach News-Journal)*

Composite sketches of Lee and Ty.

Lee Wuornos listens to
testimony of Tyria Moore.
*(Courtesy Daytona Beach
News-Journal)*

Public defenders Billy Nolas (left) and (right) Tricia Jenkins. *(Courtesy Daytona
Beach News-Journal)*

Assistant state's attorneys Sean Daly and David Damore. *(Courtesy Daytona Beach News-Journal)*

John Tanner talks to media. *(Courtesy Daytona Beach News-Journal)*

Judge Uriel Blount, Jr., confers with Nolas and Tanner. *(Courtesy Daytona Beach News-Journal)*

During trial, candy replaced cigarettes. *(Courtesy Daytona Beach News-Journal)*

Flipping her hair—a
frequent angry
gesture. *(Courtesy
Daytona Beach News-
Journal)*

"One hundred dollars is fine. That's what I told him." *(Courtesy Daytona Beach News-Journal)*

"They made me beg for my life." *(Courtesy Daytona Beach News-Journal)*

"I thought I gotta fight or I'm gonna die." *(Courtesy Daytona Beach News-Journal)*

"I'm the victim as far as I'm concerned." *(Courtesy Daytona Beach News-Journal)*

Lee communicating from defense table to gallery. *(Courtesy Daytona Beach News-Journal)*

faces of Lee

"Was I supposed to walk down the road naked with a gun in my hand? Everyone has the right to defend themself." *(Courtesy Daytona Beach News-Journal)*

"I'm only here for Richard Mallory. I'm here for one trial." *(Courtesy Daytona Beach News-Journal)*

"I've never seen the man. I don't deal with anyone that fat." *(Courtesy Daytona Beach News-Journal)*

Arlene Pralle communicating from gallery to defense table. *(Courtesy Daytona Beach News-Journal)*

Arlene Pralle and Steve Glazer after the verdict. *(Courtesy Daytona Beach News-Journal)*

Robert Nolin interviews Arlene Pralle. *(Courtesy Daytona Beach News-Journal)*

Lee hears jury's recommendation of death. *(Courtesy Daytona Beach News-Journal)*

Arlene Pralle sobs on Dolores Kennedy's shoulder. *(Courtesy Daytona Beach News-Journal)*

At sentencing, Lee tells the judge that her attorneys failed her. *(Courtesy Daytona Beach News-Journal)*

Lee is fingerprinted after sentencing. *(Courtesy Daytona Beach News-Journal)*

Arlene waits for Lee to appear. *(Courtesy Daytona Beach News-Journal)*

Lee leaves Volusia County Jail.
(Courtesy Daytona Beach News-Journal)

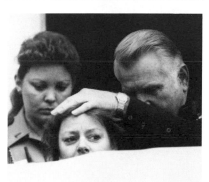

She is put into the transport car.
(Courtesy Daytona Beach News-Journal)

''Lee, bye, I love you.'' *(Courtesy Daytona Beach News-Journal)*

Lee Wuornos leaves Volusia County for death row. *(Courtesy Daytona Beach News-Journal)*

had taken a lethal turn. She was no longer satisfied with just taking men's bodies and money, now she wanted the ultimate control. She wanted all that Mr. Mallory had—the car, property, his life.

"The next day, deputy sheriffs found Mr. Mallory's automobile abandoned, in the woods, north of Ormond Beach. Approximately two weeks later, December 13, they found Mr. Mallory west on the opposite side of the road north of Ormond Beach. They found him covered with a carpet; his face had begun to decompose so that identification was not readily apparent at that time. They found four bullet holes in his body, his pockets turned inside out. He was fully clothed and his pants were zipped. Miss Wuornos shot and killed Mr. Mallory, taking his property. She had gone through his pockets, covered him up, and then returned to her motel where her lesbian lover, best friend, Tyria Moore, and she used the car to move their property to another residence. Shortly thereafter she told Tyria Moore she killed Richard Mallory and it was his automobile she had used and taken his property.

"Ultimately on January 16, of 1991, approximately a year ago, she gave a complete statement after being advised of her constitutional rights, having had a lawyer summoned to protect her rights. She told Deputy Sheriff Larry Horzepa of the Volusia County Sheriff's Office several stories as to how [it had happened]. All of the stories agree on points. She says she was hitchhiking along the interstate just east of Tampa heading in an easterly direction when she was picked up by Mr. Mallory on November 30, 1989.

"She says they travelled on the interstate, across the state toward the Daytona Beach area. While travelling, they drank and talked. In all of her stories she says that she solicited him to an act of prostitution, saying that she needed the money for rent. In the story she says he was wearing blue jeans and a shirt and without exception she says they began hugging and kissing after finding a place to park in the woods north of Ormond Beach and that they were having a good time and that it was her intent to give him sex for money. In the first story, she says that Mr. Mallory paid her in advance, but that she became concerned that he might try to take the money back and therefore she jumped out of the automobile and pulled from her bag a gun, a pistol that she had only had for approximately two days. She told him to get out of the automobile, step away and then she changed the story. Told us he stayed in the car, she didn't tell him to get out, but she shot him in the automobile while he was sitting behind the wheel. Doesn't remember whether she shot him two or three times, but, in any event, she ultimately killed him. The next story she told to the same deputy, same officer was again that she solic-

ited money, but this time she said that they had been drinking and talking and having fun for about five hours parked in the woods north of
Ormond Beach and that she decided he was a nice guy and that she usually wanted her money in advance, but he was such a nice guy she didn't
think she really needed to get the money in advance. And then they began to move toward the ultimate act of having sex. But he wouldn't take
his clothes off. He wanted to just unzip his pants. And she didn't like it
that way and they began to argue and struggle a little bit about it. Then
she got out of the car and said, "Oh no, you're not going to just fuck me.
You're going to pay me." And then she shot him as he sat behind the
wheel. In both stories when she talks about the killing, she admits he
was sitting in the automobile behind the wheel fully clothed when she
shot him. And that she was out of the car with a loaded nine shot revolver in her hand, and he with no weapon whatever. She says that after
she shot him in the front seat, he crawled out of the driver's door and
shut the door because on the other side of that doorway was a woman
who was pumping bullets into him. She says he crawled out the door and
then she ran around to the front of the car. Difficult to imagine, but she
shot him again. He fell to the ground and she shot him.

"The evidence gives several explanations as to why she killed Richard Mallory. She told the deputy that she didn't really understand
why she shot him. She also said because he didn't pay. But she also said
well because he was going to try to take the money back. Also because he
wouldn't take his pants off. She didn't want to have sex that way. Her
statements indicate that it was partly because he was middle aged. According to her it didn't make much difference if she killed him because
he didn't have any parents. The real reason as you sort out the evidence
in its totality is not all that complex. She said she doesn't really know
why she killed him. The evidence tells you why she killed him. She killed
him out of greed. She was no longer satisfied with $10, $20, $40. She
wanted it all. And she had to take it. And she did. And she used a gun
to take it. And she shot him to keep it. She also told the deputy that she
needed to kill him dead, not just shoot him because she didn't want to
leave a witness. And she had a very practical reason for that position.
She said after all, I'm a professional road highway prostitute and if I
didn't kill him, I couldn't go back out on the highway. They would find
me. And she didn't want to be caught. And she wanted to be certain
that there was no way that she could be punished and held responsible
for killing this man in cold blood and robbing him. Intent. She said she
intended to let him die.

"Ultimately, the bottom line is, the evidence in its totality will show that Aileen Carol Wuornos liked control. She had been exercising control for years over men. Tremendous power that she had through prostitution. She had devised a plan now and carried it out to have the ultimate control. All that Richard Mallory had she took, including his life. Under the law, under the law, she must pay with her life."

And then it was Tricia Jenkins' turn. Facing the jury, she cleared her throat, and grasped the lectern with meticulously manicured hands. Spectators could not help noting the contrast between the feminine, articulate public defender and the woman whose life she was fighting to save.

"Ladies and gentlemen, the evidence is going to show that when Aileen Wuornos jumped into the car with Richard Mallory on that rainy night in December of 1989, she had no idea that she was going to be travelling with him into a nightmare and that that ride would ultimately bring her into this courtroom today. The evidence will show that on the day that she met Richard Mallory, she had been to Fort Myers. She had received six rides on her way back. It was getting late and she was real tired.

"She stopped near the interstate I-4 and 75 and it was raining and she got under the overpass in order to stay out of the weather until it would clear up. She was standing in the shadows. As she was standing in the shadows, a car passed by. She saw the light and she saw it pull over and then it began to back towards her in the dark and you will hear that she was frightened. Because of the weather and because of the darkness, she couldn't tell if it was a car full of guys or what it was. She didn't think she could be seen.

"You're going to hear evidence that Lee has been on her own since she has been a very small child. You'll hear that she has been living on the road. You are going to hear that she's a prostitute living from one highway exit to the next. You're also going to hear that home for her, as the prosecutor has indicated to you, is a motel. When times are good, she rents a motel by the week. When they're lean, she rents it by the day. You're also going to hear that times were changing out on the road. Existence for Lee was getting to be very dangerous. The frequency with which she met physical abuse was escalating. Remember she started on the road when she was a young, young girl. Things were changing. Time after time after time she was raped. Time after time after time she was beaten up and she wasn't paid. Finally, she armed herself. This night that Richard Mallory stopped on the side of the road and backed towards her, she was making a decision. Do I try to get back farther in the shadows and try to hide or do I wait and see if I can get a ride with someone else. Well, ultimately he asked her if she wanted to go with him. He was going all the way to Daytona and that's where she was going. She knew that her very best friend, her roommate, the person that she was helping to support would be waiting for her and wondering why she was out so late. She was happy that she had just one ride that would take her all the way to Daytona because as I said before, it had taken her six rides to get from Fort Myers to the side of the road where Richard Mallory stopped to pick her up. So they began to travel towards Daytona. You will hear evidence that Richard Mallory was drinking and he was fixing himself mixed drinks and that he offered her a drink. You will also hear that Aileen drinks when she is out on the road. She drinks when she's out on the road because it gives her courage. It keeps her from being too nervous. So she had some beer before she got into the car with Mr. Mallory. And Mr. Mallory offered her some of his alcohol. He also offered her some marijuana. He was smoking marijuana. You'll hear that she told him no. She didn't like marijuana, but it didn't bother her if he smoked because her roommate did. But she did want to drink. She wanted to rest and have a straight shot home to Daytona. You will hear that they did continue to drink. You'll hear that she was getting concerned because he was smoking so much. You'll hear that he stopped at one point to get gas and asked her if she wanted beer and yes she did. She did want beer. At some point she indicated to him that she needed to make some money for groceries and for rent. You have heard that Lee is a prostitute and that is how Lee earns her money. Mr. Mallory said he was looking for a good time so this is perfect.

"They returned to Daytona. They arrived in Daytona late that night and they went to a secluded area. They stayed in that area until almost 5:00 in the morning, talking and drinking, having fun. You will hear that Lee had decided that she could trust him. She started feeling comfortable with him. They had not been having sex up to this point. They had been talking. You will hear that Mallory had a lot of things he wanted to talk over, problems in his life. You will hear that at approximately 5:00 in the morning, Mallory asked Lee are you ready to earn your money now. Lee said yes. You will hear that Mr. Mallory suggested that she take off all of her clothes. That way he would be assured that she was not going to run away or gonna rip him off. Lee, once again, as I told you before, thought she could trust this person. So she agreed and she began to take off her clothes. At that point, Mr. Mallory said I'll be right back. I've got to get something out of the trunk. Lee thought that was fine. Mr. Mallory got out of the car, he opened up the trunk. Lee folded up her clothes and put them in the back seat. She waited a good while;

soon she heard the trunk close. She was embarrassed. Mr. Mallory opened the door. He also opened a nightmare for Lee. This wasn't the nice, calm person. Again he had been smoking all night long and he had been drinking all night. You will hear evidence of bondage, rape, sodomy and degradation and Lee was a victim of that. Ultimately, after a fixed period of time, Lee was able to get away. During the period of time that she was being subjected to the abuse that Mr. Mallory was inflicting, he told her I've done it to other women. As I told you before, Lee had begun to carry a weapon. Lee had a weapon in her purse, on the floor on the passenger's side of the front seat. Lee got that weapon and she shot Mr. Mallory. She got out of the car and Mr. Mallory was still coming toward her. She said, 'Don't come any closer, don't come any closer or I will shoot again.' He was cursing her. He was wounded. He was angry. He said he was going to kill her and he kept coming and she shot him again.

"You will hear testimony that she was terrified. She didn't know what to do. She decided she needed to get out of there. She wanted to take the car and get away. She drove his car, totally nude, frantically, driving to get away from the situation that she had just been involved in. She drove for a good distance, again nude, driving, trying to get away, running. Ultimately she found a place to stop, she got dressed and she was trying to figure out what to do. She knew she couldn't go to the police. She knew she couldn't tell anybody. Who was going to believe her. She was a prostitute. Mr. Mallory was a business man. She knew they wouldn't believe her. As you recall, she went to her girlfriend's. Actually both of them were living in this motel. They had been living together for several years at this point. And she told her about it. And she told her that she should defend herself. That she shouldn't be treated like that. However you're going to hear that Ty has kind of changed her mind about that. You're going to hear that she changed her mind when there was a composite on the TV and you're going to hear that Ty agreed to assist law enforcement and come down to Florida and help them catch her friend, her love, and you'll hear that she did that. She came down to Daytona, law enforcement put her in a motel, paid for all her expenses, basically gave her whatever she wanted, beer, cigarettes, shopping, to stay in that motel, wrote a note to Lee, told her where she was going to be and asked that she call her collect at the motel. And for a period of either three or four days, she worked on Lee to get Lee to say that she had done this and that Ty didn't have anything to do with it and didn't know about it. Finally, after Ty threatened to kill herself, after Ty had told her that her family was being threatened, she finally convinced Lee to tell law enforcement about it. Now you're going to see a video of Lee talking to law enforcement. Contrary to what the prosecutor has told you, you are not going to hear several stories about what happened. You're going to hear her say, I will protect Ty, I will do anything, I will even die for her and you'll hear her give one version of what occurred. And you will also hear her say I was so drunk—I was just so drunk. She will say I was drunk royal. During the time that she was out in the woods with Mr. Mallory, her constant knowledge of impending danger was blurred by alcohol. She was really drunk. And she apologizes to the law enforcement. I'm confused, I can't remember anything. I was just so drunk. But you will hear her tell one version of what occurred that night. You will hear that he got violent with her.

"Ladies and gentlemen. Lee Wuornos is not guilty of first degree premeditated murder and armed robbery. She defended herself. She had had enough. Not one more time could she take it. Not one more time."

The prosecution flew into action. They called to the stand Volusia County Deputy Sheriff John Bondi and asked him to tell the jury the manner in which he had found Richard Mallory's abandoned automobile, and describe the items found at the scene of the crime.

"On December 1, 1989, in the course of routine patrol, on or about 3:20 p.m., I discovered an abandoned vehicle in a wooded area on John Anderson Drive...I conducted an inquiry around the vehicle looking for a driver, failed to find anyone in the area."

Bondi took the registration number and discovered that the car belonged to a Richard Mallory.

"Do these photographs clearly and accurately reflect the scene as it appeared to you on December 1, 1989?" John Tanner asked the witness.

"Yes, sir."

Bondi described the items buried near the scene as two plastic tumblers, a brown paper bag containing .750 liter bottle of Smirnoff vodka, blue nylon wallet, driver's license, credit cards, vehicle registration to the Cadillac, red car caddy and other assorted papers. A white cloth was used between the items and top layer of soil in the "shallow pit" where they had been buried, he said. Sort of "haphazardly" laid out, he agreed. And, yes, a sneaker had also been located.

"Do you recall a wire hanger being found at the scene of the crime?" Billy Nolas inquired.

"Yes, sir."

"Mr. Tanner didn't ask about that, did he?" Billy asked. "What was the condition of the wire hanger?"

"My recollection was that it was intact," Bondi said.

"Where was it?"

"The wire hanger was found in an area approximately ten feet south of the car."

All other items were thirty yards to the rear or east of the car down the trail.

"And there was also a beer bottle," Billy continued.

"Yes sir."

"What kind was it?"

"Budweiser."

Bondi's attempts to locate the decedent fell far short of the expectations of Billy Nolas.

"This was all relevant to a suspicious abandoned vehicle registered to R. Mallory. That was the extent of my case," said Bondi.

All items located at the scene were admitted into evidence.

James Downing, the Daytona Beach medical examiner, described the removal of the body of Richard Mallory to a local funeral home on the night of December 13, 1989. Ordinarily, bodies were sent to Halifax Hospital, but the decomposition of this body was too severe, he said.

Photographs of the scene where the body was found and the remains of Richard Mallory were identified and Downing explained to the jury the standard procedure of placing the body on a sheet and then transferring it to a body bag.

On the following day, the clothing was removed and sealed in a bag.

"I don't believe he had any underwear on," Downing told the jury.

"I did not notice the zipper," he added when questioned as to whether or not Richard Mallory's zipper was closed and fastened.

Mallory's hands were sent for fingerprints and his death was certified by Dr. Arthur J. Botting.

The photograph of Richard Mallory's decomposed body had not been admitted into evidence. The judge questioned the wisdom of allowing the jury to view the remains. As the picture made the rounds of the defense table, Lee Wuornos sighed heavily.

Deputy James Malady, one of the first to arrive at the scene of the crime, verified that the pants pockets had been turned inside out and the zipper was up and the pants fastened.

Jeffrey Russell Davis, currently a parole officer for the Volusia Correctional Center, met Richard Mallory through his mother, Jacqueline Davis, and was still employed at Mallory Electronics on the evening of November 30, 1989.

David Damore questioned him: "Were Richard Mallory and your mother still seeing each other?"

"No, sir," Davis replied. "By that time they had separated. I do not know why they had separated."

"Did your mother tell you what she thought of Richard Mallory?" Billy Nolas cross-examined.

"No, sir. She did not involve me in her personal relationships," Davis said.

The automobile belonging to Richard Mallory was studied by the Orlando Regional Crime Laboratory, said Daniel Radcliffe, crime lab analyst.

Shown photographs of the automobile's interior and trunk area, he identified it as that which he had analyzed.

"The upholstery of the back of the seat on the driver's side was removed by scalpel and placed in a manilla envelope to be tested for blood. Results showed that they were blood," Radcliffe said.

Linda Miller of the O.K. Pawn Shop described the day, December 6, 1989, when Aileen Wuornos, using the alias of Cammie Marsh Greene, pawned Richard Mallory's 35 millimeter camera and radar detector; Jenny Ahearn, fingerprint expert for the Florida Department of Law Enforcement, described her identification of prints belonging to Aileen Wuornos under the aliases of Cammie Marsh Greene and Lori K. Grody.

"Were you able to determine whether Lori K. Grody and Cammie Marsh Greene are one and the same?" questioned David Damore.

"The print on the pawnship ticket, the inked fingerprint of Cammie Marsh Greene, the inked fingerprint of Aileen Wuornos all belong to the same individual," replied Ahearn.

"The state stipulates that Lori Grody, Cammie Marsh Greene and Aileen Wuornos are one and the same," stated Damore.

After four days of searching Rose Bay, the rusty gun belonging to Aileen Wuornos was located in the southeast corner, between the sea wall and the first set of pilings supporting the bridge, said Lt. Carl Clifford of the Volusia County Sheriff's Department.

Balancing the gun between the thumb and forefinger of his right hand, John Tanner placed it into evidence.

Chapter Seventeen

It was a difficult day for Arlene Pralle.

Although families of the victims had been assigned the front row on the spectators' side of the gallery, she had been assigned nothing.

The security guards made it clear that a spectator getting up to go to the bathroom would be bumped for the next person in line. And the hallway was filled with residents and tourists hoping to get a glimpse of the serial killer and her adoptive mother.

Those who noticed found the adoptive mother standing in line with them.

"We were going to Universal Studios today," explained one tourist. "But when it looked like rain, we decided to come here instead."

Rules established by the guards demanded that the courtroom be vacated at lunch time. Although the media was assured of return seats and the victims' families could come and go at will, no such privileges were available to the mother of the defendant.

Shirley Humphreys, wife of victim number five, Charles Humphreys, sat in the front row with her daughter and several close friends.

"I had to see her face," Shirley, gaunt and tired, said to the press. "You can't imagine what she has done to my family."

Shirley and Charles Humphreys had just celebrated their thirty-fifth wedding anniversary prior to September 12, 1990. Shirley had been battling cancer for years.

"He was always in the driveway ten minutes after six," Shirley remembers. "At 6:30, I thought it was car trouble. At 7:00, maybe he stopped for a beer. At 8:00, I panicked; I got the highway patrol. . . . The Wildwood Police Department started a search. The next day my son came. I sat here and waited.

"I woke up at 2:30 the next night. I heard the knock on the door and knew right away what it was.

"He died a very hard death. She shot 'em in the gut. They don't die right away. The police told me she said, 'I finally shot him [in the head] to put him out of his misery.' I did get back his glasses, pen and pencil, wedding ring, wristwatch—all covered with blood. Maybe the prosecution will put her out of her misery. I don't mind if she meets Old Sparky."

The trial of Lee Wuornos for the murder of Charles Humphreys was scheduled for May. It would be second in line.

Shortly before the morning recess, an NBC reporter asked Arlene to step outside and talk to the press. Hesitant to leave her seat, Arlene asked that the reporter get someone to hold it for her. When the substitute moved in, the guards moved forward.

"I'm just a seatwarmer," the NBC cameraman objected when the guards asked him to leave.

"I'm not asking you to move, I'm telling you," one of the guards threatened.

Arlene was disheartened not only by the difficulty in maintaining a seat, but also by problems with Lee. Her angry face, demanding attitude, flailing hands and softly pounding fists were apparent to the jurors. And there were other visible signs of her fury. Lee would flip her hair back and yank her collar closer to her neck. These actions were visible to the jurors, and obviously troublesome to them.

"She's killing herself," Tricia told Arlene.

Lee Wuornos had her own agenda. She wanted to talk to the media. She wanted to take the witness stand. She wanted to write her own book. Only then would the world believe that she had killed those men in self defense.

"I only went to those interviews in New York to appease her," Arlene said. "She promised if I did that, she would behave."

"Whichever of us sits next to her in the courtroom can't take part in the trial," complained Tricia.

By the end of the third day, Arlene was ill. But there were good things. Jeff Brazil, reporter for the *Orlando Sentinel*, had offered her a room in the home he shared with his wife and children, and the guards at Volusia County Jail had reserved the aisle seat on the second row of the spectators' side for her.

"She looked so sick, we felt sorry for her," one of the guards told the press.

It was apparent on the following day that Lee had received her toiletries. Her hair was curled and she wore a slight bit of makeup. With her punishment lifted, she had been able to talk to Arlene the night before.

On this day, Letha Prater, middle-aged sister of Troy Burress, was also seated in the front row.

"I don't care about her childhood," Letha Prater told the press. "Everybody has problems in their childhood....She hated men. She used him for money, then she killed him....I know she's well guarded, but if she wasn't they wouldn't have to worry about puttin' her away—I'd do it for 'em."

The trial for the murder of Troy Burress was scheduled to follow that of Charles Humphreys.

Dr. Arthur J. Botting is a medical examiner who specializes in pathology. John Tanner wanted him to tell the court just how Richard Mallory died.

After the body was brought to the morgue at Halifax Hospital, it was examined in both the clothed and unclothed state, said Dr. Botting.

"We examined the exterior of the body, and in doing this, we noted that there were gunshot wounds on the upper part of the body, specifically involving the right arm, the right side of the chest, and the left side of the chest. These were both on the front side of the chest. The body was partially decomposing. The head and neck had been reduced to skeleton remains and the upper part of the chest was, the soft tissues in the skin, were undergoing degeneration.

"Were you able to determine a cause of death with regard to the decedent, Richard Charles Mallory?" Tanner inquired.

"Yes, sir. Two bullets that struck the left lung caused a tremendous amount of hemorrahaging. That was the fatal mechanism," he replied.

"All right, sir. Being a medical doctor and in particular a forensic pathologist, I would like you to, if you can, describe the mechanism of death with hemorrahaging in the lungs. How does that come about?"

"Objection, Your Honor," Bill Miller interjected.

"Objection overruled," said Judge Blount.

Tanner wanted the jury to see and feel what Richard Mallory had experienced during his death throes. Bill Miller hoped to prevent that.

"The lung has a very rich blood supply and when the bullet struck it, it tore up a lot of small blood vessels, and this allowed the rapid escape of a large amount of blood. Plus the fact that once the chest wall and or the lung were perforated, this would allow pressurized air to enter the chest cavity, which is normally sealed, and acts as a vacuum. And this would impair respiration as well. So you've got two very vital things working against the normal functions of the lung, vital functions.

"Could you describe what is occurring physiologically to the individual's body. How does death..."

"Objection, Your Honor."

"Objection overruled."

"There is a point that is reached where so much blood is lost that you cannot maintain an efficient, an effective circulation for the brain and for the heart and life ceases."

"And would you describe to the jury in your opinion as forensic pathologist was death instantaneous?"

"No, sir."

"With regard to the individual what would the effect upon the individual's ability to breathe be?"

"Objection, Your Honor."

"Objection overruled."

"It would be impaired. But they would still be able to breathe."

"For a while."

"Yes, sir. In fact, I think that they would be trying very desperately to breathe under the circumstances."

"Objection, Your Honor."

"Objection overruled."

"Do you have an opinion based upon your medical experience and training as to how long an individual or, in fact, in particular Mr. Mallory would live with these wounds before he would die?"

"Objection. Specificity."

"Overruled."

"Within a reasonable space of time."

"I would say roughly ten to twenty minutes," Dr. Botting concluded.

Cross-examining Dr. Botting, Bill Miller attacked the amount of alcohol found in the body of Richard Mallory. It was important for the jury to believe that he was drunk and out of control.

"He would have been at the lower levels where the influence would be recognized," Dr. Botting stated.

"All right," Miller countered. "This body had decomposed somewhat, had it not? And is it your medical opinion that decomposition would have no impact on the blood alcohol level of the decedent?"

"That's right," the doctor agreed.

"Decomposition indicates the presence of bacteria does it not?" Miller asked.

"Among other things."

"And bacteria break down alcohol, do they not?"

"Yes," said Dr. Botting, "they do. But on the other side of the coin there are some bacteria that can produce ethanol."

The only positives that the defense managed to extract from Dr. Botting were that he could not determine the position of the assailant, the sequence of the shots, or what might have happened between the shots.

Ward Schwoob of the Florida Department of Law Enforcement explained the process of inventorying the objects found in Lee's storage bin and removing latent prints from those items.

Complaining of "missed meal cramps," Judge Blount attempted to recess for lunch, admonishing the press for clustering on the front steps of the jail or in the parking lot. From now on, said the judge, do your interviewing on the steps of the courthouse across the street.

But the prosecution still had a few witnesses to dispose of and, promising to take only a few more minutes, called Donald Champagne, retired from the Florida Department of Law Enforcement. Champagne identified the .22 caliber, nine-shot pistol which had recently been dredged up from Rose Bay.

"It was badly rusted and deteriorated when it was recovered," he said.

"Is that the kind of weapon used to kill most people?" John Tanner asked Champagne.

"In my experience, yes, it is used to kill people," Champagne agreed.

Asked to study the four bullets from Mallory's body, he stated that they were all fired from this kind of weapon, but could not identify one with the other because they were damaged and poorly engraved.

"Isn't it true," Jenkins asked, "that a .38 is cheaper and could kill more people, while a .22 is used primarily for target shooting and to kill small animals?"

The pistol used by Lee Wuornos is a six groove with a right hand twist, a popular weapon, Champagne replied.

"I cannot say with scientific certainty that those bullets were fired from that weapon," he stated.

"Now," chided Judge Blount, "can he go for real?"

Chapter Eighteen

N o one could say for certain where the rumor began, but somehow the media knew that Tyria Moore was scheduled to testify
for the prosecution that afternoon.

The "opening act" after lunch was another crime lab analyst, this
time reporting on the gunpowder residue on the shirt of Richard Mallory.

The gallery fell silent when Tyria Moore entered the courtroom to
testify against the woman who had been her lover and companion for
more than five years.

Clothed in a casual, but colorful pant suit, the short figure strode
confidently toward the witness chair, her head erect, her face grim.

The last time that Lee Wuornos had watched testimony by this
woman, she had wept. What would she do now? the press wondered.

David Damore addressed the witness.

"How is it that you knew Aileen Wuornos?"

"I met her in a bar."

"Did there come a point in your life that you and she formed a relationship?"

"Yes, we did."

"How long did that relationship last?"

"Four and one-half years."

"Can you describe the relationship to us in regard to living arrangements and working arrangements?"

"We lived as lovers and I worked quite a bit and she worked."

"Did you earn a salary?"

"Yes."

"Did you get a pay check?"

Damore continued to support the idea that Tyria had shared in the
household bills. Then he asked about the morning of December 1, 1989.

"Where were you when you first saw her."

"I was in bed. It was early in the morning when she came in. I was
still asleep.... Well, she came in and she had a car outside and said that
we were going to move. And we moved that day."

"Did she tell you about anything that had happened?"

"No."

"Did she say anything to you about anything odd happening. . .any-
thing horrible happening?"

"No."

"Describe Lee Wuornos as you observed her."

"Very busy. Getting stuff out of the motel room, moving it into the
car. She seemed fine. She was able to help, you know, she helped me
pack the rest of the stuff. We both packed the car."

"Did she seem as though she had been drinking?"

"Yes, I knew she was drinking. I could smell it on her."

"You spoke to each other and she answered back in a coherent fash-
ion?"

"Yes."

"Was there anything about her actions that morning that you can
tell the jury about that were out of the ordinary?"

"Not that I recall."

At the defense table, Lee Wuornos looked at the woman she had
loved. The woman did not look back.

"Did she say anything out of the ordinary about the last couple of
days...or the night before?"

"No. Later that evening, I know we were sitting watching TV and
she told me she had something to tell me. We were sitting on the floor
watching TV. . . .She seemed fine. . .She came out and said I have
something to tell you. And I asked her what. And she said that she had
shot and killed a man that day. . . .I didn't want to believe it. I was probably in awe."

"Did you ask her anything about what she just told you?"

"I don't believe I asked her any questions about it. I might have replied something like I don't believe you or something along that line. . . .
Later, she was telling me that she had put the body in the woods under a
piece of rug. And that she had dropped the car off up in Ormond Beach
on John Anderson Drive."

"Did she tell you why she shot him?"

"No."

"And did Miss Wuornos have any articles at that time, that evening
that were not something that you had seen before?"

"Yes. There's only a few things that I can really remember from that
particular car because she had given me a jacket and a scarf. I remember
a box with a bunch of papers in it. . . .I wasn't really paying attention.
She was going through them and she tried to show me a piece of paper
and a picture of somebody. I didn't want to look at it. . . .I remember seeing the name Richard on a piece of paper that she was going through

. . . . She seemed normal. Going through the stuff, throwing things away and keeping things. . . . I remember a suitcase and a jacket and there was a big blanket, a comforter, brown and tan.

"Just by looking at her, could you tell whether or not she was injured?"

"I saw no signs of injury."

"How long did you remain living with her after she told you she had shot this man?"

"Approximately a year."

"At any time during that period as lovers, as roommates, as friends, did she ever confide that the man she had shot had done anything to her?"

"No, she didn't."

"Did she ever tell you that she had been raped by this man?"

"No."

"Did she ever give you an explanation as to why she shot him?"

"No."

"During that period of time, you talked about many things?"

"Yes, we talked quite a bit."

"Was this a close relationship between you?"

"I believe it was."

"And she never ever suggested that the man she told you she shot December the first and used his car to move to the Burleigh Avenue address had done anything to her on the morning of December the first, 1989, did she?"

"No."

"During that period of time, the time that she told you that she shot the man on December the first, 1989, back to when you first met her, did she ever indicate to you that she had been beaten and raped and robbed by people that she was going out and prostituting herself to while you two lived together?"

"No."

"Did Aileen Carol Wuornos own a firearm?"

"Yes."

"Did she tell you why she got the gun?"

"She said it was for her protection because she hitchhiked."

"Do you see the defendant, Aileen Carol Wuornos, in the courtroom today? Can you point her out to me?"

For the first time, Tyria Moore looked straight into the eyes of Lee Wuornos.

"She's sitting right there," she said, pointing directly at Lee.

Under cross-examination, Bill Miller questioned the witness.

"Now you've talked about the fact that you shared in some of the expenses of the home and things like that. That you worked from time to time. In fact, during that four and one-half years, approximately half that time you were unemployed, isn't that true?"

"I really don't know."

"Well, there were numerous times when you were unemployed."

"I didn't say numerous. There was a couple of months at a time I would go without jobs."

"Lee rarely told you much about her work. . . . And that was in part because you told her you didn't want to hear it. Is that true?"

"That's true."

"And you didn't want to hear it because you were jealous of her work. Is that true?"

"I didn't want her to do it."

"You didn't want to share her with other men."

A collective chuckle swept through the courtroom. Other men? Apparently unaware of the reaction, Tyria responded.

"That's true."

"And she did tell you she'd been raped a few times, didn't she?"

"Previous before I met her that she had been raped and beaten."

"And didn't she tell you that every single day, somebody abused her? Nearly every day there would be at least one person."

"Verbally."

Bill Miller was trying to portray Tyria as a woman who had taken advantage of Lee Wuornos, been aware of what was happening, and then fled when the going got rough.

"When did you decide to leave and go home?" he asked.

"I believe I left the beginning of December."

"Nearly a year later, you decided to leave."

"Correct."

"That was after you had seen the composite drawings on television and you thought you were a suspect. And what were you thinking at that time?"

"I really don't know what I thought at the time. I know I was scared."

"Why were you scared?" Miller asked.

"Because I know I was driving the car when it happened, when I wrecked."

Defense and prosecution knew, if the jury did not, that Bill Miller had just led Tyria Moore into Williams Rule territory. He recovered quickly.

What about the period of time when she was encouraging Lee to confess? What was she doing in the motel room with the investigators? Didn't they tell her what to write on the note to Lee? And wasn't that note sent so that Lee would call her?

"I really don't remember if they told me to write or if they just gave me the basic information."

"Do you recall them occasionally passing you little notes suggesting that you work on her in this way or when she's crying you should hit her harder then? Those kind of things?"

"I remember a few notes being passed, yes."

"And in order to get her to say what you wanted her to, you lied to her. And during all those conversations that you had with her, she said that she would do anything for you, that she would die for you...eventually Lee indicated to you that she was prepared to make a statement... after eleven calls during three days."

"I believe so—yes."

"When you got back up North, you heard from Mr. Munster..."

David Damore leapt to his feet. "Object your honor. Outside the scope of direct. We have to protect the record."

"Court sustains the objection," the judge agreed.

"Your Honor, with all due respect, we think this goes to the bias and interest of this witness," countered Miller.

If he could lead Tyria into the area of the contract with the Marion County investigators, he could discredit her testimony.

But the judge wasn't having any. This subject had not been brought up under direct examination and he would not allow it to be brought up under cross.

"His objection was you go beyond the scope of direct. And I sustained the objection."

Miller returned to Tyria.

"On the way to Daytona to the motel, you prepared a list of places you had lived with Miss Wuornos during the four and one-half years you had lived together and indicated where you were employed....Rose Giansanti was one of the officers that was with you. You have had many conversations with Miss Giansanti and had a discussion about your testifying with Miss Giansanti and you talked to her about the kind of things you would have to testify."

"I don't remember."

"In light of the court ruling, I have no further questions," said Miller.

"May we approach the bench or make an argument outside the presence of the jury?" Miller requested.

"Have the jury step in the jury room for a moment," said the judge.

A few moments later, both the jury and Tyria Moore were escorted out of the courtroom.

Miller took the reins.

"Your Honor, this specific line of questioning has to do with the bias of interest of the witness. It relates to a movie deal situation which has been involved in this case."

"You know you're telling me something that I haven't heard before because I've had the benefit of not reading these newspaper accounts and not viewing the television and I don't know anything about a movie contract and I haven't heard it from this witness stand," Judge Blount replied.

"I was leading into that. I think that it can be explained to expose the bias and interest that this witness might have in saying everything she did," Miller continued.

"We're talking about the direct examination that I heard from the witness as sworn and was in the courtroom. That's what I'm talking about. If you want to go beyond that feel free to call the lady as a witness of your own," replied the judge.

Tyria and the jury were brought back into the courtroom and David Damore returned to the questioning.

"Now, let me ask you this. You were asked about the composites. When you were describing the auto that you said was wrecked, what car were you describing?"

"Objection, Your Honor," Billy Nolas said.

"Your Honor, that door is wide open."

"I know its wide open. But I'm having concern with it at this time until further hearings are held."

The jury was escorted out of the courtoom for the second time that afternoon.

When the attorneys approached the bench, the state asked to hire a Volusia County psychologist to interpret the tests performed by the defense's psychologists.

The judge gave permission, "but," he warned, "we're not stopping the trial.

They then returned to the question of Tyria Moore's bias.

"I'm starting to lose where we are," Billy Nolas complained.

"Just check with me," Tanner shot back. "I'll let you know."

With the jury and Tyria returned to the courtroom, Miller resumed.

"You heard from Bruce Munster in the early part of January . . . and he suggested that you get a lawyer . . . and that lawyer's name was Bradshaw. In case someone came to you about book and movie deals and Mr. Bradshaw was assisting Mr. Munster with his book and movie deals."

"He asked if I would like to use the same attorney."

"Mr. Munster is an investigator."

"Right."

"You called Miss Giansanti about this."

"Yes."

"And she was one of the officers in the motel room. You wanted to talk to her about something...and when you did that you talked to her about some monetary figure—$50,000....Now you have testified that you trusted Rose Giansanti and you still do."

"She's been very helpful."

"And you told Rose Giansanti, 'Do you know what I could do with $50,000?' "

Chapter Nineteen

Four motions for mistrial marked the testimony of Lawrence Horzepa, who identified himself as an investigator with the Volusia County Sheriff's Office investigating homicides and suspicious deaths.

Horzepa told the jury about his involvement in the apprehension of Lee Wuornos after days of surveillance. He related the follow-through with the pawn shops and moved into his role in her confession.

The confession was a delicate area because it had involved the murders of seven men. Lee Wuornos was on trial for only one.

Horzepa had come to court equipped with notes of his interaction with Lee Wuornos during the confession.

Defense had the right to see those notes, declared Tricia Jenkins.

"These are typed references to information that you received from my client," she said.

The notes were typed with handwritten messages on the side of the paper. Those messages had been added by Larry Horzepa. In one passage which stated "She advised she was almost harmed" by Richard Mallory, Horzepa had scribbled "Don't use."

Horzepa said repeatedly that Lee had never told him that she had been raped by the men she killed.

Horzepa's report on his conversation with Jackie Davis had been withheld from the defense until the Friday before the trial, the defense said.

It was important to contact Davis and learn more about the behavior of Richard Mallory.

"It is an attempt by the defense, your honor, at character assassination of the murder victim," complained John Tanner.

And, he pointed out, the report on Mallory was a "statement by a third person."

Jackie Davis is available for questioning, Tanner continued. If you really want to put her through this testimony.

"We've been trying to find her for some time," said Tricia.

The entire defense was dependent on Richard Mallory's treatment of Lee Wuornos and the attorneys wanted to back up the plea of self defense with evidence of his erratic and abusive behavior.

Judge Blount ruled Davis' statement hearsay and told the defense team that they must call her as a witness if they wanted to pursue this avenue.

Questioned further, Horzepa continued to deny that Lee had told him anything about rape or extreme abuse on the part of the victims.

"She advised me that whenever 'someone would hassle me, I'd whip out my gun and let them have it,' " Horzepa offered.

From the defense table, Billy Nolas addressed the judge:

"Your Honor, at this time the defendant would move for a mistrial based on the questioning... in which the prosecution asked the witness as it relates to this, the Mallory investigation. I think in light of how carefully we have been skating to try to avoid any reference to any other homicides and in light of how the jury has been seeing us skate around it, that by now I feel certain that they are at least very suspicious that there is more than one homicide involved here."

Judge Blount asked the jury to retire once more. Then he leaned forward to address the attorneys who stood before him.

"Counsel, what I am concerned about now is, I think we've reached the stage where everything's on very thin ice in regard to the Williams Rule matter. And I think we ought to hear it out right now. Because even though doors have been opened, I have been very particular about testimony not being allowed until a ruling is made so you know which way I'm coming from."

"My point, judge, is counsel specifically asked questions to elicit the testimony regarding the composite and wrecking of another car. Defense counsel brought that out in cross examination," reminded Damore.

"I know. I heard that. That's what I'm saying. I think we need to resolve the Williams Rule problem right now before we proceed further. Because you see you people have had the benefit of discovery. I have not. But I think we're skirting into Williams Rule because I believe it's going to be somebody else's car."

Damore continued. "Judge, at a minimum I would like to at least... counsel was very quick to let it be left in the jury's mind that maybe this witness had wrecked Mr. Mallory's car. He didn't bother to clear that up.

"With the court's permission, what we would like to do is lay out evidence to show you similarities."

The state had prepared two charts. They had been dealing with the chart which only contained information relating to the Mallory murder. The second chart outlined the circumstances of all seven murders to which Lee Wuornos had confessed.

"Judge, I made note for the record that Miss Wuornos' confession has previously been made public throughout the state of Florida. So any chart that might be produced which would establish her guilt after her confession of those murders seems to me to be a rather bogus argument on the part of counsel," said Damore.

"Objection to bogus argument, Your Honor, and let the record reflect Mr. Damore has. . .," countered Nolas.

"Your objection is noted. I don't need all this comment," the judge interceded.

"Yes, judge," responded Nolas.

"Now, let's get serious for a change." Judge Blount took charge again.

Damore proceeded. "We see here, judge, the evidence of the dates that the bodies of each of these men were found. It also establishes that each of the men that was murdered by Miss Wuornos was a white male . . . . And the age group ranged from thirty-nine to as high as sixty-five.

And then it was time to hear from John Tanner.

"Your Honor, we'd like to assist you in determining the similarity of pattern. . . . In this particular instance, what I can establish is pattern by this defendant of intentional killing along the highways of the State of Florida. It goes specifically to her self defense argument. It is relevant to that issue. It is relevant as to the issues of the identity of the murder—of the modus operandi of the defendant. And it is also relevant to establish the use of this particular weapon. And it will also be established, judge, as an anticipated defense, that Tyria Moore was not present during any of these homicides and was in fact on some of the homicides, not within the State of Florida.

"One of the reasons we had not attempted to introduce the video tape is because it would have had to have been edited, spliced and butchered to the extent that it would have been difficult to have a meaningful flow without having the surrounding information.

"Let me just briefly touch upon what she said about the various killings. You already heard how she described her killing of Mr. Mallory.

"We'll go on to David Spears.

" 'Okay and we were nude and everything and we were screwin' around and all that stuff, gettin' drunk and everything and, uh, then he . . . he wanted to go in the back of the trunk and all I remember is that, I think there was some kind of a lead pipe or somethin' like that and we were in the back of the trunk. . .'

" 'Munster: "Back of the trunk?'

" 'Truck, I mean, yeah. And. . . and when I got back there, he started gettin' vicious with me and I jumped out of the truck and he jumped outta the truck, ran to the. . . to the car, I mean, to the door, opened the door, grabbed my bag, grabbed the gun out, and I shot him...quick as possible. I shot him at the tailgate of the truck. And then he ran around to the driver's side tryin' to get in the truck towards me, which was weird, towards me, and I just ran into the truck toward him and I thought, what the hell you think you're doin', dude, you know...you know I...I am gonna kill you 'cause you were tryin' to do whatever you could with me. And I shot 'em through the...through the door and then he was kinda ...went back and I went right through to the driver's side and shot 'em again, and he fell back. And that's all I remember on that one.'

"And then she goes on to Charles Carskaddon," Tanner continued. "That's the man whose body was found in Pasco County on June 6.

" 'That guy, huh...the drug dealer...he had $20. He wasn't going to give me any more money. The one with a .45 on top of his hood. He crawled in the back seat and I crawled in the back seat.'

"And they're about to have sex, according to her," Tanner interjected. 'And he said, "you fuckin' bitch" and all that stuff and I thought you fuckin' bastard. I shot him in the back seat and then I got out and kept shooting. I shot him more than...over nine times. 'Cause I was pissed when I found the .45 on top of the car.'

"Then on Peter Siems, Your Honor, this is the man whose body has not yet been recovered from south Georgia. On June the twenty-second, he was reported missing from Marion County. She says: 'Oh, let me see ...third guy...I had a problem with...uh...let's see...I think the next one's the one I'm talk...he was a Christian guy or somethin'. I...I didn't know he was a Christian guy. He was nude...this is the one in Georgia, I think, and he had his...he had...he took a sleepin' bag... took it out in the woods and when we got nude, I had taken my bag with me that time, 'cause I said, "Well, if we're gonna go out in the woods, I'm not gonna give him an opportunity to rape me." '

"Now you know this is a woman who solicits sex with each of these men and goes out there and takes off her clothes. But she says she's not going to give them an opportunity to rape her.

" 'And that's the time this guy gave me a problem, too. And so, I whipped out my gun and I said, "You know, I...I...I don't wanna shoot you." He said...he didn't say anything, he just looked at me and he said, "You fuckin' bitch." And I said, "No, I know you were gonna rape me." 'Cause he was gettin' physical with me again and I knew. And he... and he said, "Fuck you, bitch," and started to come at me and he was, you know, tryin' to get the gun from me. We...we struggled on that one. And he tried to get the gun from me and stuff, we're strugglin' with the gun and everything else and a couple bullets shot up in the air and finally I ripped it away and I had the gun in my left hand and I put it back in my right hand and I shot him immediately...and I'm positive the only one I left in Georgia is that missionary guy...I remember the missionary guy. I shot him once.'

" 'So you had to kill him and silence him...basically, is what it boiled down to,' Horzepa had said.

" 'Yeah. But it also was in bitterness of what you were doing to me. See what I'm saying? Like...hey, dude, you're gonna rape me, you're gonna kill me, whatever you're gonna do, it's not gonna happen 'cause now I'm on the other end of the stick now, see.'

" 'You're in control?'

" 'Yeah.'

"Troy Burress, he was a delivery man who drove a sausage truck in Leon County. His body was found August the fourth. She goes on to talk about him.

" 'I remember him. He's the one...he has to ask me what...he was gonna kill me.'

" 'How many times did you shoot him?,' Horzepa had asked.

" 'God, let me see. Let me see. I shot...I shot...he was...he physically attacked me and he was...he laughed. He pulled out a ten dollar bill and said, "This is all you fuckin' deserve, you fuckin' whore" ...like that. And I said, "Wait" ...and then he just...he threw the fuckin' money down and I was standing in front of the truck here, and he had the door open here, and he just came...he didn't know that I had a gun or anything. He came at me. We were fighting. I mean, we went all the way into the weeds and everything...fighting. And, uh, when I got away from him, and I ran back to the truck, and I had my gun in the back, and I ran in the back real quick, and he...now, we're still fighting and he realizes I got a gun. Now, I finally got a...fighting, and somehow he...I kicked him or somethin'. He backed away or something or I pushed him or somethin' like that and he backed away and I pulled my gun out and I said, "You bastard," and I think I shot him right in the stomach or somethin'.'

" 'Okay, did you shoot him again after that?,' her interrogator continued.

" 'Yeah, 'cause he...oh, yeah, I shot 'em, and he turned around... turned around and he was gonna start runnin' and so I shot him again in the back. If I remember right. God, let me see, let me see. He started running. He was running towards me and I shot him, and then he started to go away from me, and I shot him again because I, well, you know, the bastard, he's gonna rape me and shit.'

" 'Did you have to chase him to catch him?'

" 'Oh, no, he didn't even run very far.'

"She goes on to talk about Dick Humphreys who worked for the HRS Department. His body was found September the twelfth, 1990 in Marion County. She says: 'And I pushed him back and he walked up to me and he started struggling with me and then I shot him and he stepped back and he started to stumble and he fell. He got back up and I shot him from there. Then he went back and started goin' toward the trunk and I shot him again.'

" 'How many times did you shoot him?'

" 'I think I shot him three times.'

" 'Three times?'

" 'I think. Oh, yeah, he stumbled and fell. Oh, yeah, I remember... 'cause he pissed me off and everything. I felt sorry for him 'cause he was gurgling. Well I shot him in the head and tried to put him out of his misery.'

"Walter Antonio, retired police officer, your Honor, whose body was found in Dixie County November the nineteenth. The last killing we know about.

" 'How many times did you shoot him?'

" 'Twice, I think.'

" 'Okay. Now, how did you feel when you thought he was a cop?'

" 'At first, I...'cause that one guy, that HRS guy tellin' me he was a cop, I said to myself, this...he's a...that guy was an HRS guy. So this is another faker. He's just tryin' to get a free piece of ass. And that's all I thought. Yeah, it pissed me off.'

" 'Well, when you shot him the first time, what did he do?'

" 'Mmmm, well, when we were struggling with the gun and everything else, again, he fell on the ground and he started to run back...run away. And I shot 'em in the back...right in the back.'

" 'What did he do then after you shot him in the back?'

" 'He just kinda looked at me for a second and he said...he said somethin' like, uh...shit. What did he say? I think he said, "You cunt" or somethin' like that. And I said, "You bastard," and I shot him again.'

" 'And then what happened?'

" 'Then I just got in the car and took off.'

" 'Did he say anything more after you shot at him?'

" 'No.'

" 'Did you shoot him in the back again?'

" 'Mmmmm. I think I shot him in the back one more time. Shot him near the head or somethin' like that. I just kinda randomly shot. I kinda turned my head and shot.' "

"Initially, if you look at the chart, well, let me get to that in a moment," Billy Nolas began.

"When a court has a Williams Rule issue to determine because of the fundamental importance of the right to a fair trial that Your Honor is aware of when that type of issue is before the court, the initial question before the court is what is the evidence being admitted to prove. The second issue deals with prejudice and the necessity of the evidence to the state's case. The argument (used by the state) is basically a propensity argument. And that's the way the jury is going to hear it. That's what is going to happen when the jurors in this case hear that evidence. We do not try people in this country on propensity. We do not try people on their character. And we do not try people on anything other than the crime alleged in the indictment. What you will see the state doing, should this evidence be admitted, is in essence to present a case of propensity prosecution. There is no other way to do it, I would submit, given the evidence at issue."

David Damore chose to leave the courtroom. He wanted to make it clear to the jury and the spectators that Billy Nolas was presenting a frivolous argument. Passing the media, he commented, "I won't miss anything."

Returning a few moments later, he addressed the same people.

"I didn't miss anything, did I?"

Nolas was just wrapping up his argument against admission of the similar fact evidence.

"Secondly," he said, "the collateral crimes evidence will become a feature of this trial."

Judge Blount leaned back in his chair.

"I've heard sufficient argument of counsel. I think you're where I can prepare a ruling. That subject to the testimony to be proffered, which we accept the representation as stated, it does not appear to me from what has been spoken here this morning that the testimony to be proffered is too remote. That it would be relevant to the allegations contained in the indictment. That it would be established to show an establishing of a plan, scheme or design to identify the defendant, a plan or pattern followed by the defendant committing the crime that is alleged in the indictment. And would not solely be used to prove character propensity. Accordingly, the similar fact testimony will be accepted by the court."

It was a major blow to the defense. Everything they had hoped to suppress was now open season.

The jury was readmitted to the courtroom.

"Ladies and gentlemen of the jury, the evidence that you are about to receive concerning evidence of other crimes allegedly committed by the defendant will be considered by you for the limited purpose of providing motive, opportunity, intent, preparation, plan, knowledge, identity, the absence of mistake or accident on the part of the defendant and you shall consider it only as it relates to these issues.

"However, the defendant is not on trial for a crime that is not included in the indictment that has been read to you."

The state then recalled Larry Horzepa to identify the chart which included all seven victims.

"Could you tell the jury what it shows?" asked Damore.

Horzepa was pleased to cooperate.

"This shows the central area in the northern area of Florida. On this particular map here, we have a small circle 1 and a small circle 1A right at the Daytona Beach area and I-95 approximately at the Ormond Beach area. Circle No. 1 indicates the area where the body of Richard Mallory was found and Circle No. 1A indicates the area where Richard Mallory's vehicle was located. . . ."

Damore and Tanner were elated at the judge's ruling. They shook hands. They patted each other on the back. And they called in a succession of witnesses to elaborate on the involvement of Lee Wuornos in the murders of Charles Humphreys, Troy Burress, David Spears, Walter Gino Antonio, Peter Siems and Charles Carskaddon. Ballistics, fingerprints, possession of items, all were placed into evidence.

Lee Wuornos spoke animatedly to her attorneys. She wanted a press conference, she said. She wanted to go to the United States Supreme Court, she added.

In the jury box, the school teacher watched Lee's behavior, a pensive expression on her face. The equestrienne turned her cool gaze on the defendant, and the pharmacist leaned back in his chair and, ever so slightly, shook his head in bewilderment.

In the gallery, two guards canvassed the spectators looking for Jackelyn Giroux. Sue Russell shrank into her seat. Information leaked out that Jackie was being subpoenaed as a witness. Arlene told those near by that Jackie had an attorney who was going to try to prevent that.

Later in the afternoon, Arlene learned that Lee was being called before the board because she had complained about a strip search. Would this result in lock-up again? Arlene wondered.

The families of the victims were the last to leave the courtroom. In their presence, David Damore leaned over the bench to speak to Arlene.

"These are the people you should be praying for, not Aileen Wuornos. These are the families of the people your daughter killed."

It was in keeping with Damore's reputation as the "instrument of society's retribution."

Reporters crowded around the attorneys outside the jailhouse. They wanted to hear their feelings about the judge's decision on the Williams Rule.

"We think it's crucial to producing evidence touching upon intent, common scheme and the identity of Wuornos as perpetrator of all the murders," said Tanner.

"Obviously we didn't think it was appropriate," retorted Tricia Jenkins. "If she is convicted, it will definitely be an issue on appeal."

In the parking lot adjacent to the jailhouse, Shirley Humphreys' dog, Boy, recently released from the captivity of the car, scampered happily around the open area. For Shirley and her daughter it had also been a long day and they climbed wearily into the car to head home.

Chapter Twenty

J udge Blount's ruling set a new playing field: jurors could now expect to hear details of all seven killings claimed by Lee.

"Sledgehammer!" thought the state. "Appeal!" thought the defense.

"I can't believe this! I'm up on one case!" whispered Lee to Arlene. She shook her head and hissed at her lawyers through clenched teeth. Her hands punctuated her remarks with brisk karate chop movements.

Tanner had been prepared to rest his case had the ruling gone the other way. But now he had an open field. He could play the damning videotape: Lee's flippant documentation of her own bloody handiwork.

Sample: "I felt sorry for him because he was gurgling. I shot him in the head to get him out of his misery."

No juror, no human being, could remain neutral after viewing such a confession, he thought.

From here on out, the defense was swimming upstream.

"We do not try people on character," Billy Nolas complained at day's end. "We do not try people on anything other than the crime charged in the indictment."

But the damage to the defense was done as soon as the words, "motion granted" passed the judge's lips.

The state began a steady and well-planned hammering. Cop types from five counties marched to the stand. There were ill-at-ease redneck deputies. Good old boy detectives, nervous in cheap suits. Self-assured coroners, one a Hispanic woman. Snappy firearms experts. Grim crime scene technologists.

They served up photos, stolen goods, bullets, a gun, charts and diagrams. This was the hard jigsaw evidence meant to expand Lee's activity from that of a single violent episode to a statewide killing spree.

The puzzle wasn't a seamless fit, but it was enough to sink the defense's hopes. Juries tend to be fascinated by technical cop testimony. And it's difficult to crack the testimony of an experienced pathologist when it comes to bullet trajectory.

The jury grasped the state's main point—that most victims were robbed of cars and personal belongings, and shot in the torso with a .22. Deputies described how the bodies were found. Doctors detailed how they died.

The murder of Charles Humphreys was the most brutal. He had been shot seven times, once in the back of the head.

The defense was successful in excluding as evidence bloody color photos of maggot-covered bodies at crime scenes and disassembled victims on the autopsy table. It was frustrated, however, in stopping the ghastly catalog of evidence concerning the other killings. So it turned to legal technicalities.

Billy Nolas objected constantly as the police officers and experts testified. He once even objected to a smile from David Damore. Five times Nolas leapt to his feet and demanded a mistrial. Once he complained about a reference of Judge Blount's concerning "when this case gets to the Supreme Court," an obvious prediction of conviction and appeal. Nolas also pitched a legal fit over an indistinct utterance Damore made within the jury's earshot.

Blount angrily crushed the objections and mistrial arguments, calling them a "shotgun attack." The exchange grew nasty when Nolas claimed prosecutors hadn't provided him with the police witnesses' reports, a blatant violation of procedure. Damore fought back.

"Every single one of those reports has been provided to them," he steamed at the judge. "I'm not going to use the 'L' word, Your Honor, but that's a mistake in fact."

At another point, Nolas became agitated over Damore's reaction to a question he asked of an expert witness.

"Objection to Mr. Damore making a face and rolling his eyes, Your Honor," Nolas cried. "This is not kindergarten!"

"I didn't see him," growled Judge Blount.

The best the defense could get out of the string of cops and experts was that while all victims had been shot with a .22 caliber pistol, the bullets couldn't be traced to the weapon identified as Lee's—it was too rusty to test fire.

During a break, Arlene confided that jail officials were now allowing Lee the use of a toothbrush, hairbrush and other items previously denied her.

"As long as they're treating her right, she's a lot less stressed out," Arlene happily reported. "Now we're kind of rolling with it."

While Tanner was saving the best . . . Lee's videotaped confession . . . for last, he was crafty enough to relieve the dry police technicalities with human testimony.

Stefan Siems, the twenty-four-year-old son of missionary Peter Siems, took the stand to testify how in June 1990, his father had planned to visit him in Arkansas. First, however, Peter was to visit his mother in New Jersey and call Stefan from there. The call, Stefan said, never came.

Peter Siems, it turned out, barely made it out of Florida. According to Lee, his body, still undiscovered, lies rotting somewhere across the state line in the piney woods of Georgia.

Stefan Siems identified some luggage and a radio as belonging to his father. Earlier witnesses had testified how the items were found in the storage locker Lee had rented under an alias.

The hitherto dry testimony chased away many courtroom spectators, and the balky air conditioning system began to chill the room. Spectators, mostly retirees, huddled in coats or drew blankets over their laps.

At the defense table, Lee had been provided with a sweater. She chattered with her lawyers, scribbled in a legal pad or flipped through the pages of a law book. During a break, she stood, turned to local reporters, grinned and waved.

Peter Siems' niece, Kathleen Siems of Stuart, Florida, proffered her testimony outside the jury's presence. She was confused, however, about the actual time she last saw "Uncle Pete." It was in June 1991, she said—a full year after his disappearance.

Damore attempted to prod her memory with leading questions.

"Objection, objection, objection!" shouted Nolas.

The witness was not allowed to testify before jurors. Damore was unperturbed. "Sometimes it goes easy, sometimes it goes hard," he said later.

On the following day, state witness number forty captivated jurors with his tale of a frightening highway encounter with an enraged Aileen Wuornos.

Trucker Bobby Lee Copus took the stand. Heavyset, in blue jeans, and speaking in a thick cowboy drawl, Copus was the very stereotype of his profession.

In November 1990, Copus was driving his car from his Lakeland home to Orlando to pay an insurance bill, he said. He stopped at a truck stop in Haines City, southwest of Orlando.

"As I was coming out of the truck stop I ran into that young lady right there," Copus said, pointing to Lee. A trucker, he said, introduced her as needing a ride to Orlando.

Copus agreed, never guessing that his fidelity to his wife of thirty years was about to be tested, possibly at the cost of his life.

Lee told the trucker she needed to get to Daytona Beach by a certain time to pick up her two children at a day care center. Once in Orlando, she said, she could call her sister for a ride the rest of the way home.

Copus drove to his bank, withdrew an estimated $4,000 for his insurance bill and tucked the money into his sun visor. He continued to Orlando on a country road.

"And that's when she propositioned me," Copus testified. "She said she needed $100. She really dumfounded me for a minute. I thought she was a woman in distress."

Copus refused to cheat on his wife, despite Lee's guarantee that "I'll give you the best blow job you ever had in your life."

Twice more Lee insisted he stop in a nearby orange grove. Twice more he refused. She became increasingly angry.

"When she propositioned me the third time, she wasn't the same person," Copus said. She opened her purse for a comb, Copus watching every move of the blonde beside him.

"I seen what I thought was a small caliber pistol in her purse," he said. "At this point I was really scared. I just wanted her out of my car in the presence of a lot of people."

Copus gambled on a trick. He pulled to a truck stop phone booth, told Lee he would drive her all the way to Daytona Beach and gave her $5 to call her sister. As soon as Lee got out, he locked his car doors.

Lee flew into a rage.

"What I saw was a woman in total frustration, mad as hell," Copus said. As he drove away, Lee hurled threats, as well as a confession, after him.

"Copus, I'll get you, you son-of-a-bitch!" she said. "I'll kill you like I did the other old fat sons of bitches!"

"It's an experience I'll never forget as long as I live," Copus concluded.

The trucker was immediately followed by another motorist whose life was possibly spared because he resisted Lee's temptation.

James Dalla Rosa said he picked up a hitchhiking Lee in late 1989 or early 1990. She showed him a photo of two children and said she was a high-class call girl who lived in a $125,000 home. She pulled out a plastic case with various business cards.

"She said, 'These are some of my customers—judges, attorneys, state's attorneys, police officers,'" Dalla Rosa recalled. "I felt very uncomfortable with the situation. I didn't feel that everything was as advertised."

Lee quoted him her fees: $100 for a tryst in a motel, $75 for sex in the woods, and $30 for oral sex in the car. "She said, 'I prefer to go to the woods,'" Dalla Rosa testified.

When the driver spurned Lee, she became agitated, moving jerkily, bouncing in her seat, snatching at her purse. "She became angry after I was not receptive of her offer. Her demeanor changed tremendously," Dalla Rosa said.

He dropped off the angry woman near the interstate. "When she exited the car, she slammed the door of the car and didn't say anything, not 'Thanks' or anything," Dalla Rosa concluded.

Having exposed jurors to the grim technicalities of Lee's crimes, and the stories of those who survived her, the state was now ready to cap its case with its most damning evidence: the killer's own confession to Mallory's death.

Television monitors filled the courtroom on Thursday, January 23, 1992.

It was obvious that the confession tapes of Lee Wuornos were going to be shown to the jury. With the entry of the Williams Rule, the spectators had every reason to expect the full three hours of the tapes.

As the prosecution and defense dickered over the position of the twenty-seven-inch monitors, Judge Blount quipped:

"I sat in this courtroom for twenty-two years and I never found any counsel that agreed on anything yet. Is the entire tape going to run?"

"It is your honor," replied John Tanner.

Within the next few moments, this was reconsidered by the prosecution who felt that, "In view of Williams Rule objections and being aware of the potential for appeals, perhaps the collateral evidence should not be included."

John Tanner spoke to the judge:

"[Since] perhaps this series of killings may become too much of a question, we are offering only statements on the Mallory homocide, eliminating the generic statements."

By law, he added, testimony about the other cases could not overshadow the one at hand.

To the defense team, the offer was a mixed blessing. If they demanded that the entire tape be played, they could lose the right to appeal the Williams Rule. On the other hand, by using the edited version, all of Lee's statements about self defense, and most of them concerning her undying devotion to Tyria Moore, were excluded.

"We have a difficult decision to make in this regard," Nolas admitted to Judge Blount, "but it would be untenable for us not to agree to the condensed tape."

"That's your decision, sir," the judge replied.

As the courtroom lights dimmed, David Damore cracked to one of the reporters: "I know with all these ladies next to you, we better leave some lights on."

None of the family members of the victims were present to see the confession of Lee Wuornos. Without references to the other six murders, the tape, spliced and edited, lasted only about twenty minutes.

The prosecution had succeeded in editing out most references to other homicides. The tape ended with Lee's admission that "I don't care about me. I deserve to die."

Lee sat motionless throughout the presentation. At its completion, she was smiling, relaxed, reaching for a piece of candy from the plastic bag always kept on the defense table.

Arlene had never seen the confession and those around her watched her expressions.

"How do you feel about your daughter now?" a spectator asked her.

"Those men were animals," she replied.

Larry Horzepa was recalled to the stand by John Tanner.

"The original tapes ran over three hours, is that correct?"

"Yes," replied Horzepa.

"Did you edit those tapes?"

"I did."

"Did you edit to matters concerning the homicide of Richard Mallory?"

"Yes, I did."

"Did you exclude any generic reference to Richard Mallory? Did that appear to be the tape that truly and accurately depicts the conversation with two other parties concerning Aileen Wuornos on January 16, 1991?"

"Yes," concluded Horzepa.

"Does this tape deal only with statements from Aileen Wuornos after her attorney is present?" asked Billy Nolas. "The tapes don't show that Lee cried for forty-five minutes before confessing."

Horzepa assisted the prosecution in establishing a pattern for the homicides of seven men by Lee Wuornos. All had emanated from the Daytona Beach area.

He related to the jury that Richard Mallory's body was located 11 miles from Daytona Beach, his automobile 12 miles; David Spears' body 112 miles, his truck 41 miles; Charles Carskaddon's body 94 miles, his vehicle 66 miles; Peter Siems' body had not yet been found, his vehicle 57 miles; Troy Burress' body, 64 miles, his vehicle 56 miles; Charles Humphreys' body 68 miles, his automobile 170 miles; Walter Gino Antonio's body 147 miles, his vehicle 39 miles.

Billy Nolas questioned Horzepa's use of Daytona Beach as the centralized area from which the action had sprung.

"What if you had used Zephyr Hills, Homassasa Springs, Oleander?" All places where Lee and Ty had lived.

Billy placed his arm around Lee, sobbing into the pink Kleenex which had been placed at her disposal.

"During that year, she lived in the Daytona area. This is where she was hitchhiking from when she made her forays onto the interstate," declared Tanner.

Returning to the witness, he asked Horzepa:

"Where did you get your information?"

"From Miss Moore."

"Who did she live with for the past four and a half years?"

"Miss Moore."

John Tanner turned to Judge Blount.

"The state rests, your honor."

"The jury will be in recess until 9:30 tomorrow morning," responded the judge.

The defense table was littered with crumpled pink tissues. Lee turned to look at Arlene. She raised her hands in a gesture of surrender.

Tricia approached her client.

"We'll spend the afternoon together," she said calmly.

On the railing before the spectators, the photo of Richard Mallory's decomposed body, considered too gruesome for jury consumption, had been trimmed to a pie shape. All it revealed was Mallory's pockets and the zipper of his pants. The former turned inside out. The latter securely fastened.

Outside the courtroom, Tricia Jenkins addressed the reporters.

"I'm not at all sure if we'll present a case. That'll make Lee very happy, I know," she joked.

"The defense could be as short as one hour and as long as two days," she added.

"Will Lee testify?" asked several members of the press.

Tricia smiled. "Now come on."

Chapter Twenty-One

Lee Wuornos had an air of tranquillity about her on the following morning. Wuornos watchers noticed it immediately. Speculation was that she had won her fight with her attorneys to testify in her own behalf.

Steve Glazer was among the spectators that morning. He had come in from Gainesville to file suit against the Volusia County Department of Corrections for their treatment of the defendant.

Dr. Elizabeth McMahon, one of the psychologists hired by the defense to testify in the penalty phase, if there was one, sat quietly in the back row. Within a few moments, she was asked to leave. As a potential expert witness, she could not watch the upcoming testimony.

Billy Nolas addressed the court, asking that the judge reconsider his motions for mistrial based on the Williams Rule evidence which had become a feature of the trial.

"Most of the trial," he said, "has nothing to do with Richard Mallory."

He also asked for a judgment of acquittal based on various errors in the testimony of state's witnesses.

The judge denied both motions.

He did, however, agree that the state could not refer to confidential statements made by Lee to her psychologists during cross examination.

The box of pink Kleenex sat perkily on the witness stand. It was no longer speculation that Lee Wuornos was about to testify.

"The defense calls Aileen Wuornos to the stand," said Tricia Jenkins.

All eyes followed the carefully groomed figure to the witness chair.

"Please state your full name," Tricia began gently.

"Aileen Wuornos."

Lee looked pretty and calm. Her hair fell softly around the collar of the tailored white blouse. The cross lay against her chest. This was the moment she had been waiting for. The moment when she could tell the world what had happened to her on the night of November 30, 1989, in the woods with Richard Mallory. None of them could doubt that it was self defense after they heard her story. She had been thinking about it for a long time.

"Can you hear me?" Trish asked. She knew, as did most of the court-room, that Lee had trouble hearing.

"Yes."

"Because if you can't hear me at any time, let me know. You might come a little closer to the microphone."

Lee adjusted the equipment. She wanted to make certain that every-one heard her.

"How old are you?"

"Thirty-five."

"Where are you from?"

"Troy, Michigan."

"When did you leave home and what for?"

"When I was fourteen years old."

"Where had you been living just prior to when you were fourteen years old."

"With my grandparents."

"Why did you come to Florida?"

"Because when I was younger, I was sleeping out in the streets and it was too cold."

"How did you come to Florida?"

"On the train."

"Did you come with a friend? How did you come?"

"By myself."

"How did you support yourself during those early years?"

"I had a couple of jobs that paid seventy-five cents an hour, but basi-cally I prostituted."

"When did you start becoming a prostitute, Lee?"

"At the age of sixteen."

"And how did that happen. How did you end up getting into that particular profession?"

"Well, I was hitchhiking and guys would pick me up. And they would ask do I want to make money. And they would pay me as much as $60 an hour. And that was really good money, so I took the offer and be-came a hitchhiking prostitute."

"Were you always in Florida?"

"I was all over the United States."

"And how old were you when you finally came to Florida to settle?"

"Well, I was sixteen when I came to Florida, but I settled here at age twenty."

"Have you ever had any children?"

"Yes, I had one son."

"And how old is he?"

"He should be twenty-one."

"And how old were you when you had him?"

"I was fourteen."

"And did you give the child up or what happened?"

"My grandmother made me give the child up. My parents. My grandparents adopted me."

"Then you thought of your grandparents as your parents?"

"Yes, they adopted me."

"How often over the last few five years, let's start four or five years ago, how often did you go out during the week to hustle."

"Well, I would go out anywhere from three to seven days, depending, basically four days for sure."

"And how many men would you say you had contact with during the course of the day."

"I would say anywhere from three to eight."

"Were all of those contacts sexual?"

"Yes, those were sexual contacts."

"And did you have contacts with men on the road that weren't sexual?"

"Yes. I worked from exit to exit."

"Explain that. You worked from exit to exit."

"Well, I would spend the whole day and night on the road for two or three days and I just worked one exit to another and the guys would pick me up as a hitchhiker and a lot of guys asked me and if I asked them and they were interested, fine, and if they weren't I would get off at the next exit and try again."

"There came a time when you met Ty, Tyria Moore. When was that?"

"In 1986."

"Describe your relationship with Ty."

"I met her at the Zodiac and from the first day I met her we fell head over heels with each other. The first year we had a sexual relationship, but the second year we became more like sisters. I loved her very deeply. We didn't care about the sex part."

"Did your hustling stop once you got into your relationship with Ty?"

"No. Matter of fact she quit her job because I made $150 a day and she made only about $150 a week so I said why don't I take care of you. . . . I was a white slave, but I didn't know it at the time."

"Did you go out more often?"

"The last year she didn't like trailer living and I was able to provide enough for her. She wanted me to go out more often. She said or else she would break up with me and find another girl to take care of her."

"Did you talk about your experiences on the road with her?"

"No."

"Why not?"

"She didn't want to hear them. She didn't care what happened to me."

"Did you try to talk to her about Richard Mallory?"

"I did, but she didn't want to listen."

"And during the times that you were with Ty, did she ever work?"

"When I met Ty she was working at El Caribe. The only salary job she had was as a laundry worker for two months."

"Was she working when you split up?"

"She got fired."

"Why?"

"She beat up her boss."

"So during these periods of time were you supporting her?"

"Yes."

"What were you spending your money on?"

"I wanted to save up for a house and every time I came home with money, she wanted to go to the mall and buy clothes. I had a bra with safety pins. One time she spent $200 in quarter machines for stuffed animals. I just took care of her. I didn't really care about myself. I bought her a lot of clothes. Or we would go to the bars. Whatever she wanted, she got it. I loved her very much."

"Did you like to drink too?"

"Yes."

"Did you drink a lot?"

"We made sure that we kept the drinking even so one didn't have more than the other. That's how close we were."

"But you drank when you were out on the road?"

"Yeah. I drank anywhere from two to six beers, sometimes more."

"Why would you drink on the road?"

"It was like my tranquilizer. I was shy. I was embarrassed about my body. I was scared. I knew it was my profession. It was the only thing I knew how to do."

"Did you accept rides with men of all ages?"

"I didn't go with young men. They were more aggressive. Always stoned. I don't do drugs."

"Prior to meeting Richard Mallory, had you ever been hurt when you were out working on the road?"

"Yes."

"Can you tell me something about it?"

"Yes. A couple of guys raped me. I did not have a weapon and I got hurt."

"When you were a young girl, just starting out, were you ever physically hurt while you were out on the road?"

"I was hurt a couple of times. In Indiana a judo instructor had beaten me up so badly that you cannot describe my face. Took me about two months to recover."

"Why didn't you quit working the roads?"

"I tried to get the church to help. Said I had to be part of the congregation. Didn't have my GED. I tried to be a corrections officer, but I didn't have a car. I needed $3,000. I tried and tried and tried to help myself. I tried the government military field, but didn't pass. The only thing I could do was be a prostitute and I lived here and there and everywhere. I had an apartment once that I lost."

"Do you remember catching a ride with Richard Mallory."

"Yes."

"Do you remember, when did you meet him?"

"The end of November 1989."

It had been raining off and on all day and the pavements were wet and slick.

Lee had been in Fort Myers for a few nights, hustling, and was trying to get home to Daytona Beach and Ty. In her purse was $250, enough for the apartment on Burleigh Avenue that they wanted to rent. She had been travelling since 6:00 a.m., and it had taken her six rides to get to the Tampa area. Her clothes were damp and she was tired and she was still a long way from home.

"I was waiting for it to stop raining, under the viaduct. When it slowed down, I decided to walk toward the light so that if a car stopped I could tell whether it was a girl or a guy."

As night fell, the headlights of approaching cars were reflected in the pools of water which collected under the I-75 overpass. Sprays of water splashed against her legs as the cars passed, soaking into her clothes.

The Cadillac drove past her, then stopped and backed to where she was standing.

"I saw one head, so I thought 'All right' and I walked to the car and opened the door."

"Did you stop for me?" she asked the driver.

Richard Mallory had left his video store a few hours earlier and headed for a rendezvous at Daytona Beach.

"Yeah," he said. "You going to Orlando?"

"No, I'm going to Daytona," Lee replied, still standing outside the car.

"This is your lucky day because I'm going all the way to Daytona," Mallory offered.

"I thought, this is great, and I got in the car."

"Lee, let me ask you something," Tricia said. "At this time, the time that you met Richard Mallory, had you started carrying a gun?"

"I carried a gun for six months before at least. I can't remember when."

"And why were you carrying a gun?"

"For protection. Security."

It was warm and dry inside the car, and Lee sank gratefully into the seat next to Richard Mallory.

"How about a drink?" he offered, glancing at his blond companion.

"What is it?" she asked. She liked his looks. She wouldn't mind getting it on with him, except she was so tired.

"Vodka, and I have orange juice," he said.

"Back on the road he asked me if I wanted marijuana and I said no, but I didn't care if he smoked it because it was his car. He asked me what I did and I told him I had a pressure cleaning business and he said he had a video store. He said he knew girls in topless bars and he would pay $2,000 per [photo] session. He talked about politics and religion and he talked about his store a lot. And he kept asking me if I knew anyone who would be interested and I said no.

"We finally arrived at Orlando and he asked if I wanted a beer because I had told him I don't drink mixed drinks. I drank beer in Fort Myers. I had $250 and I needed to get back and get an apartment."

"What did you do once you got to Orlando?" Tricia asked.

"He bought a six-pack. Stopped for gas. Past Orlando we went to the bathroom. He talked about his problems—his ex-wife and having problems with a lady, losing the video store."

"Did you proposition him?"

"No."

"Why not?"

"I was too exhausted. I had enough money and I wanted to get home."

"What happened next?"

"We stopped to go to the bathroom. He kept talking to me about his problems."

"You're a good listener, Lee. You're like a psychologist or counselor or something and you give good advice. How about if we stop somewhere. You're really helping me," Mallory offered.

"I dunno. I really need to get home."

"Just maybe an hour—I'll take you home then."

"Well, it's getting pretty late and I don't have a key," Lee conceded. "If the dogs start barking it'll wake up the manager. I guess we could stop for awhile."

"How long had it taken you to get to here from where he first picked you up?" Tricia continued.

"About two and a half hours."

"What happened after you stopped?"

"Do you know where we can park around here?" Mallory asked as he exited off I-4. "We gotta go somewhere private cause I don't wanta get busted."

"So I directed him to Quail Run. We drove there and were talking for at least one and a half to two hours. We talked about everything. He still asked me about the photos and all that stuff. I was drinking beer and he was drinking his mixed drinks. And he was still smoking pot."

Mallory kept talking about his ex-wife, about his problems with that marriage, and about the woman he had just broken up with.

"How come you know so much about married people? You told me you're single and you got a roommate," Mallory asked.

"I guess I gotta be honest with you. I'm a hooker."

She liked Richard Mallory. He'd told her so much about his life, it seemed all right to share hers.

"Sex? You mean sex? I thought we were eventually gonna get it on together, but you don't do it for free. You do it for money. You don't do it for free," Mallory chuckled.

"No, I don't. This is my job. This is what I do for a living."

"How much do you charge?"

"$100 an hour, and then after an hour I don't say you have to give me another $100 if the guy's all right. I'm not greedy. I don't care about making anymore. $100 is fine."

"If I gave you $100 we could spend a couple of hours together?" Mallory leaned closer.

"Well, I have to wait for dawn now anyway. It's too late to go home." If only she weren't so tired. But they needed the money. She and Ty always needed more money.

Mallory looked out his window. "Where can we go? It's wide open here."

"So he fixed another drink and smoked more pot—he had this pipe thing—and I grabbed another beer. I told him I use rubbers—it's mandatory so we might have to stop at a gas station. He said he had some. So we started down the road. We couldn't see to get to the trail so we got a flashlight from the glove box. Put the light on the dashboard."

Richard pulled the car into the wooded area and stopped. It was obviously a dumping ground, but it was secluded. No one would find them here.

"Hey, I got an idea. Why don't we both get undressed," Lee suggested.

This was the way she operated. If they both took off their clothes, neither of them could run out on the other.

"Wait a minute, I gotta get rubbers out of the trunk and a blanket. Don't wanta get anything on the seat."

Lee began to undress, piling her clothes into the back seat. She could hear the trunk close and saw Richard come around the side of the car. He was still dressed.

"Hey, you got your clothes on. Not fair, Richard. We agreed we'd both be nude and I'm the only one who is."

Richard slid into the car, switched on the dome light and looked at Lee.

"Not bad," he assessed.

"I dunno. I got stretch marks and a beer belly. Come on, get your clothes off and let's get started. It's cold in here."

He smiled and leaned across her, rolling down the car window.

"Yeah, it's cold. I love cold weather."

He began to unbuckle his pants. He was still smiling, but it was not friendly. There was something frightening about his face.

"What if I told you I don't have enough money? I have enough for breakfast and gas, but that's it?"

"No way, Richard, no way. I'm not here for my health. Sorry, but I guess we have to call this off."

Lee turned to the back seat to retrieve her clothes.

"I turned to look at him and he wrapped a cord around my neck."

Lee paused in her testimony.

Very gently, Tricia encouraged her client to continue.

"Tell us what happened after you felt the cord around your neck."

"I'm going to tell you right now, I'm nervous. This is hard for me...." Lee ran her hands across her forehead and took a deep breath.

"I told him I wouldn't have sex with him."

"Yes, you are bitch. You're gonna do everything I tell you to do and if you don't I'll kill you right now. It doesn't matter to me. Your body will still be warm for my high cock." His voice was different now, threatening, commanding.

Richard tightened his hold on the cord, choking Lee. His face was close to hers now and she could smell the liquor and marijuana. His eyes blazed.

"You wanta die, slut?"

"He told me to lie down on the car seat. He tied my hands to the steering wheel. He was sitting in the driver's seat. Then he told me to slide up and went to the passenger's seat. I was crying my heart out. He said he loved to hear me in pain. He loved to hear me cry. It turned him on."

Richard was naked. He was on his knees in the passenger's seat. He grabbed Lee's legs and lifted them in the air. Grunting, he plunged his penis into her rectum. She had never had anal sex. She had always hated the thought of it. It hurt. Still he kept pulling out and plunging back in. Finally, still hard, he dropped her legs and mounted her, thrusting into her vagina.

Afterwards, Richard picked up his clothes from the ground outside the car, walked back to the driver's side and removed the keys from the ignition. Lee could hear him go back to the trunk. She watched him as he returned, carrying a cooler filled with bottles of water, a tote bag with a white and yellow towel.

"I said, 'What are you doing?' He said, 'I'm full of surprises.'"

"He got out a bar of soap, toothbrush, rubbing alcohol and visine. Then this guy began to take a bath. He began pouring the rubbing alcohol all over himself. He said the last sluts he had were full of disease. Then he put his clothes back on. Put things back in the tote bag except alcohol and visine, which are on the dashboard. Walks back to the passenger's side and says, 'This is one of my surprises.'"

Richard lifted Lee's legs again, but this time he poured the visine and rubbing alcohol into her rectum. It ran down her buttocks, red with the blood which had resulted from his attack. Leaning over her, he poured alcohol into her nose.

"I was really pissed and yelling. He put the tote bag in the trunk and sat on the front of the car, listening to the radio. I'm freezing to death. I think he's going to kill me."

"I can see you moving. You're not gonna get untied unless I untie you. Finally the cold weather got to you." Richard's voice drifted in through the open window above Lee's head.

"It must've been about an hour. Finally he untied me from the steering wheel and put the rope around my neck. He's still saying all kinds of jazz about what he wants to do to me. He told me to turn toward him, lie down and spread my legs. And I guess he's going to zipper fuck me. He had his clothes on. He was holding the cord around my neck like reins. I thought I gotta fight or I'm gonna die."

Lee was close now to the area where her bag lay on the right side of the floor. If she moved quickly, she could remove the gun from the bag. She raised her left arm and pushed Mallory away from her, spitting in his face.

Richard Mallory stared at her, his face reddened with rage.

"You're dead, bitch!" he screamed, each word puncturing the stillness of the woods.

Gunfire pierced the morning quiet.

Lee opened the passenger door and backed out quickly. Mallory, wounded, his eyes wide, went out the driver's door. He staggered around the front of the car, toward her.

"Don't come near me or I'll shoot you. Don't make me have to shoot you again," Lee cried.

"And he started coming at me and I shot him."

"What happened after you shot him," Tricia asked her client.

"I thought what am I gonna do with the car? I dragged him away from the car, went to the ignition to get the keys, looked through his pockets for his keys, turned on the headlights, checked his pulse. I took nothing from his pockets except keys. I didn't want the birds to pick at him so I covered him with carpet. I drove to Quail Run, nude, crying and shaking. I had a little blood on me so I got out the stuff he got out and cleaned myself like he had. Drank a beer and tried to decide what to do. Put everything in the tote bag. I will have to lay low. Scared they're going to find the body. It was 6:30. I got rid of the prints that I could. I hurt all over. My crotch hurt, my vagina, nose all hurt. Freaking out. Got to take a shower. Got to get back to Ty and get rid of the car. I don't know what to do. We had Maggie, the dog and a cat, Tyler. I knocked on the door. When Ty opened the door I could see they had destroyed the curtains and a chair. We were supposed to move that day and I thought if the manager sees this, he will call the cops. We had everything ready to move so I told Ty a guy had loaned me his car and he was waiting at a motel. She asked me what the hickeys on my neck were from and I said I must have slapped a mosquito. We moved stuff to the apartment along with the moped and 12-speed bike. I drove her back to the motel. She took the moped to work. I took the 12-speed to John Anderson. Went through his wallet to see if he really was Richard. Dug hole and put things in it. Just threw stuff out."

"Did you take anything out of Richard Mallory's wallet when you were going through it?"

"He only had about $38—$42, something like that."

"Did you take it?"

"Yes."

"Did you take any credit cards?"

"No."

"What did you do then?"

"I got on my bike and started riding and threw the keys in someone's yard."

"Had you ever had anal sex prior to this time with Richard Mallory?"

"Never."

"When Mallory started getting violent, did you try to calm him down?"

"I couldn't say anything to Mallory because he was choking me."

And then it was John Tanner's turn to question the witness.

The defense team had dreaded this moment. They had always doubted that Lee would be able to stand up under cross-examination.

"You saw the confession tape in its entirety, didn't you?"

"Yes sir."

"You didn't make one mention of anal rape or being tied up or having alcohol poured in your rectum, did you?"

"Every time I tried to tell him about what was happening, he interrupted me and asked me how many times was he shot, what kind of items did you take, did he say anything after he was shot. And where did you leave his car. I never got a chance to express anything. I was always interrupted."

Tanner accused Lee of telling several different stories to Horzepa.

"I'm trying to tell the truth today, what actually happened."

"Hard to keep the stories straight, isn't it?" Tanner responded sarcastically.

Tanner's remark brought an immediate response from Billy Nolas, which became a heated exchange with David Damore.

Interrupting, Judge Blount threatened to gag both of the young wranglers and, to prove his point, told his bailiff to have someone bring a roll of masking tape. Several minutes later, a deputy obliged by placing the tape on the bench before the judge.

"You just were cut off," Tanner continued. "You didn't have a chance to tell him. Before Detective Horzepa began the interview, you said you wanted to tell him all the facts and circumstances surrounding Mallory's killing, didn't you?"

"I don't recall that."

"Well, what did you think your purpose was when you were sitting there telling him about the Mallory case."

Tanner was his cutting edge best when attempting to break down a witness.

"My main purpose was to confess that Ty was innocent....I was hysterical...I was in shock...and they had forced me to talk thinking they were going to arrest Tyria Moore if I didn't answer their questions on this case...I was only there to confess about Ty's innocence. I had just got done talking to her on the phone....I was totally out of it."

"Oh, so it wasn't because the detective cut you off. Now you're saying it's because you were totally out of it. Which was it?"

"They cut me off and I couldn't remember."

"You can remember being anally raped. If you'd been anally raped, couldn't you?"

"I wasn't interested in telling them certain things. I was only interested in Tyria Moore and I was mad that they had threatened me that if I don't talk to them, they will arrest her. So I was pretty well belligerent and stubborn...I'm just here to confess about Tyria. I'm not here to confess about the murder because I was trying to clear her that there weren't two women... there's one woman."

"You didn't understand about the anal rape and the alcohol...you didn't talk about that because the detective cut you off."

"That's right."

"Or you didn't tell it because you forgot about it, or...the third reason you gave is that you were just there to talk about Ty Moore and you were stubborn."

"There's a lot of reasons."

"Well how about the rest of them."

With the mention of Tyria Moore, Lee's demeanor changed noticeably. It was apparent that she would have very much liked to tell the jury what she had already told Arlene. That she hated Tyria Moore. She had trusted Tyria. And Tyria had turned against her.

"The reasons are I'm there to confess that Tyria Moore is innocent ...I lied because I loved her so much...I'll be more than happy to explain that Tyria knows more than she's saying; that she knows it's self defense...I will tell you all about Tyria Moore."

John Tanner was not interested in having Lee talk about Tyria to the jury. It could open too many doors best left closed.

"... Any other reasons you didn't tell the detective?"

"I couldn't remember because I was in a state of shock thinking about Tyria. I told you over and over and over and over I'm only here to confess for Tyria...and I was totally focused on Tyria...."

"I walked in there and he talked to me fifteen minutes before the

tapes...were on. It was not on at all. Nothing was on...and he threatened me."

"He threatened you?"

"Yes, he did....When I walked in there, they said, I told them I was
there to confess and I want to really tell you about Tyria and I was telling
them I'm just here to talk about Tyria and they said well, that's not going
to do any good because if you're just here to talk about Tyria and not
about the case I've got Tyria Moore in custody and I'll have her appear in
Volusia County Branch Jail and I'll have her indicted for first degree
murder as well as you....I called her under the direction of the police."

"The police had her set up so they could record your telephone calls,
didn't they?"

"Tyria Moore knows more than...she knows it's self defense and
she's not saying anything because she's involved in books and movies
and she doesn't want to lose her family....I know her very well...and
she's willing to lie for that...and she's also worried about being arrested
as accessory to the facts."

The frustrations that Lee felt about Tyria Moore rushed out.

"You said it would jeopardize Tyria Moore if you told the self defense
story. How would that jeopardize her?"

"... No, I'm talking about she doesn't want to say it's self defense
because I believe she is involved with millions of dollars books and movies and she doesn't want my acquittal because if I get convicted, she gets
the money and so does Mr. Horzepa, Munster and a lot of you other detectives and police officers that are involved in this and also that she is
concerned about her family, she loves her family...she's acting like she
doesn't know anything...I got 289 lies in her deposition...why is she
lying so much?...I believe she is lying about a whole lot of things to
keep herself from being accessory to the facts...she's afraid to tell anything, she's even afraid to say it's self defense because then she was
knowledgable about the situation."

Lee was beginning to lose control. The anger she had felt toward the
investigators, toward Tyria, was urging her on.

"Was there anything else that you say she knew that would incrimi-
nate her except for the self defense story?"

"I couldn't tell her because I didn't want her to get too involved....
she saw the bruises...asked me a little bit about the situation."

"You told Detective Horzepa she didn't know anything, didn't you?"

"I was covering for her totally."

"You didn't tell her that you killed him did you?"

"Yes, I did."

"Oh, when did you tell her that?"

"Fourteen days after he was on TV."

"Did there ever come a time when she believed you?"

"Yes, after I started telling her...that day that you saw the bruises on me...that day Richard Mallory had raped me really bad....she loved me very bad and I loved her very bad...and I didn't want to just sit there and tell her what happened....I told her I was raped, and she asked a few questions...and she said don't tell me any more....I don't want to hear any more. She was really pissed off...she was really mad at Mallory."

"How close were you to Tyria?"

"Very. Two peas in a pod...right arm, left arm..."

It was painful to remember how close they'd been. Lee flinched at the prosecutor's next words.

"You trusted each other."

"Yes."

"What broke up the relationship?"

"When we saw the sketch on TV. I told her you're going to have to just leave me."

"Are you not going to answer any questions about the other six murders?"

Billy Nolas shot up from his seat.

"On our advice, she will not answer that question. Those cases have not been tried."

Lee returned to the subject of Tyria.

"I never knew she had a black heart like she does. Right now she could help me out....she knows I was raped and she knows I defended myself."

She described to the jury how she avoided talking about the murders during her telephone conversations with Tyria, in case they were being taped.

"In case she's lying to me, I'm not going to say anything that will put her in jeopardy or put myself in jeopardy."

"It [the rape] was not brought up until months after your arrest, correct? It wasn't brought up with Detective Horzepa, was it?"

"It sure wasn't. He didn't give me a chance to say it."

Tricia Jenkins interceded: "Lee do not answer about other cases. They have not been tried yet."

"In fact, during three days of phone calls before then, sixty-five times you said it was either mistaken identity or Ty was innocent. Correct? Over and over again," Tanner hammered.

"...I felt just in case she is lying to me, I had better not express anything on that phone that would get her in trouble."

"You didn't want to tell her about the rape because it would implicate her."

The familiar anger of Lee Wuornos was striking back.

"I'm not lying. I'm up here telling the truth and I think I'm the only one that's telling the truth...especially when I learned about all these books and movies."

"Let's talk about that. You've talked to some news people about this, haven't you?"

"I did? Jackie Giroux? We're filing a lawsuit."

"Movie producer type person? Did you talk about if any money was to be made out of this, you'd like Lee to have it, didn't you?"

"Lee?"

"I'm sorry. Ty."

"If I said anything to her in a letter, which I don't understand how I could have wrote to her while I was in jail because as soon as I got through talking to the detective, they stuck me in solitary confinement lock down, shoving pills down me and got me messed up on drugs forcing me and I didn't have any pen or pencil or paper to write and you keep saying that those letters came in January in jail, but I don't remember writing any letters."

"Who's this who is forcing drugs down you?"

"They had me on vistaril. They had me where I didn't have any commissary not a Bible or a book nothing to read 24-7 in a square little room with nothing to do but come up and say do you want your pills and it will help you to sleep....I was taking 2800 milligrams a week, sixteen pills a day. They almost killed me."

Tanner was enjoying himself. The witness was visibly rattled.

"Was Detective Horzepa forcing you to take pills?"

"It was a plan, I believe."

"Were you on drugs when you made your confession?"

"No, but I was coming down off of alcohol. It was the detective's idea."

"Did you see the video tape of yourself? Did you see evidence of yourself shaking? You were lighting cigarettes."

"I was trying to keep it together."

"You never once said that your victims tried to rob you?"

"You never know how many you're going to have. You just keep hustling until the day is through."

"And you were charging how much for the sex act? You made anywhere between $600 and $1000 a week."

"Well, you're right..."

"You're capable of holding other jobs, aren't you? You've done other work."

"I don't have the qualifications for other jobs. I've always been fired and I've never been able to hold a job. The only thing I know how to do is prostitute."

"You get paid more for that than anything else you've ever done. Good money. You like it."

"Well, I like the sex and I like some of the clients—they become like my brothers. But it's a job. That's just part of being a prostitute."

Tanner couldn't resist it.

"Kind of a rolling road party, wasn't it?" he asked.

"Your Honor, objection," Tricia rose to her feet.

"Objection sustained," Judge Blount retorted.

"You've got to watch it and be careful and keep a level head on your shoulders," Tanner continued.

"It's a job. It's not exciting."

"Then there came a time when you decided to arm yourself or carry a pistol."

"I carried it for protection."

"How many times during the four and a half years you lived with Tyria Moore did you have to defend yourself?"

"I was raped three times."

"Did you have to use a gun to defend yourself? How many times before you killed Mr. Mallory?"

"I didn't have a weapon."

"But if you had, you'd have used it earlier. Would you have shot the men who raped you before Mallory?"

"They made me beg for my life. I wouldn't do anything to them unless they were mean to me. We talked about religion, politics. Everyone prostitutes, even housewives. And the men, they're out there saying to us prostitutes... here we are. If they kept their money in their back pockets and their wallets in their pants there wouldn't be any prostitution. We're just out there making a living. I never worked bars, truck stops, rest areas, streetwalk, I did strictly hitchhike prostitution. If I walk in a bar and I meet a guy and we want to go to bed together that's just like prostitution. So here let's say he offers me money and we don't hurt each other...what's the difference. We've agreed upon sex with each other, the only thing is he's giving me a little money to help me and I'm helping him. It's like friendship. Here's a loan."

"So you think you have the right to disregard the law?"

"Well, I tell you, it's the only thing I can do anyhow. That was my job. I wasn't hurting anybody out there."

"Well that's not true is it?"

A wave of laughter rippled through the court.

"I wasn't hurting anybody out there. I'm the victim as far as I'm concerned. He had no reason to rape me. He had no reason to do any of those things. I didn't provoke him."

"You say that you were the victim in every case where you hurt someone?"

Lee was receiving signals from defense counsel. He's trying to trick you those signals said.

"I'm only here for Richard Mallory. I'm here for one trial."

"I'm only trying to find out why you killed six other men. Isn't it a fact that you had a habit of hitchhiking the highways and selecting middle-aged men, men above thirty-five, thirty-six, on to their sixties?"

Tanner was baiting her now.

"I worked the major highways...out of the Daytona Beach area. I've worked the whole Florida state."

"It was your pattern, was it not, to tell them that you were a prostitute so you could make money?"

"They propositioned me many times. Lot of times guys pulled over strictly for sex. I'm sure every other girl out there gets propositioned by guys. Lots of times I didn't have to ask them. They asked me."

"Well, we heard Bobby Copus talk about you asking him."

"He didn't pick me up. I never saw him. I think furthermore that Jackie Giroux knows him. That he called her up something about a movie. He is boldfacedly lying up here to get to the media attention. I don't work truck stops. And I don't ride with truckers."

Lee's voice was rising. She was getting angry. It was exactly the reaction that Tanner was looking for.

"You deny that you went over to him and asked for a ride saying that you needed to get back to your children where your sister was?"

Lee was growing increasingly irritable. Her patience with the tenacious John Tanner was waning. He was messing with her. She leaned forward in her seat.

"Guess what. My sister...I haven't seen her since 1976."

"I didn't ask you if you told the truth. I'm asking if that's what you told him."

"I've never seen the man. I don't know who he is. I don't deal with anyone that fat. He's too big a guy. I wouldn't trust being with him."

"You didn't holler after him: You fat old son of a bitch, I'll kill you, too, like I killed the others."

"He never picked me up. Especially at truck stops. I don't work truck stops. I think truckers are too dirty. He said I had a purse. The police officers got my purse. It's a brown one. My gun does not fit in that purse and you can check it."

"You generally carried your gun in a little bag, didn't you?"

"I carried my gun in a tote bag. He says a purse."

"You even practiced with that to see how quick you could get it out, didn't you? Did you ever tell anyone that?"

"When I get home I'm too tired. I just set the bag down or in the closet and go to sleep."

"You never practiced to get it out fast to shoot fast?"

"No of course not. Someone made that up royal."

"You know Dr. McMahon?"

"Yes."

"Your Honor, we ruled on that," said Tricia Jenkins. It had been determined by the court that nothing Lee Wuornos told the psychologists could be used against her in court.

"If I weren't a convicted felon, I'd have bought a gun. They say, 'Go ahead and get killed. We don't care.' We have to protect ourselves- . . . .Some convicted felons are very decent people."

"And some of them shoot men to death in cold blood, too, don't they? Did you ever shoot a man in the back of the head in cold blood?"

John Tanner was referring to Walter Gino Antonio, Lee's seventh victim. Antonio had been shot in the back repeatedly.

Lee shook her head.

"I'm not going to answer that question. It has nothing to do with this case."

"So you're even a victim of the law," Tanner continued.

"We have to have a way to defend ourselves. Lots of them have turned to the Lord and are decent people. I didn't shoot anyone in cold blood. I'd have been out there decaying.

"I threw the gun away nearly a year later on the advice of Tyria Moore."

Lee was talking too much, and by so doing, she was falling into Tanner's hands. The more she talked, the less sense she made.

"You say Tyria Moore advised you to throw the gun away?"

"She used to tell me, you got a gun, you got rubbers. Be sure and clean the car out if anything like that happens again. I don't want anyone to hurt you."

"If he was shot while you were lying down, why didn't the bullet go upward?"

"I thought he was so decomposed you couldn't tell," Lee snapped. "Every incident is different. Depends on the situation involved. Nothing can be level to one person."

"You can tell it all if you want."

Tanner smiled coaxingly. He knew how much Lee could hurt herself if she began to refer to the other murders.

"I felt like what he did to me was unnecessary so then I took his property. I felt like he owed me for what he did."

"Didn't you tell Detective Horzepa maybe it was self defense and maybe it was stupid and what I did, I don't know why I did it."

He emphasized the word "maybe."

"I believed no one would believe that I was raped and I had to defend myself. They'd say I'm a prostitute and we don't care."

"You were naked, cord marks around the neck, bleeding from the anus where you'd been raped, the alcohol, a cord with which you had been tied and held by the neck and no one would believe you were assaulted?"

"Was I supposed to walk down the road naked with a gun in my hand? Everyone has the right to defend themself."

Tanner shook his head incredulously. "And you didn't even tell your best friend."

During the lunch break following Lee's testimony, Arlene told reporters that "I thought she did really well on the stand because she's so shy. I was afraid she would break down. No matter what happened, if she didn't testify, she would always wonder 'what if.' "

The defense team scooped Arlene up and took her to lunch. Lee's testimony had been a disaster, they said. It pointed out clearly why defendants should not take the witness stand.

In another part of DeLand, three female members of the jury lunched.

"I'd rather be shot than raped," one of them revealed to her companions.

As the afternoon session began, Lee looked tired and pale. The pink tissues were returned to the defense table, but the emotion was drained from the defendant and she sat quietly, turning once to see Arlene in her usual seat.

"I love you," Arlene mouthed silently.

Lee nodded and smiled wearily.

When the judge was seated, Billy Nolas asked once again for a mistrial.

"The jury has been substantially tainted," he told the court.

Jackie Davis had been seen in the courthouse and it was obvious that she was to be questioned by the defense. They had not had an opportunity to depose her and asked to question her in closed court.

After notifying the jury that they would not be called for a few minutes, the judge allowed the defense to bring in the trim, red-haired woman. Davis, the prosecution pointed out, had an injury which had left scar tissue on her brain and there were certain instances that she could not remember. The defense must take this into account, they said.

It was obvious from the outset that Jackie Davis did not want to talk about Richard Mallory. She spoke slowly, her manner guarded. Whatever she had told Larry Horzepa, it had been tempered by the months since.

Yes, Richard Mallory had been charged with burglary, she said. He had entered a house, a woman was there, he had put his hand in front of her and she screamed.

Davis waffled on Nolas' question about Mallory's incarceration. Mallory had been in a rehabilitative program was her understanding from what he had told her.

Yes, he was paranoid, she told Nolas. He had been involved with an ambassador's wife and was certainly paranoid in reference to this woman. He thought he was being followed. He had wanted to have plastic surgery and get his nose fixed, presumably so she would not recognize him.

Mallory had two personalities, Jackie Davis said. One was very easygoing and generous. The other was withdrawn.

"Do you remember that you told Larry Horzepa that he was obsessed with washing himself," asked Nolas.

"No," Davis replied.

He had all kinds of tapes, pornographic ones, too, she admitted, but denied that when he was smoking and drinking he was difficult to deal with. It was true that he did not have male friends.

"I had an accident and have some scar tissue and some kind of memories I don't know," Davis admitted.

"You've been getting a lot of discovery here, but what do you want to do with it?" questioned Judge Blount.

There seemed to be no point in putting Jackie Davis under oath. It was apparent that whatever she had told Larry Horzepa about the volatile nature of Richard Mallory had slipped her mind.

"Your Honor, at this time the defense will rest," Tricia Jenkins announced.

"It's the only time I've had a nightmare at night and wakened up the next day to find the reality worse," Arlene confided to a friend that afternoon.

The prosecution recalled Larry Horzepa.

"On January 16, 1991, you interviewed the defendant, Aileen Carol Wuornos. Tell the jury whether or not that interview was videotaped."

"Yes, it was."

"Can you tell the jury how long that entire tape runs."

"A little over three hours."

"Could you describe her demeanor throughout the tape."

"She was slightly nervous at first."

"Did you at any time intentionally cut her off and not let her explain?"

"No, sir."

"Before the videotape came on, was she in the room with you before the recording began?"

"No, sir."

"The very moment that she was in your presence that day, the tape was running?"

"Yes, sir."

"Was your every word and action and her every word and action and that of Deputy Munster recorded on the audio video tape?"

"It was all recorded."

"Did you at any time that day or otherwise arrest Tyria Moore and seek her prosecution if Aileen Wuornos did not confess to this murder?"

"No, sir."

"Did you ever threaten Aileen Wuornos with the arrest of Tyria Moore?"

"No, sir, I did not."

Closing arguments were set for Monday morning, the judge told the court. Did the defendant have any questions concerning procedure?

"I don't think so," said Lee standing before the court. "I trust my lawyers real good."

David Damore felt strongly that Lee's testimony had damaged the defense.

"I think she hurt herself very badly on the witness stand," he said. "It gave the jury an opportunity to really get to see her a little bit and fear her and watch her as opposed to being shielded by just sitting there at the defense table and occasionally crying on cue."

Outside the jailhouse, John Tanner talked to the press. It was obvious that he was pleased with the prosecution's position.

"I think we've presented a credible case that should bring just results. Again, I have to be careful how I characterize evidence. The defense will have two shots at closing. They have the first statement, we respond and give our view, they have rebuttal. I'll do closing. The judge's not limited us. I rarely go much outside of an hour."

Down the street, nearer the parking lot, Tricia Jenkins told the crowd that the defense team would be working all weekend.

"I don't know what the prosecution is going to do," she added.

Chapter Twenty-two

B ill Miller had been selected to present closing arguments for the defense. Tall and fair-haired, Miller was the least volatile of the defense team. He was a gentle man and he addressed the jury in a quiet voice. At times the gallery strained to hear his words.

"We have listened to testimony of this case over a two week period. Our job now is about to begin—to discover the truth. To discover the truth, and by the truth what happened on December 1, 1989. You are to decide but one issue—that is whether Aileen Wuornos felt that she had to take Richard Mallory's life on December 1, 1989.

"So much of what you have heard has nothing to do with the death of Richard Mallory. In order to do your job properly you have to remind yourself that there will be other jurors and other judges to determine what happened in those cases. You must consider Richard Mallory and nothing else."

Miller discussed the role of Dr. Botting, who had performed the autopsy on Richard Mallory.

"He could not tell you how far away Richard Mallory was. He could not tell you the sequence of the shots. He could not tell you what happened before Richard Mallory was shot. In short, Dr. Botting could tell you nothing about self defense—the real issues of this case."

Still frustrated by Jackie Davis' failure to repeat the statements she had made originally to Larry Horzepa, Miller reminded the jury that Richard Mallory's lifestyle indicated that he might very possibly have been abusive to women.

"The state wanted you to hear from Tyria Moore that Lee Wuornos had come to her and told her she had killed a man," Miller continued. "Tyria Moore was a suspect. She had wrecked a car and had known for over one year that Lee Wuornos had shot Richard Mallory. You have to ask yourself what does that tell you. She did know it was in self defense. But she only started to care when she saw this might affect her and not only Lee Wuornos. Tyria Moore pulled Lee's emotional strings during phone calls.

"Lee Wuornos would do anything for Tyria Moore. Lee Wuornos would die for Tyria Moore. And Tyria Moore knew this and knew it well.

Tyria Moore, as a witness, and for obvious reasons, would try to please law enforcement."

Miller discussed the synopsis presented by Larry Horzepa which included the section where Lee, during the confession, talked about being hurt, and the handwritten note accompanying it which advised "Don't use."

"Don't let the jury hear, don't let you hear, you who are to decide what happened in this case. But not to hear why. The why is the only issue in this case. . . .

"The tape speaks for itself. Lee Wuornos said over and over and over again in January 1991, that she defended herself. But Larry Horzepa, just like Ty, didn't want to hear about it.

"You remember Mr. Nolas asked Mr. Horzepa on the stand: Why didn't you or Mr. Munster ask why she felt her life was in danger? Why didn't you ask what Mr. Mallory was doing to her? And Mr. Horzepa's response was: 'Well, I wanted to let her talk. I didn't want to interrupt her.'

"Half of the time in the last two weeks, you have been listening to testimony that had nothing to do with Richard Mallory.

"We don't know what such an experience did to Lee's mind and if she would ever be the same again. . . . Maybe something snapped in Lee after that, but those are questions for other juries and other judges.

"Far from being a predator that Mr. Tanner described, Lee Wuornos is a victim. Victim of a brutal attack—a violent attack.

"If she seemed angry with Mr. Tanner, consider that Mr. Tanner is asking you to sentence her to death."

As he returned to his seat, Miller touched Lee briefly on the shoulder.

"I don't think jury service is any less important than service in the armed service," John Tanner told the jury.

"This is the only opportunity I will have to talk to you. I would prefer an open exchange so the jurors could ask questions, but that's not the way we do it.

"You will receive jury instructions. . . . Lawyers' arguments are not evidence, what I say is not evidence. The evidence comes from the witness stand and the exhibits. You should not decide this case on sympathy for Richard Mallory or Lee Wuornos—you should decide it on the facts. Reasonable doubt, we discussed that during jury selection, is not some mystical, hard to understand concept, but it certainly doesn't put the burden on the state to prove anything beyond any doubt always. Especially when it comes to matters of a crime unwitnessed by anyone except the victim and the defendant. Premeditation is long range planning, conspiracy type crime. The kind of planning that would take days or weeks or hours—may only be the time between picking up a firearm and firing it—or may be between the first and second shot." Tanner paused. He wanted to give the jury time to digest what he had just told them.

"The verdict form you will receive has two parts. One deals with robbery—six options, guilty of armed robbery; guilty of robbery with a deadly weapon but without a firearm; guilty of robbery without a firearm or deadly weapon; guilty of robbery without a weapon; guilty of petty theft; or not guilty.

"The second deals with murder—guilty in first degree, premeditated and felony murder as charged; guilty of only first degree, premeditated murder; guilty of first degree, felony murder; guilty of second degree murder; guilty of second degree murder with firearm; guilty of third degree murder; guilty of third degree murder with firearm; guilty of manslaughter; guilty of manslaughter with firearm; and not guilty.

"Aileen Wuornos has been portrayed as a victim by the defense. She is not a victim in any sense of the word. She is not a victim because she is a prostitute. She has chosen to be a prostitute.

"This is not a victim prostitute. This is not a child wandering the streets... this is a grown woman, a healthy woman, capable of making an honest living if she wanted....

"It's not unusual to have similar fact evidence.... You've heard that other juries and other cases would render verdicts on the other killings and that's entirely true. You are not here to find her guilty or innocent on the other killings. The verdict that you will be asked to render will be for the case of Richard Mallory.

"This case is divided into two portions—we have chosen to separate guilt or innocence and, if a verdict of guilty, a penalty phase. Penalty should not be in your vocabulary, let along in your mind, at this point.

"Miller said that all these other cases had absolutely nothing to do with the murder of Richard Mallory. That's incorrect. Similar fact evidence—evidence of other crimes is relevant and material and properly and legally should be considered when ruled by court on criminal cases and even civil.

"The case involving Mr. Mallory is the case on trial. This is the only case—but with regard to second victim, Spears, third, Carskaddon, fourth, Siems, fifth, Burress, sixth, Humphreys and last, Antonio, automobile locations, where bodies were found, are all key issues.

"What did these men have in common? All of them were white males between the ages of thirty-nine and sixty years old. All travelling major thoroughfares in Florida, all travelling alone, each of them made one fatal mistake. They picked up Aileen Wuornos. In each of those cases she propositioned them for sex and she also killed them all in isolated areas. She shot every one of them in the torso, a couple were also shot in the head. All gunshot wounds, all .22 bullets from the same pistol, everyone had property stolen and their vehicle taken, and again it was wiped clean in cases of Mr. Mallory and Spears. Mr. Carskaddon's vehicle was stripped on the side of the highway. License plates removed on five of seven. All vehicles left abandoned in a range of 12 to 170 miles. Property of three of five were found in the warehouse. This illustrates pattern, method, criminality, intent and plan to carry out robberies and murders. She picked, selected, targeted a type of individual....

"Why would Ty Moore come in as Wuornos said and lie. They were very close, they were good friends, lovers, close as peas in a pod. Miss Wuornos says Ty knew it was self defense and she might get in trouble if she told it was self defense. How would that cause trouble? If anything, it might give some moral justification to the fact that Ty Moore didn't come forward and tell that in December...she believed her girlfriend had been raped and had horrible things done to her. That would be a plausible story if it was true. It's not true. Because she never told Ty Moore.

"You'll make a lot of money by lying about this self defense thing, she said. Well, that's not true. It would be a much more interesting story, more saleable story, if the poor prostitute simply did her job and some guys did horrible things to her and she killed in self defense. That's a good story. That would sell a lot of books and movies.

"And she says that Horzepa cut her off, but her lawyer was sitting there. Would any lawyer allow the police to cut off his client so she couldn't tell the story if she had a story to tell?

"There is not one shred of evidence that she was tied up. I thought the coat hanger would be involved. She did tell us something. She said what she deserved. She never told anything about rape. Never said Mr. Mallory raped her. Certainly never said she was tied to the steering wheel. In fact, I recall I asked her about this anal rape thing and she said, 'no, that's a different one—that's a different man.'

"Virtually everyone in court was lying, she says. Even Bobby Copus she says is a liar because he wants publicity.

"Had she had a gun two months or two days?...Something about having a gun changes some people.

"Ty Moore should have come to the police. Ty Moore should have reported it and maybe, just maybe, it would have stopped right there. Ty Moore is not on trial. This is the murder trial of Aileen Wuornos.

"This is because people don't want to be involved. We have to be involved. You have to be involved...Ty Moore...could have saved six men's lives. That doesn't hold her up to be anything respectable or honorable. If she had been told about anal rape, it would have given her some moral justification for not saying anything. It was bad enough that she didn't come forward. At least she didn't sit on that witness stand and lie to you and protect this woman who killed Mr. Mallory.

"This is a murder out of greed. This is a woman, who, by her own testimony, made between $30,000 and $50,000 a year and squandered it. Moved out of power and control to an obscenely simple way to have it all.

"Is there any answer to the whys—how did this happen? Not for this jury. Not for this time and not for us.

"She chose her life. She chose the time and the place and she has left you no reasonable choice under the evidence of this case except to find her guilty in the first degree and for armed robbery."

It had grown warm in the courtroom and the men at the prosecution table had removed their coats.

Lee's anger was apparent. Bill Miller's wrap-up did nothing to dispel it.

"I would agree with John Tanner that your services are vitally important," Miller began.

"...Demand of Mr. Tanner proof, not speculation. Demand of Mr. Tanner evidence....Maybes don't count in a court of law....The state has given you nothing. Demand more.

"...Lee Wuornos had every right to shoot Mr. Mallory....she was raped, she was brutalized and, despite her profession, she had a right to defend herself."

The state's rebuttal was rapid fire.

Larry Horzepa stated that, "When someone gave her a hassle, she had to kill them because she didn't want to leave a witness."

Jenny Ahearn, fingerprint expert, identified Lee Wuornos' fingerprints on the handgun in connection with the 1981 armed robbery conviction.

Deputy Susan Hanson repeated her conversation with Lee Wuornos on January 18, 1991, at Volusia County Branch Jail. Lee Wuornos had said to her: "Sometimes I feel guilty; other times I feel happy—like a hero or something."

Intent. Prior conviction. Lack of remorse.

And then it was over.

Judge Blount explained the jury's responsibilities in terms of the verdict forms. If Lee Wuornos was found guilty, she could be sentenced either to death or to twenty-five years without possibility of parole.

As the jury filed out, Lee sobbed uncontrollably, comforted by Don Sanchez, the pony-tailed defense investigator. For many years Sanchez had been a cop. He had come out of it with an amazing empathy for defendants.

While the jury deliberated, the courtroom was cleared. Media people looked for interviews, the attorneys gathered into clusters. Speculations were made as to how long it would take the jury to reach a verdict.

Outside in the hallway, a fair-haired, middle-aged man approached the two women writing books about Aileen Wuornos.

"I've been doing research at Stetson University," he said. "I've found a Bible passage which shows that Aileen Wuornos is not guilty. It's all part of the Kennedy conspiracy and I'd like to talk to you about it."

Not now, they told him. This is not the time. Call us. Cards were handed out followed by a hurried exit.

"This is the same man who has been trying to talk to the defense team," Arlene said. "He's crazy."

It took exactly ninety-one minutes for the twelve members of the jury to reach a decision. The verdict surprised no one except, perhaps, Lee Wuornos and her adoptive mother.

Pamela Mills, the schoolteacher, had been elected foreperson. She presented the verdict to the bailiff. He handed it to the judge. The judge read it and passed it to the clerk. No one envied the pretty girl with the long dark hair.

"We, the jury, find Aileen Wuornos guilty of premeditated, felony murder in the first degree," she read to the court.

Lee's stricken expression was duly recorded by photographers, as were the tears of Arlene Pralle in the company of her attorney, Steve Glazer. The courtroom was strangely silent except for the sobs of the woman who had adopted a killer.

Court was in recess until the following morning, declared Judge Blount, at which time the penalty phase would begin.

As the jury was dismissed from the courtroom, Lee watched them, her face darkening.

"I'm innocent!" she exploded. "I was raped! I hope you are raped, you sons-of-bitches and scumbags of America!"

The echo of her outcry reverberated in media across the nation.

Statements from attorneys and other interested parties following a verdict are an essential ingredient to media news.

"Can you imagine what she's like with a gun?" asked Tanner. "You've seen the real Aileen."

"How do you feel about the verdict?" a reporter asked him.

"I'm satisfied. I believe justice has been served."

"We will be presenting mitigation or reasons to save her life," said Tricia Jenkins.

"I loath, detest and despise her," offered Shirley Humphreys, wife of the fifth victim.

"I'm elated. Hope this sets a precedent. I would like to see her get the death penalty."

"I can't believe it," said Arlene Pralle. "How could they find her guilty?"

Chapter Twenty-three

"The verdict of this phase is advisory," Judge Blount explained as the trial moved into the penalty phase. "But it carries great weight. It need not be unanimous, but the majority of the jury must vote to recommend the death sentence, a minimum of seven jurors. . . . The burden is still on the state and you must consider the evidence you've heard to this time."

Aggravating and mitigating circumstances were explained at great length. "It will be up to you to determine whether there are any mitigating circumstances that exist that outweigh the aggravating circumstances," the judge continued.

"Based on the evidence you have heard, the aggravating circumstances which you may consider may be based on any of the following referenced by the evidence: the defendant has previously been convicted of another capital offense or of a felony involving the use of threat of violence; the crime to which the defendant is to be sentenced was committed while engaged in committing robbery with a firearm; the crime was committed in a design to inflict a high degree of pain; the crime was committed in a design that was cold, calculated, premeditated.

"If you find the aggravating circumstances do not justify the death penalty, your advisory sentence should be a life sentence without possibility of parole for twenty-five years.

"Mitigating circumstances must not be proved beyond a reasonable doubt. They include: The crime for which the defendant was convicted was committed while she was under the influence of extreme mental or emotional impairments; when the crime was committed she did not have the capacity to appreciate the finality of her conduct or her ability to conform her conduct to the requirements of the law was substantially impaired; the age of the defendant at the time of the crimes, and any other aspect of the defendant's character or record and any other circumstances of the offense.

"In these proceedings, it is not necessary that the recommendation be unanimous. Before you ballot, you must carefully weigh and realize that a human life is at stake."

Billy Nolas prepared the jury for the mitigating factors which the defense team planned to present. Their only hope lay in the jury's recognition of Lee's illness.

"You have observed Lee's behavior," Nolas began. "Why is Lee the way she is? This is the part of the case where you get those answers.

"She did not simply fall from the sky. There are things that she was born with and things that happened to her along the way...a world which has made her what she is."

The world of Lee Wuornos is a chilling place, a malevolent place, an angry, out-to-get-her place, a threatening place full of perceived terrors, testified the three psychologists during the next day and one-half of the penalty phase. She perceives the world as having evil spirits, ghosts, things that are beyond our face-to-face control. She distances people by seeing them as angels or demons. And she functions, they agreed, on the level of a very small child.

She has basic, primitive, child-like coping mechanisms that evidence themselves in a lot of complaining, temper tantrums, naive attempts at manipulation and attention-seeking self mutilation, the experts agreed.

She keeps trying to show the world how desperate she is.

Lee Wuornos, they said, evidenced a mild degree cortical dysfunction on the left side of her brain, the language side.

Dr. Elizabeth McMahon was the first expert witness to the stand. A tiny woman with large expressive eyes, her hair cropped short, Dr. McMahon explained her qualifications to serve as an expert witness. Neuropsychology, clinical psychology, the study of human behavior, deviant from the norm, private practice in forensics. She had performed the necessary neurological, psychological and intelligence tests on Lee. She had then passed those findings on to Dr. Harry Krop and Dr. Jethro Toomer, who had spent lesser amounts of time interviewing the subject.

"I was called by Tricia Jenkins and asked to evaluate Aileen Wuornos on five different occasions, for a total of 22 hours, on February 26, March 8, December 23, January 8 and January 19," said Dr. McMahon.

"The structure of Lee Wuornos' brain is normal, but it does not function properly, like sand in a gas tank....The condition is chronic, static, doesn't change and interacts with other problems," she continued.

The injury was a result of head trauma and was apparent from the early testing shown in her school records.

Lee Wuornos is also a borderline personality, the doctor said. A borderline personality is defined by eight classic symptoms, she explained, and Lee Wuornos evidenced them all: A pattern of unstable and intense interpersonal relations; impulsiveness; unstable moods; inappropriate intense anger; recurrent suicidal threats; marked and persistent identity disturbance; feelings of emptiness or boredom; frantic efforts to avoid real or imagined abandonment.

This, combined with the dysfunctional background, produced an unhappy, discontented woman who cannot cope with the world.

"Lee is always in a state of living on the edge. There is a sense of danger, striving just to get her physical needs met," said Dr. McMahon.

"She has some sense that other people are doing it okay, but she's not.... Miss Wuornos is probably one of the most primitive people I've seen outside of the institution. By that I mean that she functions at the level of very basic...a small child. Always making an attempt at some sense of security, some sense of contentment."

Billy Nolas produced a picture and held it before Dr. McMahon.

"Take a look at that and tell us what that is."

"That is the last picture that Miss Wuornos drew... in response to my request to draw anything you want."

Lee had drawn a picture of a crucifix. The defense wanted the jury to see it, but the state had objected.

"Objection, your honor, this is irrelevant," said Damore.

"Did you rely on these tests?" countered Nolas.

"Yes," responded Dr. McMahon.

"They are projective tests and they told me that I was dealing with an individual who was not psychotic, who was in touch with reality, but who distances people and sees them in the forms of angels, lizards, ghosts, malevolent. When she becomes emotionally aroused, her ability to make good judgments goes out the window."

"Paranoid," Dr. McMahon said. And depressed. In need of affection and basic closeness. Angry.

"Was the result of the projective testing consistent with the borderline personality disorder and the cortical dysfunction from which Miss Wuornos suffers and has suffered from the time she was a child?" asked Nolas.

"Yes", said Dr. McMahon.

David Damore was anxious to cross examine the doctor.

"In your clinical opinion is Miss Wuornos insane?" he asked.

"No, she is not."

"In your clinical opinion, does she know right from wrong?"

"In most instances, yes."

"She knew when she shot Richard Mallory over and over and over again that what she was doing was wrong legally."

"At that moment," said Dr. McMahon, "I do not think that was a relevant consideration."

Damore's questions hit furiously, hardly allowing the doctor to respond.

"The truth of what happened out there doesn't matter?" Damore asked.

"It matters in so far as if it is at great variance with Miss Wuornos' perceptions."

"Then her perception is more important than the truth," countered Damore.

"I believe she told the truth as she believed it to be."

"Having a borderline personality dysfunction does not make someone a killer," stated Damore.

"Not in and of itself."

"What are the chances of rehabilitation?"

"Low, not good, but possible," admitted the doctor.

"In the real world, we have no real possibility of her ever changing," Damore challenged.

"I am not saying there is no chance," Dr. McMahon responded patiently.

"Get her answer to the question. Don't be argumentative," Judge Blount warned.

Damore switched to Lee's relationship with her grandfather.

"He struck her on the back and on the face with a belt buckle," Dr. McMahon said. "She says her father told everybody he hated her guts. I asked her why and she said she didn't know—perhaps it was because she was Diane's daughter."

"Statements from Barry Wuornos indicate that is false," Damore said. "Lori Grody verifies the same account that Barry Wuornos gave."

Lee's needs were not getting met at home. She could not confide in her family. She had no one to "stand behind her and help her." She was afraid to tell anyone that she was pregnant. No one was there for her as a child, continued Dr. McMahon.

The prosecution had been attempting to portray Lee as cunning and manipulative and Damore moved into that line of questioning.

"Isn't it true that she was good at manipulating?" he asked the doctor.

"Not all that good at it," she replied. "She doesn't have any healthy adaptive interpersonal skills essential to manipulation."

"In the first interviews she did not tell you about the rape?"

"That's true," admitted Dr. McMahon.

In fact, it had been the third interview before Lee had begun to talk about the abusive treatment of Richard Mallory.

"The first time, she didn't say it was because he tried to rape her?" Damore repeated.

"No, she did not say this specifically to Mr. Mallory. I'm hesitating because she has said to me at various times that all of those men tried to rape me, but she did not say this in that account. . . .

"I asked her to define rape," Dr. McMahon told the jury, "and she said if they hurt her or had sex without paying. What I later realized is that Miss Wuornos has a particular way of dealing with clients and that is that they must pay her first. So if she says they had sex without paying, it's because they didn't pay her, she refused and would not have sex with them and they insisted.

"During rapes, once she had mace and once tear gas and they had been taken away and once a shotgun was held on her. She was forced to have sex and was very frightened."

At the prosecution table, John Tanner was busy with his legal pad. In large letters, he had written the following, underlining and exclamationing it with red pen:

1.   She loved her guys!
2.   She loved the money!
3.   She loved the penis!

During Damore's cross examination, Tanner handed him the pad, and the questions changed dramatically.

"Did Miss Wuornos tell you that she was a prostitute, loved men, loved the sex with men and enjoyed the clients? Made good money?"

It was an opening for Dr. McMahon to talk about Tom Evans, the man who had contacted the defense about the five days and nights he had spent with their client.

"She liked tactical contact. She spent more time with the men than was necessary, hugging, kissing, holding hands. And she enjoyed it even from a stranger. It was a way of obtaining it without close personal sustained relationship."

After her testimony, Dr. McMahon sat with Arlene for a few moments. Arlene had been anxious to hear the psychologists so that she could better understand her wayward daughter.

"You are giving her what she should have had when she was a little girl," Dr. McMahon said. "If she had this when she was a child, I'm telling you none of us would be here. If you keep doing this, little by little by little you're going to see changes in her. It'll be a long road, but it will happen."

The doctor had suggestions.

"When she gets ugly, before the discipline, during the discipline and after the discipline, keep telling her, 'I love you. I love you. I love you.' Be consistent. Draw the boundaries and the structure and stick to them."

Chapter Twenty-four

The following morning, as the trial moved into the second day of testimony by the psychologists, Arlene Pralle found herself seated next to a tall, heavy-set man who introduced himself as Lee's cousin. He did not mention his name. From the defense table, Lee waved and smiled and he waved back.

He had been in town, he said, and wanted to stop by.

At recess, Arlene asked defense counsel if she could invite the young man to lunch.

"Shortly after that, he disappeared and I never saw him again," she said.

Defense counsel, having learned of his relationship to their client, introduced him to the psychologists who were serving as expert witnesses. During questioning, they found that he would back up Lee's perception of her grandfather. They would not put him on the stand, but could incorporate his statements into the findings of the psychologists.

"We are a product of everything that has gone before us," Dr. McMahon had said to the jury before ending her testimony.

What had gone before Lee Wuornos, according to Dr. Harry Krop, a clinical psychologist who specialized in sexual abuse, was a biological mother, Diane, who had evidenced promiscuous behavior, conceived Lee and abandoned her. Diane had grown up with a father who was physically and sexually abusive, and she turned her baby over to him.

Lee's biological father was a violent individual with sexually deviant characteristics who had killed himself in prison.

The grandparents with whom Lee was left were dysfunctional people.

"Lee's cousin describes her grandfather as a Jekyll and Hyde type of individual, a severe alcoholic, very critical of Lee always, and when he was drinking he was violent and physically abusive. He committed suicide," Dr. Krop said, repeating the information recently given to him.

Her grandmother was an alcoholic who was ineffective in raising Lee or intervening when her grandfather abused her.

"Both male father figures committed suicide and both mother figures were ineffective," said Dr. Krop. "And her brother, Keith, the person to whom she was closest, died of cancer.

"Lee has had the fantasy of being part of a healthy family. Of coming home to people who love her." She evidenced strong guilt feelings about her family, he added.

Dr. Harry Krop is an expert in psychosexual matters, having started a sexual abuse program in 1977 to treat sex offenders and molested children.

Sex has been a major theme of Lee's life, starting when she was a child, he said. In cases where sex is prevalent at an early age, the result may be hyposexuality, where there is a withdrawal from this function, or, as in Lee's case, hypersexuality. For Lee it was a means of being accepted by others, and she became sexually aggressive.

"All of Lee's relationships have been dysfunctional," he continued. They are intense involvements with a great deal of jealousy, often manifesting in physical confrontation.

"People like Lee have trouble adapting to the world," he said. "They are always trying to have the world adapt to them."

The highlight of Dr. Krop's testimony came during a discussion of Lee's intelligence tests. According to Dr. Krop, she was rated "low dull normal, which was borderline retardation."

At the defense table, Lee burst into laughter. The jury watched her curiously.

Billy Nolas walked back to the defense table and stood behind her, his hands on her shoulders.

"Look at her," he said to the jury, "she's laughing." Lee has just heard that she has extremely limited mental capacity, and she is laughing, continued Nolas.

"Is that typical of the borderline personality?" he addressed Dr. Krop.

"Yes," responded the doctor. Their way of coping is inappropriate, he added. "It is difficult to accept they aren't normal."

Referring to an early school report, Dr. Krop read:

"For the girl's welfare, it is important that she receive counselling immediately."

Dr. Jethro Toomer confirmed the findings of the two psychologists who had testified before him.

"Lee dealt only with negatives from the very beginning. There was a lack of nurturing, lack of support, critical ingredients in terms of later life . . . . When an individual does not have access to that kind of nurturing you set the stage for certain deficits which are going to be manifested. . . with Lee, the impulse control mechanisms meant to defer gratification are not there.

"Her lack of self concept or self esteem caused her to seek to ingratiate herself to try to compensate for deficits. Please like me. Please accept me. I am seeking acceptance, but I'm not worth acceptance," he continued.

"When she is reminded of past abuse, past betrayal, her behavior breaks down." Dr. Toomer added.

"Looking at the world through the eyes of Miss Wuornos, if she perceives abandonment or abuse, she has a break in control because she doesn't have break mechanisms.

"Any variations in the stories about what happened in the murders is consistent with the borderline personality disorder."

John Tanner questioned Dr. Toomer. The prosecution had decided to call only Barry Wuornos to the stand, but wanted to make certain that Lori Grody's statement about life in the Wuornos household was available to the jury.

"With regard to her report on her family situation, did you talk to Lori Grody about what went on in the home?" Tanner asked the doctor.

"No, I did review the statements provided by her."

"Lori Grody in her statement said they had a comfortable home, stable household, and that Miss Wuornos had been provided for by the grandfather after her mother had abandoned her," stated Tanner.

"Lori Grody also said that Miss Wuornos was disliked by the people in her environment and they went out of their way to heap abuse on her," countered Dr. Toomer.

"I'm just asking you about the family," Tanner admonished. "With regard to the sister, really an aunt, the grandfather served as a father, and the grandmother served as a mother . . . . she said that Aileen was rebellious and had a quick temper. With regard to discipline, the usual discipline was grounding or spanking . . . no excessive discipline. No report of sexual abuse of Aileen Wuornos by the father . . . . There weren't any favorites."

"I understand that that was her perception . . . that was included in her statement," responded Dr. Toomer.

"We did find out that the grandfather kinda drank when he came home after work," admitted Tanner.

"I don't recall that there was a specification that it was after work, but that he drank."

"But he was not violent or abusive," stated Tanner.

"That was her perception," agreed the doctor.

Discussing reports of family members, Dr. Toomer revealed that Lee had, some years ago, called Lori Grody to tell her that she "saw the Lord at the front of her bed." It was a light that she believed to be the Lord, she continued. Lori had spoken to Barry about the possibility of having Lee committed.

"She first began manifesting symptomology at age ten or eleven. It would not surprise me if it went back beyond that.

"There were a number of cries for help that were never heeded," Dr. Toomer said, "so her behavior just grew worse as time went on....she suffered the effects of the borderline personality disorder...that's a long-standing disorder, lifetime disorder."

"With regard to the cerebral dysfunction?"

"Cerebral dysfunction, cortical dysfunction...brain damage."

"She doesn't suffer an injury that could be seen on a catscan, for instance?"

"It may not show up on a catscan, but it would be apparent in a neurological exam," said Dr. Toomer.

For a day and a half, the psychologists portrayed Lee as "a very unhappy, discontent individual who cannot cope with the world...whose possibilities of rehabilitation lay in extensive counselling at least three times a week with someone familiar with borderline."

To which David Damore responded:

"The truth of all these psychological reports depends on the stories given by Miss Wuornos. Isn't it true that her lies may result in inaccurate reports?"

And to the question of what really happened in the woods with Richard Mallory, the psychologists answered collectively:

"She told the truth as she believed it to be."

It was apparent to those concerned that Dawn Botkins, Lee's friend during her early teens, was not scheduled to appear as a witness. Arlene, at the request of defense counsel, had contacted Jackie Giroux to seek her help in reaching Dawn. She could not understand the change in tactics. Lee, who had counted on Dawn as her defense witness, was furious with her attorneys.

"The defense rests, your honor," Tricia Jenkins said and the issue was resolved. There were to be no character witnesses for Lee Wuornos.

Dr. George Barnard, forensics psychiatrist, took the stand for the prosecution.

"In my opinion, at the time of the crime, she was legally sane and there was no medical disorder or defect," said Dr. Barnard.

He agreed with the psychologists' findings that Lee suffered from a borderline identity disturbance, but argued that the findings were non-statutory mitigating circumstances and did not meet either of the statu-tory requirements. He did not agree that at the time Lee Wuornos shot Richard Mallory she was under the influence of extreme mental or emo-tional impairment or that her ability to conform her conduct to the re-quirements of the law was substantially impaired.

Court adjourned for lunch after the testimony of Dr. Barnard.

At the water fountain during recess, an elderly woman approached Arlene. "What would you do if she were released?" she asked.

"I would take her to Van Nuys, California, for counselling," said Arlene. She had picked the spot months ago. It was the same place she and Robert had gone for counselling years ago.

"Then I would take her to the farm and we'd never leave the farm," she added.

"Would you have to support her?" the woman asked.

"Of course, I'm her mother," Arlene replied.

Chapter Twenty-five

"I'm Aileen Wuornos' brother."

From the defense table, Lee turned to look at Arlene, a puzzled expression on her face. What did this mean? They had all agreed that if the prosecution decided to call either Barry or Lori to the stand, the defense would bring in Dawn to deflect the testimony. But Dawn had not been called and, contrary to expectation, Barry Wuornos had just taken the stand.

David Damore was questioning him.

"You were raised by your father and mother, Miss Wuornos' grandfather and grandmother in the same home, is that correct?"

"That's true, that biologically they are her grandmother and grandfather, but legally they adopted her," acknowledged Wuornos.

Barry Wuornos was short and heavy, in his forties. He had been Diane's younger brother and Lori's older one. He described the household in which Aileen Wuornos grew up:

"It was a normal lifestyle, pretty straight and narrow family. Very little trouble in the family while Aileen was growing up. They picked her up when I would say she was two years old. Father was a kind of a disciplinarian."

"What was your impression of your father?" Damore asked.

"Well, he was a very strong character...a gentle man...laid down strong rules."

"Did you ever see him beat her? Was he the kind of man who would beat a child?"

"Absolutely not," Wuornos replied.

"Tell us in your own words the interaction you saw between your father and Miss Wuornos from the time she came to your house until you left for the service."

"It was a very good relationship until she reached the age of nine or ten, about the time I left for the service...things began to get a little tight for Aileen discipline-wise. She got caught for shoplifting. The only discipline he ever put down were groundings—no spankings that I ever saw. I got a few myself, but none for Aileen," he paused, "that I ever saw."

"Would you describe her grandfather as being abusive?"

"Not at all. Normal spankings, but general rule was grounding for two days, three days."

"After you left for the service, did you stay in touch with Miss Wuornos?"

"Well, I stayed in contact with my mom and dad."

"Did your mother and father provide her with a home, shelter, food and clothing?"

"Oh, yes."

Damore began to question the period during which Lee had been severely burned.

". . . Was medical care denied to Miss Wuornos?"

"She did go to the doctor for a period of eight months and received salves," Wuornos stated.

"Mom took care of those things. She was a very quiet, studious laid back woman, very in the background. Much easier going than my father and no punishment of any kind came from her. My father worked at Ford and Chrysler as an engineer, was a janitor for a while and then worked in quality control. . . . He was strong on school. He was disappointed because I started at the university and dropped out to go into the service."

"Was Aileen treated differently than any of the rest?" Damore asked.

"Not that I ever saw," replied Wuornos. "One time she was going to be spanked and she brought up the fact that she was adopted and she said, 'Don't lay your hands on me. You're not even my real dad.' From that time, I never saw any attempts on the part of my dad to physically spank her."

At the defense table, Lee was visibly angry at Barry's denial of his father's abusive treatment. She wrote furiously on the legal pad in front of her.

"When did she learn that she was adopted?" Damore continued.

"She was ten or eleven at the time. How long before that she knew, I don't know."

Barry Wuornos stated that he had never spoken to any of the psychologists for the defense.

"Who have you spoken to?" questioned Tricia Jenkins in cross-examination of the witness.

"Various reporters, investigators, a woman, Jackie something. . ."

"Giroux?"

"That's it—Giroux. We turned all those people away from the door."

Wuornos neglected to tell the jury that he had also turned Tricia away from the door. In fact, he had threatened her that he would call the police if she bothered him again.

"Did the sergeant you spoke to tell you why they needed information?"

"She had just been picked up for—at that time, I don't think she had been charged with any of the murders. She had been involved with some car burglaries."

"Did you ever ask them to let you talk to Lee?"

"No. It never occurred to me. I think I asked him if she was incarcerated. She's been in trouble. I figured this was another time. I didn't know she had lawyers at that point."

"Lee's mother was your sister. What was she like?"

"Now?"

"Then."

"She was like a normal older sister. She had run-ins with her first husband, naturally. We picked up Aileen at the age of two. And she was in trouble at that point, but before that she was a model student at Troy and she got mixed up with Leo Pittman....She was with Leo—an on and off marriage."

"What about Aileen's father?"

"I knew very little about Leo. I remember he was trying to date Diane. He was pretty abusive. I remember one day he threw me down and threatened to choke me if I didn't give a message to Diane. He was generally a criminal type....He was sent to prison and later killed himself."

"How old was Diane when she left home?"

"I think she was fifteen or sixteen when she got married."

"How old was she when she had Aileen?"

"That was two years later. It wasn't discussed much in our family—it was a very sore spot. All I know is that it was a troubled marriage and why she left and how she left and on what conditions I don't know."

"Did Lee do well in school?"

"Yeah, I think she did well in school until she reached the ninth grade. She had great artistic ability...through letters in the service I heard that she was getting into trouble."

What about the rest of the family, Tricia continued, what were Keith and Lori like?

"Keith had a rebellious streak. He had a temper, but he was a good kid—a kid you could trust. Lori is more like me, laid back, calmer."

What was the extent of Lauri Wuornos' alcoholism? Tricia asked.

"Not more than one bottle of wine a day," Wuornos stated. And how, she continued, did Lauri Wuornos die?

"Came home one day and dad wasn't there. Went into the garage and he was dead."

"Did you ever ask the prosecutors to let you talk to Lee?"

"No."

"I have no further questions, Your Honor," Tricia concluded.

"The state rests," said John Tanner.

In retrospect, the words "Not that I ever saw" seemed to be the key to Barry Wuornos' testimony.

Lee did not look at Wuornos as he left the stand.

"It's my daughter they're playing games with," Arlene said of defense counsel. "It's obvious they were ill-prepared."

"The question is," said John Tanner as he presented his closing argument to the jury, "whether she knew what she was doing and chose to do it in spite of its wrongness, in total disregard. . . . The psychologists don't think she's like most folks. Did we need the psychologists to tell us that? Everyone of them agreed that Aileen Wuornos, at the time of the killing, knew right from wrong.

"Mental impairment is the defense of last resort," Tanner said. "The entire framework of this defense mechanism called mental impairment . . .is based upon Aileen Wuornos' story."

Aileen blames everyone else for the murder of Richard Mallory, Tanner continued—her parents, her job, Richard Mallory himself.

"This is not about forgiveness," Tanner continued, "it's about her refusal to accept responsibility from the start. She led her lifestyle and she chose to kill.

"One view of what happened is by Aileen Wuornos. . .the other view is evidence, facts and truth. Aileen Wuornos said Richard Mallory should die because he's cheating on his family, she had to pay bills, at his age it made no difference because he had no family. It became obscenely simple for Aileen Wuornos to kill. In one moment Richard Mallory was eliminated and by that act of her will, he was no more. . .simply was no more.

"And you know this is true. Aileen Wuornos deserves the ultimate penalty provided by the state of Florida."

Tricia Jenkins gripped the lectern as she looked into the faces of the twelve jurors. Her voice trembled and she was near tears. "I must convince you that she should live," Tricia told them, "and that is a difficult task. How do I explain what it's like to people who are normal, people who are unimpaired. How do I help you understand how it feels to be impaired...everything is filtered through impairment.

"I don't know what to do or say to convince you that Lee should live. I only know that she should. You have learned about Lee Wuornos in a vacuum. Everything you know has been given on this witness stand. I can't tell you what the three of us have learned over many hours. You must decide based on the courtroom.

"We're here because late on the night of November 30, 1989, Lee Wuornos and Richard Mallory met on the side of a highway. We have all been here and we all know that was a tragic meeting...and it went back to the day years ago when Lee stepped to the side of a road and stuck out her thumb....She carried around the luggage of abandonment, forfeiture of childhood....She did not know how and does not know how to satisfy her own basic needs."

In the jury box, the equestrienne wrung her hands and the teacher swallowed back her tears.

"Richard Mallory is dead and that is a terrible, terrible thing," Tricia continued. "Richard Mallory is dead and he should not have died. We are asking you to understand Lee's involvement in light of who she is. Do not evaluate Lee's action on that night in terms of what another person would or would not have done. This is about Lee. Lee, who dealt with her experience with the insight of a damaged, primitive child. In her mind, by her perception, she thought she was in danger, she was threatened. It was the only thing she knew how to do.

"The last few days," Tricia concluded, "Lee has had to accept that nothing will ever be all right again. When she leaves this courtroom for the last time, she goes without hope. Whether the sentence is life imprisonment or death, Lee has lost her life. Even if you are merciful, you will simply be giving her the mere right to live. Please go back there, please, and decide that that is punishment enough."

Throughout the closing arguments, Lee had wept silently. A pile of crumpled pink Kleenex lay scattered across the defense table.

As the jury deliberated the fate of Aileen Wuornos, questions surfaced in the jailhouse.

Why had Dawn Botkins, Lee's friend during her early teenage years, not been called to the stand? How long would it take the jurors to reach a decision?

In the hallway, David Damore told those within earshot: "If this were a man, they'd be out in ten minutes.

"She's so ugly and overweight, even those who patronized her didn't want to pay."

Damore had made it clear from the beginning that he felt Lee Wuornos killed for money. "Mallory was probably passed out drunk and she shot him," he offered.

One hour and forty-eight minutes later, court was called back into session. The jury had reached its decision.

A piece of lined yellow legal paper was delivered to the defendant from her adoptive mother. It asked Lee to "Be good. No matter what. So we can be together tonight. Please. I need you."

Tears filled the eyes of many of the jurors as they took their seats for the last time in the jury box. Their recommendation to the judge, in a twelve to zero vote, was death for Aileen Wuornos. When polled, many of their responses were nearly inaudible.

Swaying on her feet, Lee was supported by Tricia and Billy, while Bill Miller removed his glasses to wipe his eyes. In the second row, on the corner seat which she had occupied during the entire trial, Arlene Pralle sobbed on the shoulder of a friend.

Privately, Tanner turned to his wife, Marsha, in the courtroom: "I'm glad we restored this man's name [Lauri Wuornos]. We've been trying to do this."

Outside the jailhouse, he spoke to the press:

"John, did anything happen during the course of the trial to make you change or modify your opinion of who Aileen Wuornos is and what her motives were?" asked a reporter.

"Well," said Tanner, "her determination to slander and try to destroy the reputation of the man she killed, Richard Mallory, and her determination to ruin the good name of her grandfather added to my conviction that she was totally without remorse or any hope of repentence at this time. She could have come into the court and pled guilty and asked for mercy without subjecting the families, including her own, to a vicious, groundless attack.

"I saw a lot of crying at the table by Miss Wuornos during the closing arguments by her attorneys," he continued. "If those were genuine tears and not staged tears, she may at this time be faced with the reality that she is responsible for the terrible destruction that she wrought. Not just her own family, but the families of seven innocent men."

Billy Nolas also dealt with the press:

"You put people in a situation which our society should not put people in. We have people coming out and unanimously voting for the death penalty and crying while they do it. I don't think we should put our jurors in that situation. I don't think we should put anyone in that situation. But we do, and we have to deal with it."

"You'll be representing her in the May trial?" a reporter asked.

"Yes, we'll be representing her in the next three trials, two in Marion County and one in Citrus County," Billy responded.

Marsha Tanner approached Arlene in the hallway. The two born-again Christians confronted each other. Nowhere in the scripture does it speak against the death penalty, Marsha said. "Don't forget an eye-for-an-eye."

The last twenty-four hours had been hell for Arlene Pralle. Her father had called her the night before: "How can you defend this person?" he had asked her.

And Lee had wakened the Brazil family at 4:00 a.m., to scream at Arlene that she was part of a conspiracy against her. Despite Arlene's protests, Lee had hung up on her and called back forty-five minutes later. Jeff had picked up the phone and calmed Lee and the conversation had ended quietly, but Arlene was nearing the breaking point.

"Where's your miracle?" the press asked.

"She isn't dead yet," Arlene replied.

The main focus was why Dawn Botkins had not been called to testify. Arlene was furious with the defense team and did not hesitate to vent her feelings to the press. In the parking lot, she attacked the attorneys. What were they thinking of—they had promised to bring in Dawn. Lee had had no one to defend her on the stand. Tempers were short on all sides.

Tricia told the press that Lee had been hopeful of a life recommendation. "She's very, very emotional about it. We're all very, very sad."

Billy Nolas talked about Lee's expectations. "She knows that there will be court tomorrow, and when you're dealing with somebody like Lee, that's as good as you're going to get," he said.

"Did she take the stand against your wishes?" a reporter asked.

"That's not an issue for public discussion," Nolas responded.

"Are you prepared for the death sentence tomorrow in light of the unanimous message?"

"Yes, in light of our understanding that Judge Blount does not override," he replied.

"You are condemning an innocent child," Arlene told the press.

"Did you expect this?" she was asked.

"I think I was so devastated by the verdict of guilty that I didn't want to get my hopes up again. But I feel that justice is not served at all."

"You've got so many more trials to go. Is this too much for you?"

"Right now it's too much," she said sadly.

That night Arlene went to Volusia County Branch Jail for the last time. She had to pick up all of Lee's possessions and, at the same time, say goodbye to her. Tomorrow Lee would leave the jailhouse and head for prison or death row. Depending on the sentence given by Judge Blount.

This would not be a contact visit. There had been no contact visits since Lee left Citrus County several months earlier. She could talk to her through glass. It wasn't much, but it was better than nothing.

"That last night we were together," Arlene would later describe, "Lee asked me how I saw her. And I said I saw her inside as a little girl wanting to come out...never having a chance to grow up and wanting very badly to come out. 'But every time you come out,' I told her, 'you get hurt. So you're hiding.' And she started to cry. Nursery rhymes, all those normal things a kid has, she just never had. I'll tell you, when you love somebody as much as I feel for her and the maternal thing that's developed, and to watch her cry with a piece of glass between us. Nothing can hurt worse than that. I just wanted to reach out and hold her and make all the pain go away and there's this horrible piece of glass.

"Prayer and physical touch has gotten us through this entire thing. When we have prayer to rely on, but are denied the physical touch, under the extreme trauma, we were not able to pray that night. We both started crying and there was the bonding and tightness, but we couldn't talk and couldn't pray. We just stared at each other through the glass."

When they took Lee away, Arlene returned to the waiting room to pick up her possessions. Four pages of items to acknowledge and sign for. Items such as "one blue button," "four hairpins," "three pens" confronted her. Hurriedly she signed the papers, checking off the items as she scribbled her initials. And then she left the jail carrying the sum total of Lee Wuornos' life: the clothes that she had worn during trial, and two brown paper bags.

Pamela Mills, dark-haired and round-faced, had been chosen to serve as foreperson of the jury because her name was drawn early in the trial proceedings. It was not the first time she had served on a jury, but the Wuornos case was far more visible than any of her previous experiences.

A high school English teacher, she admitted that she had given little thought to the death penalty prior to her involvement in the Wuornos trial.

"You sit around a table with friends and start talking about the death penalty and you bandy it about. But you never dream that you'll actually have to make such a recommendation," Pamela told the press.

But she, and eleven other jurors did make the recommendation, and, after sentencing, the public wondered how they felt about it. Most of the jurors chose not to discuss it, but Pamela talked to the media, both local and national.

"That's the most difficult decision I've ever had to make in my life. I know I feel a whole lot different about a lot of things because of it," she said, her eyes saddened in recollection.

Reporters wondered whether the inclusion of the Williams Rule affected the outcome of the trial.

"We had testimony from some of the other cases, but I honestly feel it didn't have anything to do with my verdict. I just concentrated on the case involving Mr. Mallory," she said. Returning a verdict of guilty had not been difficult. The hard part was during the sentencing phase of the trial when the jury had to weigh whether to recommend a life sentence or the death penalty.

Pamela felt that State Attorney Tanner and Assistant Prosecutor Damore were well prepared in the presentation of their case. She had nothing to say about the work of the defense.

A somber crowd gathered inside and outside the courtroom at 9:00 a.m. the next day. There was no question in anyone's mind that within the next few hours Lee Wuornos would be sentenced to death.

In her customary seat, Arlene Pralle reviewed her notes. She had been asked by the defense team to speak directly to Judge Blount in a plea for Lee's life. And, if that failed, she would talk to the press on the subject of capital punishment.

Rumor had it that for the occasion, Judge Blount had purchased a new pinstripe suit. When he was seated, John Tanner approached the bench:

"I am saying sincerely that this is probably the most difficult time our office faces...a studied, considered decision to first ask the citizens and then ask the jurists to permit the law which requires a forfeiture of life to be activated against a citizen. It is not only personal standpoint, it is a great emotional drain on all of us involved.... nonetheless, people, through their elected representatives, believe there is a place in our society for the death penalty...where it is inequivocably justified. This is one of those cases....This is the only time that I have stood before this particular court and asked you for a sentence to take another person's life. I don't do it lightly. Aileen Wuornos has come into this courtroom with utter disregard for the destruction she has wrought on her victims ...an utter disregard for the reputation of her very family...and a cold, absolute, unwavering determination to avoid and deny responsibility. I ask you to sentence her to die."

Flanked by the defense team, Arlene Pralle and Lee Wuornos stood resolutely before the judge.

In a small voice, inaudible to most of the crowd, Arlene told Judge Blount that the woman she had adopted was a child. Dr. McMahon stated that she was the most primitive child she had ever seen outside an institution, Arlene reminded the judge. "Robert and I have adopted her and I have spent more time with her than all three of the witnesses combined, and I am in 100% agreement with their diagnosis."

School records had indicated that all those years ago, Lee Wuornos had needed nurturing, love, and, finally, psychological counselling. She had received none of these, said Arlene.

"We have a doctor and will stand behind her and will pay for the professional counselling she needed as a young child," Arlene continued.

"She never had a chance to grow up...she's still a child....I beg for mercy for the life of my daughter," she concluded before returning to her seat.

Lee Wuornos had plenty to say. She was right back where she always was—defending herself. Her attorneys had failed her, no character witnesses had appeared on her behalf, and so, once again, it was up to her to speak out in her own behalf.

"First of all, I would like to say that I have been labelled a serial killer and I'm no serial killer," she spoke directly to Judge Blount. "I am a prostitute and I've dealt with a lot of men, almost 250 men a month and I ran into these men along the way. I was not out there to hurt anyone. I had no intention of hurting anyone. In my confession, I stated that nine times. I stated thirty-seven times self defense, thirty-nine times I was raped or beaten. What I did is what anyone else would do. I defended myself and I had no intention of hurting anyone. I would not do that.

"What I am trying to say here, I told you that I was raped and that was what happened, and that is what happened in all cases I was involved in. These people did violent attack on me and I did what I had to do to protect myself.

"Now, I would like to point out one other thing and that is that the law enforcement has branded me a serial killer purposefully for books and movies and I have been treated really bad since I have been incarcerated. I have gone through a lot of physical and mental abuse which I feel was a conspiracy (throughout, Lee pronounced it "conspyracy") by the law enforcement and I also feel that the law enforcement and state attorney has a conspiracy here. And I have to say another thing. Conspiracy and manipulation was talked about by State Attorney Tanner. State Attorney Tanner was manipulating the jury. He has made a lot of things up, made up on the top of his head, which were not true and I felt he lied through his teeth. I did not lie. I was coerced into making my confession. I was threatened that Tyria Moore would be arrested if I did not talk about my confession. If I didn't answer their questions the way they wanted, she would be arrested and they asked me to implicate myself as a serial killer and every time I talked about rape they cut me off.

"I was totally under duress and delirium and I couldn't tell you anything under stress. I was trying to clear Tyria. Tyria knows it's self defense. She's lying through her teeth, telling that she doesn't know anything. She knows it's self defense and she's been offered half a million dollars after this for keeping her mouth shut.

"I'm not a serial killer. I had fifteen high school friends, two clients, a police officer, that I wanted to contact, but they were not contacted. This case—for me to testify for myself...I couldn't believe that I just got on that stand by myself....I got a raw deal."

Spectators who later tried to define the expression on Tricia Jenkins' face during Lee's testimony could not decide what was more prevalent—anger, sorrow or hurt.

Billy Nolas appealed to the practicalities of imposing a death sentence. In terms of the expense and the time, "Is it worth it?" he questioned the judge.

No one expected Judge Uriel Blount to take last minute pity on Lee Wuornos and spare her life.

Reading from the book before him, the judge explained his duty.

"Aileen Carol Wuornos, being brought before the court by her attorneys William Miller, Tricia Jenkins and Billy Nolas, having been tried and found guilty of count one, first degree premeditated murder and first degree felony murder of Richard Mallory, a capital felony, and count two, armed robbery with a firearm...hereby judged and found guilty of said offenses...and the court having given the defendant an opportunity to be heard and to offer matters in mitigation of sentence....It is the sentence of this court that you Aileen Carol Wuornos be delivered by the Sheriff of Volusia County to the proper officer of the Department of Corrections of the State of Florida and by him safely kept until by warrant of the governor of the state of Florida, you, Aileen Carol Wuornos, be electrocuted until you are dead.

"And may God have mercy on your corpse."

A collective gasp swept through the courtroom, diminishing the solemnity of the occasion. May God have mercy on your corpse? Did Judge Blount really say that? Corpse? Members of the media stopped with pencils paused in mid-air. Could they quote him? they whispered among themselves.

The incessant whir of cameras clicking accompanied Lee, her face expressionless, as she was directed to the bailiff to be fingerprinted.

Quickly and quietly the courtroom emptied as spectators headed for home and media gathered near the side entrance of the jailhouse. From here, Lee would make her last appearance before being taken to death row at Broward Correctional Institution in Pembroke Pines, Florida. Reporters made use of their time. What will happen now? they asked Tricia and Billy.

"The case proceeds to the Supreme Court. Appeal has to be filed within thirty days and a court reporter is given a certain amount of time to get the transcript together. Then the court is given a certain amount of time to compile the record. With the brief filing, it can take anywhere from eight months to two years," explained Tricia.

"There are legitimate issues in this case," added Billy. "Issues related to venue, issues related to the Williams Rule, issues related to the case as a whole. This case does have legitimate issues to present . . . not all smoke and glass."

"What about the issues that Aileen raised before the judge about witnesses not being called?" asked the press.

"I have no comment on Lee except that she's very sad," said Billy.

As reporters waited by the side entrance of the building, Arlene was denied access to the parking lot. In their haste to position themselves in the lot, no one had not asked Arlene for the comments she had prepared on the uselessness of capital punishment. Standing just outside the area with two female writers, Sue Russell and Dolores Kennedy, she tried to explain to the security guard that she wanted to say goodbye to her daughter.

"We have our orders and we're going to carry them out according to the way we got them," said the oversized black man, whose name tag identified him as G. Jackson.

"But I'm her mother," Arlene persisted.

"And we're writers," added Dolores.

"Only reporters allowed," stated the guard.

As he spoke, Mike Reynolds, the man who completed the trio of book writers present, strode past the women into the lot accompanied by an investigator.

"If we don't belong there, neither does he," Dolores said to Jackson.

"And if there's someone back there that you got problems with and you don't feel they should be back there it's too late," replied the guard.

"This is the way I've been treated in Volusia County," said Arlene.

"Seems to extend to your friends, too," said Sue.

Closer to the action, David Damore was enjoying himself.

"Lee turned on her attorneys like she turned on everybody else," he said with satisfaction. And he described the three psychologists who had portrayed Lee as a pathetic victim of life-long abuse as "phony balonies."

Word had gotten to the reporters that Judge Blount had accidentally skipped a line while reading the sentence and said "court" instead of "soul." To those present it had sounded like "corpse." What will happen to the record of his sentencing? reporters asked Damore.

"The record will read soul," replied the prosecutor. "He said soul."

There was little point in arguing.

Undaunted, Arlene and her friends walked around the block to the far side of the lot. The deputies' cars were aimed in that direction. It seemed reasonable that Lee would pass through that area on her way to Broward.

It was a wise move. A few moments later, Lee Wuornos appeared in the door and was ushered immediately into the car.

But she wasn't leaving without one last outburst.

"Bust these crooked cops and their conspiracy, please! I'm innocent!" she called out to the crowd.

"She's a chronic liar and she's determined to maintain her posture of innocence," John Tanner retorted to those around him.

Arlene was within feet of her daughter, and rushed to the departing auto.

"Bye, Lee. I love you!" she cried through the closed window.

A year ago, Billy Nolas had been on his way back to his native New York when he had been asked to help Tricia Jenkins represent Lee Wuornos. He detested the death penalty and was not willing to be part of the farewell crowd.

"This is getting morbid," he commented to no one in particular.

When the two deputy sheriffs' cars had departed, the first carrying

Lee, the second serving as a back-up, the crowd dispersed. Minutes later, some of them gathered at a local restaurant to rehash the day's events.

Seated in a remote corner of the restaurant, Arlene and her friends watched John Tanner and his family eating dinner. Before the evening was over, he approached her table.

"I've had to maintain my distance from you to do what I did," he smiled down at Arlene. "I'm sorry. My family and I pray for her soul, as we pray for my friend, Ted Bundy."

As quickly as he arrived, he departed.

"He cannot be a Christian and work for the death penalty," Arlene observed to those around her.

Later in the evening, rumors circulated that the deputies' cars had been in an accident. Shortly after pulling away from the jailhouse, the lead car, carrying Lee, had stopped suddenly. The back-up car had rear-ended it, jolting its famous passenger. Offered a medical examination by the police, she declined.

IV

To Share a Bit of This Lifetime—A Little Together

This is not a homecoming, since the home had never before existed. It is the discovery of home.

Alice Miller

Chapter Twenty-Six

The sprawling ranch-style house on Cadmus Street in Troy, Michigan has not changed a great deal since the Wuornos family moved out.

Lee remembers the house painted yellow, with a cyclone fence portioning off a substantial part of the yard. These days, the house is white and the fence has been removed. The stately trees of her youth still soar skyward, but the new, modern house next door has upset the Cadmus Street addresses, and the number has been altered since Lee Wuornos lived there.

When Lee first went to jail, she drew detailed pen and ink pictures of the house on Cadmus Street, both exterior and interior. These are now in Arlene's possession, illustrations for the book that Lee plans to complete one day. Cadmus is one in a series of short streets clustered in the northeast section of Troy, twenty miles north of Detroit. The streets dead-end each other, emptying into a large wooded area with paths that meander in and out of its sanctuary.

The houses which line these streets vary in size, style and condition, but, for the most part, they are weary and unkempt. The newest of them, a brick ranch with a paved driveway and manicured lawn, has a for sale sign outside.

Just east of Cadmus, Shelldrake Road divides the exclusive Sterling Heights area from the small cluster of bleak Troy dwellings.

To the west, Rochester Road runs through the heart of town, spilling into Madison Heights to the south and Rochester Hills to the north.

New villas and townhouses have sprung up along the road, but for the most part it is a series of strip malls, fast food restaurants and gas stations.

Like its neighboring communities, Troy owes its prosperity to the industrial activity of Detroit.

Thirty miles north of Troy, in the sleepy town of Lapeer, Michigan, Dawn Botkins lives in a small white ranch with her husband, Dave, two teenage children, and Cassie, the dog.

Dawn works in the kitchen at the Ferguson Nursing Home, "but not really in the kitchen," she said. She feeds the elderly patients, and, with infinite patience, wipes their noses and washes their glasses. "I treat them like people," she explained, and "I try to understand what they're feeling."

Dawn's right arm is bruised from being tapped with a spoon. This is the way she determines whether or not the offered food is too hot to be palatable.

Dawn understands illness. Sixteen years ago, she was diagnosed with multiple sclerosis—a death sentence which she says made her reevaluate her life.

"My mother-in-law went around telling everyone I was dying, so I thought I'd better deal with it," she laughed. "It made me look at my values."

Life is difficult for Dawn and her family. Because of her multiple sclerosis, there are many days when she cannot go to work. Her husband, Dave, works as a factory inspector, and five months ago, his overtime was taken away. "We cancelled Christmas this year because he was laid off and didn't get his Christmas bonus," she admitted.

Multiple sclerosis is an expensive disease. There are doctor bills and medication bills, lost time at work—it all adds up. The telephone has been disconnected at the Botkins residence and they are in danger of losing their home.

Slightly over one year ago, Jackie Giroux offered Dawn $5,000 to talk about her friend, Aileen Wuornos.

"She came twice. The first time she was alone," recalled Dawn. "The second time I was really sick, but I agreed to see her. She just had to understand that I was not going to get off the couch. She brought along a woman who she said was a German investor. They were going to make a movie about Aileen's childhood that would be completed in May and she would pay me $5,000 if I would sign a contract agreeing not to talk to anyone else. I told her I wasn't interested in a contract or the money, that

I only wanted to help Aileen by telling people about her life, but she insisted that I sign it."

Much later Dawn learned that the woman who accompanied Jackie was not a German investor—she was Sue Russell, Jackie's English associate.

In addition to her contract with Dawn, Jackie Giroux was gathering signatures on contracts from literally everyone who knew Aileen Wuornos, including her aunt/sister Lori Grody. They were all promised $5,000 except Lori, who was to receive $50,000, if they would refuse to give out information to other sources. So far there has been no payment.

Dawn, dark blond and slender, with a forthright approach, pours endless cups of coffee as she talks about her friend, Aileen.

"At first, when I talked about testifying for Aileen in court, Lori considered doing it too, but then she got money hungry, and her husband wanted the money. And then there are lots of things she doesn't want people to know. She was always pampered and now she's going to go with the flow. Lori and I have had some really big arguments about this. I love Lori a lot, but I can't allow this to happen to Aileen."

When Dawn first learned about Aileen's arrest, she wrote to her attorneys, Raymond Cass and Donald Jacobsen.

"I never heard from them," she said.

Finally, Tricia Jenkins and Don Sanchez came to see her to talk about testifying for Lee in the Mallory case.

"I wanted to do it. I wanted to tell everyone what a terrible life she had had. I knew I would be nervous, but I would do it. I even borrowed a dress so that Aileen would be proud of me and the jury would know that she had respectable friends. The dress is still hanging in my closet."

Why Dawn Botkins was never called to testify for her friend remained a mystery. Did the defense team get themselves in a bind by failing to learn that Barry and Lori were in town?

"It was always understood that they would only call Dawn if the prosecution put on Barry or Lori," Arlene Pralle said. "Yet I knew that both Barry and Lori were in town to testify, and they still didn't get Dawn on that plane."

Did they decide that Dawn Botkins would not be a helpful witness? Tricia Jenkins had been quoted as saying that Dawn's testimony would not be "earth-shaking."

Or were they giving Lee an opportunity, down the road of appeals, to claim ineffective assistance of counsel if everything else failed?

Billy Nolas, when questioned about this issue, said that failure to put Dawn on the stand was a reasoned decision, not oversight. In order to protect his client, he would not explain that decision, but said without hesitation that Dawn will be called to testify at the Humphreys trial.

"It was strange," said Dawn, "because I received this telegram from Jackie Giroux asking me to call her or Don Sanchez immediately. I got her answering machine requesting my phone number at work because our home phone was disconnected and then I got a call from Sanchez telling me they wanted me to get on a plane that night. I told them I couldn't because I was at work, but I could be on the plane the next morning. I made arrangements to get to the airport and then, several hours later, Sanchez called me back and said 'something terrible happened' and they weren't going to call me. He didn't explain what that was."

During the months between Aileen's arrest and her first trial, Dawn was deluged with offers to appear on television, to talk to the media.

"I refused all the television offers because I thought I was going to testify. I did talk to a few reporters, but now I wish I had talked to everyone.

"I don't think the jury could have given her the death penalty if they had known about her life."

Dawn and Lee became friends shortly after Eileen Britta Wuornos died. Dawn does not identify with the name "Lee" because, in those days, she was always called Aileen.

"I don't remember how we met," she admitted, "but it must have been through Lori and Keith because we all hung out together. I remember the kids kept saying, 'You gotta meet this chick who had the baby.' They knew all about her, that she was a prostitute and there was never a time when any of them accepted her. When I first heard them talk about Aileen, I didn't even know what a prostitute was."

At 14, Dawn had been "kicked out" of school. Aileen had dropped out too, so they spent their time together.

"We hitchhiked all over the place, went to the race tracks where she taught me to short-change, and the pool hall, and lots of times to the shopping mall. We even went to California once, and we had some pretty scary experiences on the road."

After Eileen Britta Wuornos' death, Lauri Wuornos "lost it", said Dawn. "He left the family home in Troy and moved to a small house in Utica where he spent his days sitting in a chair drinking.

"Neither Aileen or Keith were allowed in the house," Dawn recalled. "So they lived on the streets.

"The Kretsches had a bunch of old cars in their yard and Aileen and Keith would sleep in them. The Kretsches had a bunch of kids and Lori would go in and clean for Mrs. Kretsch and she'd let Lori sleep inside, but never Aileen. Sometimes Lori and I would sleep in the cars, too. The difference was, we had a choice. We could go home. Aileen and Keith couldn't. There wasn't one."

Sometimes Keith and Aileen would sleep at Dawn's house. "I had the basement to myself and they could come and go," she said. "My parents didn't exactly like it, but they didn't prevent it. My mom had a problem with Aileen because she would stop by and ask to take a shower. Once she even asked if she could use her toothbrush."

Lee's interpretation is somewhat different.

"I was hardly ever allowed at Dawn's house," she disagreed, "because her mom didn't want me there."

Reflecting on how she and Aileen became such good friends, Dawn said, "I think it was because I was such a tomboy. I had no interest in boys and so there was no competition between us. We just had a good time together. She had so much guts. I really loved and respected her. I think I'm the only one who ever really, truly loved her."

The other young people did not share Dawn's feelings about Aileen.

"She was never accepted by any of them. They knew about her and they made fun of her and they were terrible to her."

Dawn's husband, Dave, remembers Aileen.

"We were so mean to her," he admitted, "because she was tough. She was street wise. Raised like an animal and she acted like an animal. I feel bad about her now."

Dawn remembers time after time when Aileen was abused by her peers. But the worst, she said, occurred at Barry's house.

When Aileen was nine years old, Barry went into the service. When he returned, he bought his own house.

"When he was away, Lori stayed there, and we decided to have a party. Aileen went out and prostituted to get booze and 'weed' while Lori and I cleaned the house all day. When Aileen got back, we got dressed up and put on make-up and Aileen was so happy because at last she was going to be accepted.

"The kids came and someone must have called her a name and she got mad. The next think you know, they had thrown her out the back door and wouldn't let her in. Lori said, 'I can't believe this is happening,' and Keith and my brother, Ducky, just sat there and watched. Nobody helped her. I should have been out there with her."

Dawn remembers, too, the day the kids invited Aileen to a party in the "pits"—part of the field where they often hung out.

"A bunch of us were in a car, driving through the field, and we could see Aileen up ahead carrying the beer. The guy who was driving said, 'Watch this.' He opened his door and knocked Aileen down with it, grabbed the beer and took off. I just kept thinking, 'I hope she knows I had nothing to do with that.'

"I knew about the baby and I knew about the prostitution, and Aileen knew that I knew, but we never talked about it. I respected her too much to ask and she never wanted to include me in that part of her life. When she was leaving to go prostitute, she would just say, 'Catch you later, Dawn,' and she would go off alone and I would go back to my other friends, who accepted me, but never her. Sometimes I would see her later and her hair would be mussed and she would have a look on her face that said things did not go well. Sometimes she would say, 'The asshole didn't pay me,' but that's all she would say. That's how I know that Tyria Moore was not involved in anything that she did. And I also understand why she didn't tell Tyria about Richard Mallory's abuse. Aileen operated by herself, she kept the people she cared about out of it, and she wouldn't have talked about it. That was the way she handled it."

Dawn is willing to go a step further.

"I know Aileen killed Richard Mallory in self defense," she said with certainty. Her eyes cloud. "After that, I don't know."

Dawn first learned about Aileen's arrest when the police came to her door.

"I hadn't seen her since her brother Keith's funeral in 1970. I used to think of her so often and I thought maybe she was dead. I could never understand how she survived as long as she did."

At the time that Keith died, Aileen was living in Florida with her elderly husband, Lew.

"She told me she married him for security," Dawn recalled. "When I read that she said he beat her with his cane, I laughed. I could just imagine anyone beating Aileen with a cane.

"Keith had been sick with cancer for years," she continued. "It started in his throat and just took over the rest of his body. For a long time, he was in the VA hospital, but he refused to believe he was dying. Barry never went to see him there...not until he bought the Corvette. As long as I knew Keith, he'd always wanted a Corvette, and, somehow, maybe he came into some money from the service, but he managed to buy one. The next thing I knew, Barry, who had his own house, took Keith to live with him. Keith was in the spare bedroom and the Corvette was in the garage.

"Barry was supposed to be taking care of Keith, but he was never home. I went to see Keith almost every day, he spent day after day in a hot room with no fan and no pillow—I don't think he was even fed most of the time—and I would take him things. Aileen and Lori weren't in town and I did it mostly for them—on their behalf.

"Right before Keith died, I heard that Barry gave him a bath and cried when he saw how skinny he was. He had lost his teeth and most of his hair. And it seemed to me that that was probably the only time Barry ever gave him a bath."

During the Mallory trial, Dawn kept track of the events, and she was aware of Barry Wuornos' testimony.

"He lied," she said. "Lauri Wuornos was not a nice man. I know how he treated Aileen."

In a notarized statement to the defense team, Dawn explained her feelings:

"I know for a fact that Barry Wuornos lied under oath that he was there for Aileen. He indeed was not, for she stayed at my house with Keith and Lori because they were not allowed to stay at their grandfather's house. Except Lori could. And when they were not staying at my house, they were sleeping in cars. I know. I was there. Barry was not there then and is not there now and never will be there for her. He should be ashamed of himself the way he did not take care of Aileen and Keith . . . he treated her like shit just like everyone else did."

"Aileen supplied Keith and Lori with cigarettes and anything else they needed," said Dawn. "It was all prostitution money and they knew it. No one ever tried to help her."

Dawn remembers the day that Aileen took her to the shopping mall to buy her a purse.

"I never carried one and she was determined that I should have one. She bought me a purse and all the things that go in it and when we hitchhiked home, I left it in the car. I remember saying to her, 'See, I told you I wasn't supposed to have a purse.'

"I have a lot to thank Aileen for," Dawn commented. "We were hitchhiking when Dave, my husband, picked us up. If it weren't for Aileen I wouldn't have all this." With a sweeping gesture, she indicated her husband, her children, her house.

"I feel so guilty. It keeps me awake at night. She was so full of love. How can one person take so much in life all these years?"

When Arlene Pralle entered Lee's life, Dawn was suspicious. "And jealous, I guess. I had been Aileen's best friend and now I was being replaced. But when she adopted Aileen, it was all right. I was still her best friend. She was her mom."

Dawn knows about killers and victims. Her brother, Ducky, was shot eight years ago in a drug-related incident.

"My parents are for the death penalty and they don't understand my feelings about Aileen. I could never be for the death penalty. When they caught Ducky's killer, I was glad to have him go to prison. I went to see him and asked him why. The answers he gave me were nothing, but at least I had tried.

"Aileen has had the death penalty since she was born. And all she ever wanted was to be accepted. She idolized Lori, but Lori was so mean to her. She wanted to be just like her sister, but she couldn't.

"You know," she said, with a slight shake of her head, "I always thought that Aileen would be the one who got killed.

"I remember her walking down Atkins Road in her black suede coat with the fringe, her long blond hair shining. No matter what happened, her hair was always in place. . . . And, funny thing, she always told me that some day she was going to write a book . . ."

Chapter Twenty-Seven

Lee was glad to replace the tension of Volusia County Branch Jail with the serenity of Broward Correctional Institution in Pembroke Pines, Florida. Lying midway between Fort Lauderdale and Miami, Broward is a prison for women, and Death Row is housed in a large gray building, trimmed in pink and bordered with tropical flowers.

Marta VillaCorta, the superintendent, oversees a staff of approximately 200 at Broward. Tall and slender, sandy brown hair framing her long, narrow face, there is an aura of calm about her which is reflected throughout the institution. Marta, who worked her way up from classification officer at the Department of Corrections, cares about the welfare of the inmates at Broward, and frequently counsels them and their families.

The faces on Death Row are familiar to crime story fans. Judi Buenonano, forty-eight, and popularly known as "the Black Widow" has been there since 1985, convicted of poisoning her husband, drowning her quadriplegic son and placing a bomb in her boyfriend's car.

Deidre Hunt was sent to the Row slightly more than a year ago.

Andrea Hicks Jackson is sentenced to die for the 1983 shooting of a police officer.

Virginia Larzelere, with whom Lee shared confidences at Volusia County Branch Jail, has recently been given the death penalty, and so, once more, she and Lee will be imprisoned together.

Settling into her new home, Lee described it in a letter to Arlene:

"The room is eight by ten, dull-looking pink that I've adjusted to. The ceiling is really high up, 15' maybe, which makes it look roomier. I've got a black and white TV that sits above the toilet on a varnished brown shelf. Neck and back breaking to watch until my specks arrive,'cause I'll be darned if I can see it. It's a 12-inch size screen. Fairly small. I've got a grey metal foot locker that sits on the floor from which I'm writing this. No tables. One metal chair, and an ugly lime green foot locker that sits in a corner at the foot of this metal bed for clothes and all, which after cell check I put your cards on top of to perk up the room. During cell check nothing is to be out visible but only the lockers and the bed made. Cell inspection is anywhere from 9:00 to 11:00 a.m. So nothing out until it's over."

The window in Lee's room overlooks a parking lot. It is her only view of freedom. There are no bars across her room. Instead, a steel door with a window separates her from the rest of the cell block.

For a while, Lee agreed to answer some of my questions in writing. She wrote:

"How I spend my time is in constant contemplation of writing a book about all you've ever wanted to know about jail house treatment—the profiles of perjury played against the defense by the state for political gain. . . and insufficiency of these so called "Public Pretenders" who just work for the state, for they get paid by the state. . . and to balance their funding to free counseling on the indigent, perform plea bargains, to eliminate any further financial problems. Profaning the courthouse seal, In God We Trust, with inappropriate counsel for the accused. . . . A very sad and broken system we have today. This book will probably be called 'Sound Off.'

"And for my routine of the day: 7:00 a.m., breakfast, TV is turned on. I slowly wake up with a cup of prison coffee, then clean the room on weekdays for 9:00 to 11:00 a.m. cell inspection. Normally, I sit on a pillow using a twelve-inch high, three-foot wide foot locker as a desk, and do a lot of writing, a little reading, and a little TVing. Eleven o'clock is lunch, four o'clock is dinner. Mail comes in around then. I answer my mail, watch the news, then "Wheel of Fortune" and "Jeopardy," and, hopefully, a good movie. If not, then I'll write or read. That is all I do every day."

Four times a week, Lee is taken into the yard where she can talk with Judi, Deidre or Andrea, but often she prefers to be by herself. Lately she has been arguing with Judi and Andrea and sometimes does not even wish to venture into the yard.

She spends the long indoor hours reading books on spiritual growth and writing lengthy letters to her mother.

"Man, I really hope by God's grace that someday we may get this opportunity to share a bit of this lifetime, a little together. It will be great.

"But, if not, imagine heaven. It's got to be just so profoundly beautiful and just so much worth waiting twenty or thirty more years for. Even eight or ten. You know. What ever."

She writes often about the inevitability of death.

"For you, I'll keep as alive as I can. I love you so much, I'm afraid to die right now. But otherwise, death does not scare me. I know I'll be right up there waiting for you should I ever go. He'll be beside me taking me up with him if I leave this shell. I am very sure of it. I have been forgiven and am certainly sound in Jesus' name."

"Lee's like a horse on the home stretch, not letting anything distract her," says Arlene. "And she'll keep going until she crosses the finish line —heaven."

It is 2:10 p.m., on Valentine's Day, at Maranatha Meadows. This is my fourth trip to the horse farm and by now I have learned to manipulate the front gate, the wolves no longer howl at me and Kingman looks on me as a friend.

I find Arlene curled up on one corner of the sofa in animated conversation with Eileen, the woman who attacked her years ago and stole her jewelry, credit cards and horse equipment. It was this episode in Arlene's life that was responsible for her suicide attempt.

Eileen, an attractive, graying woman 'nearing fifty' has finally divorced her abusive husband, is part owner of a horse stable, and has just won a major race. She has brought Arlene shirts with wolf designs and Palmer shirts adorned with the stable's logo.

Arlene is making plans to go to Eileen's soon and spend the night so that they can watch movies together.

"Is that okay, Dad?" she inquires.

"You know, Arlene, I'm not going to stay here forever," Palmer says in his most authoritative tone.

"Why, Dad?" she asks.

"Because he has a life of his own," I interject, thinking of Palmer's two girlfriends and intention of finding a condominium close to Arlene, but "not too close."

Eileen is discussing her life in terms of religion. She is talking at length about those people who seek money as opposed to those who seek only Jesus.

"They [the money people] will remain at a lower level, removed forever from the rest of us," she says. She is very eloquent and mentions that a local preacher who deals in healing has rid her of cancer. A friend had called to tell her that her healing had been announced on the preacher's television show. Since that time, she has been free of pain.

"Were you being treated for cancer?" I asked.

"Oh, no. She never goes to the doctor," Arlene responds.

"How did you know you had cancer then?" I asked.

"I just knew," Eileen says. "I was in a lot of pain and I knew I had cancer of the lower digestive system and colon. But I'm fine now."

Palmer winks at me and I wink back.

Palmer and I share an enormous respect for these two women, who constantly overcome adversity, and, more important, have learned the art of forgiving and forgetting. But there are limits.

When Eileen climbs into her enormous black farm truck to head home, Arlene fixes me coffee and I take it into the backyard. We have decided to sit outside so that Palmer will not have to listen. He doesn't like to hear about Lee Wuornos. But he is cutting an article out of the local newspaper concerning the state's request for the defense witness list in the upcoming Marion County trial.

The mailman has come and there is no valentine from Robert. I notice, if Arlene doesn't. There is, however, a letter from a woman in Arkansas who has read the article in *Charisma Magazine*, a fundamentalist Christian publication, and praises Arlene for her position. Yesterday there were three letters.

"I believe the Lord has called you to be the father and mother Aileen never really had and to heal the pain of those lost relationships," wrote a woman from Lewisburg, Pennsylvania.

"You have exhibited love in a field of hate—a light in darkness," said a note from Vienna, Illinois.

"You are such a good example of Jesus Christ. He does not love us because of what we have done, but in spite of what we have done," praised a resident of Browns Mills, New Jersey.

"Renewal begins in the most unlikely places—even the desert of prisons," wrote a woman from New York City.

"Before we start," Arlene says, "I have to find out why the water pump keeps running. Maybe I left a hose running in one of the horse troughs."

There are eight troughs throughout the farm for the thirty-two horses, she adds.

Arlene and I walk through the farm, checking troughs, talking to the horses. I meet them all. One used to be called Ty, but his name has been changed.

None of the hoses are running, and I ask if it could be something in the house since it is on the same pump. Then we notice the sprinkler system which is watering the front yard.

Arlene settles into a chaise lounge while I choose to sit on the ground. It is a lovely, sunny day and, looking out over the pastures, I am beginning to appreciate her love for Maranatha Meadows.

"The farm is my sanity saver," she says. "I wouldn't be able to hold on if I didn't have it. I would hate her for what my life has become."

We both know that "her" is Lee and she asks me to read the letters that she received from Lee yesterday.

They are hateful letters, demanding $100 in her account, accusing all those who have tried to help of conspiring against her, challenging Arlene's allegiance to her.

She tempers the letters with an occasional "I love you, mom," but the words seem manipulative and, in some ways, more unsettling than the abuse.

I recall an earlier conversation with Billy Nolas: "Lee had a terrible background as a kid," he said, "and then goes on the road. So Lee's not only mentally ill, she's stunted at the level of an eight-year-old. She acts like an eight-year-old. She gets upset with Arlene and with her defense attorneys. You did not hear Lee's wrath come down on Tyria. You did not hear her wrath come down on Munster. She talked about a conspiracy when she gave her little spiel, but it was not related to the targets of that, the folks with whom she was upset.

"You have an eight-year-old in a grown woman's body. A kid is a kid. A kid will stomp around and bite and kick, but when you're an adult, you can seriously harm others.

"Just think of the content of what Lee says. It's one thing to say that Bruce Munster is trying to make some money out of this case. It's true. It's another thing to say that Arlene is part of a conspiracy or Tricia is going to write a book. The content itself is on the level of an eight-year-old. These are not the imaginings of an adult who is paranoid on a grown-up level. Lee's on the level that kids are."

And I remember that this is a street child, who sees danger around every corner. Who has learned not to trust. Who will take advantage of any opportunity offered her. Because there have not been many.

We had hoped to make the trip to Pembroke Pines over the weekend so that Arlene could visit with Lee. It would be the first contact visit since early November.

"She is fine when I touch her, when I hold her," Arlene says.

Yesterday, the superintendant, Marta VillaCorta, had called to say that the visit to Pembroke Pines had not yet been approved and she will try to arrange it for the following week. Marta is scheduled to call back today and has not done so.

Arlene is edgy waiting for her call, but she knows I have questions and she is ready to talk.

Palmer has returned from his walk through the pastures and Kingman wants to join us. He bounds toward us, positioning himself between Arlene and me.

"J-e-a-l-o-u-s-y," Arlene spells out. "I've been spending so much time with the horses that he feels left out."

By now King has his head in her lap. His stance has partially removed the barrier between us.

We are talking about the relationship between Arlene and Lee and how demanding and paranoid Lee is.

"People tend to call me either crazy or neat," Arlene says, "and I hate either.

"I am not crazy and I am certainly not neat. If it weren't for God, I would smack Lee sometimes because she makes me so furious. And I want to say 'Get out of my life!' And I wonder why I am doing this!

"It's like horses—each one of them, under riding circumstances, has a different bit for different control. Some are so voice commanded that they don't need a bit. Each works his own way. The way God gets me to react the way he wants me to when I am misbehaving, what he always uses and it never fails and it never will, is the little child—the vision of the little child and the horrible abuse and he reminds me what she came from. And I say, 'Whatever you want!' "

Aside from all the conspiracies against her among her attorneys and the media, and maybe even Arlene, Lee complains in her letters that she has no mirror and no commissary. She wheedles Arlene and demands that Steve Glazer come and see her immediately. After all, she says, both Arlene and Steve will come into a great deal of money someday because of her.

It is what she has to give, but it comes with a pricetag.

Arlene goes inside to call Marta VillaCorta, and I sit with Kingman wondering what all this means.

I think of Deanie Stewart, convinced that Lee killed her brother, yet sitting at the table writing a valentine to her when I arrive for an interview.

And I think of Shirley Humphreys telling the press that she is elated with the verdict and is pleased that Lee Wuornos is going to die.

Jackie Giroux, claiming to be a friend and a sympathizer, yet she lied to Arlene about Sue Russell and her contracts with witnesses to the child abuse in Lee's past have, according to Tricia Jenkins, made them hesitant to talk to the defense or testify in court.

I remember the testimony of Tyria Moore and her failure to even look at Lee Wuornos except, under oath, to point her out in court.

Dawn Botkins, wanting desperately to testify for Lee, consumed with pain because she did not help her friend years ago before it was too late.

Bruce Munster, who saw a string of dead men and equated it to a Hollywood movie.

And Arlene Pralle, whose life is guided by the vision of a small, blond girl with a tortured expression.

Arlene returns from the house and she is smiling.

"What a wonderful woman," she says, speaking of Marta.

"Lee has been a disciplinary problem and stole cigarettes from another inmate. Marta realized that no one had given Lee commissary. She went to see Lee and apologized and when she left Lee shook her hand. I explained to her that she'll be better after I get to see her because I have a soothing effect on her. She said she realized that. And I may get to see her next week! I told Marta that once Lee and I are together, she'll make life easier. And it's true. When we get together and pray, she's a different person. The attorneys saw it with their very own eyes during the attempted plea bargaining. Lee was ready to assault Tricia Jenkins physically. She was so aggressive toward her and I just held her and didn't pray out loud, just kept saying, 'Jesus, Jesus' right in front of Tricia and those guys, just holding her, tears coming down my cheeks. She all of a sudden turned from anger to total tears, apologized to Tricia. They've seen it. There's something when I touch her. When I pray with her. God uses me as his channel. Billy says he's seen the living God working through me and it blows him away because he's never seen anything like it."

It is time for Arlene to feed the horses and for me to go home. She bundles up and drinks a cup of tea before tackling the job. I stay a few more minutes to talk to Palmer about father-daughter relationships and he tells me he thinks often of the nights he walked the floors with Arlene when she was little. She had a painful throat condition, and Carol did not have the stamina to stay up at night with a sick child.

When I leave, Palmer walks ahead of my car to open the gate leading out of Maranatha Meadows. When I am gone, he will lock it for the night. As I depart, I see the bird sitting on the telephone wire. Arlene had pointed it out weeks ago.

"It sits there and watches me when I go out," she says.

Arlene's world is bordered by fences. Lee's world is restricted by bars.

And I wonder: Is this you, Lord?

Epilogue

On the last day of March 1992, Aileen Wuornos stood before Judge Thomas Sawaya in the Marion County Courthouse in Ocala, Florida and pleaded no contest to the murders of Charles Humphreys and Troy Burress in Marion County and David Spears in Citrus County. At the proper time, she will repeat this plea in the Pasco County murder of Charles Carskaddon. No contest is not a plea of guilty. It simply means the defendant wants no more trials. She will not contest the charges made against her.

A repentant Lee told the judge that she wanted to tell the truth. That she wanted to make her peace with God. And that she wanted no more of the criminal justice system, its crooked cops, its opportunism, its greed, its lies.

Intermittently, she broke into tears.

"With the help of my beloved new friend, Arlene Pralle. . . . it is now planted firm my love in Christ within my heart," she said. "So, therefore, in order to get myself completely right with God before I die, I am coming forward today, in all honesty. . . .

"I plead today no contest in self defense," she told the court. "And I also plead no contest to end all trials. . . . I am very sorry, what has happened. I am sure, without a doubt, God has forgiven me of my consistent prostitutional career I used to carry on. As well as forgiven me of all these killings. . . . Well, I do hope that the families of the victims can understand, that I also do grieve over what I've done. It hurt me to have to kill 'em. For it is each and every day, a hard thing to live with, with all that happened. I am sorry. That I had taken their lives away from you."

And she ended, once and for all, speculation about the motives for the murders.

"I wanted to confess to you that Richard Mallory did violently rape me as I've told you. But these others did not. Only began to start to. And the psychological trauma, from the worst rape I've ever gone through before in my life, left me in a set frame of mind, in never allowing it to ever happen again. Once they even started, it was fight, and hopefully win. And each one used physical force or a weapon to prove to me they were going to carry out a rape, or even kill afterwards...which I wasn't about to wait around to see.

"I just right flat out killed them," she concluded.

The Marion County hearing had been scheduled to consider Steve Glazer's motion to replace Jenkins, Nolas and Miller as Lee's lawyer. The plea was unexpected by everyone except Steve and Arlene, who had for weeks been aware of Lee's desire to plead no contest to the court.

All three members of the defense team were present at the hearing. None of them had contacted Lee during the two months she had been on Death Row. None, says Arlene, had returned the repeated phone calls placed by Arlene and Steve. Nevertheless, they told the press that Steve's entry into the case was "unconscionable."

"By no stretch of the imagination is this in the best interest of Aileen Wuornos," said an angry Billy Nolas.

Not fighting at all was a serious mistake, said Nolas. Even if a jury in Ocala found her guilty and imposed the death penalty, it would be better than not fighting it. Now, the judge will not hear her side of the story, abandonment by her parents, abuse throughout her childhood, a hard life on the streets.

"This is very unusual," Nolas added. "Something an attorney should never do."

"She is essentially killing herself with the assistance of her lawyer," said Tricia Jenkins.

Bill Miller commented to Arlene that the action had "sealed her in her coffin."

"I told Bill that if any of them had returned my phone calls during the past two months, we could have worked this out. I kept trying to tell them that Lee wanted to plead and no one would listen to me," said Arlene.

Even the judge was hesitant to accept the plea.

"You're entitled to a trial. Let the jury decide about this," he said.

"The jury can say whatever they want. God knows I killed these people," said Lee. "That's why I'm doing this."

Lee had been brought to court with her hands cuffed in front of her, fastened to an unwieldy machine at her waist, which attached to the waist chains. Her arms were discolored, deep impressions visible from the tight enclosure. The apparatus had been placed on her as she left Broward for Marion County and she had lashed out at the guards. That night Arlene was not allowed to visit her, and the guards promised that the rest of the punishment would take place when she was returned to the jail for sentencing.

No visitations and no phone calls and only two showers a week, they told the press.

Jackie Giroux's parents were in the audience.

"If they did to an animal what they are doing to her, they would be arrested," said Alva Lusky, who had come to the hearing on behalf of her daughter.

Jackie and Arlene had talked. Jackie had caught up on her promised $60 a month payments to Lee, but she had no real money from her investors yet, she said. Now the deal hinged on casting the production. She wanted Jamie Lee Curtis to play Lee. And Andy Garcia to play Lauri Wuornos.

"I promise that Lee will come out looking like a heroine," she told Arlene.

As further reasons for her plea, Lee cited the actions of the police and the prosecutors.

"I am fed up with a great number of the deceptions that have been carried out in these cases...for ladder climbing, limelighting."

Attacking the anticipated movie about the Marion County cops entitled "Overkill: the Aileen Carol Wuornos Story," Lee referred to the "script of this sick and vile, made up horror flick these law enforcement officers have created. And this movie portrays a man-hating lesbian, who only killed to rob or robbed to kill....I never kept their cars, or all of their belongings. I told them I threw them out. Basically every single thing. With exceptions to the stuff I pawned. And their honor cards, each one had, with other cards galore. I had, and could of withdrew their money out of the bank, as a matter of fact, $200 at a time. I also had their codes, which were written down in their wallets. Yet I didn't. I never drew any of their money out of the bank. And some after the assault only had $20 on 'em. Now if I was this deranged monstrous slaughterer the cops are labelling me as, why didn't I? And since they have also claimed I robbed to kill and killed to rob, why didn't I withdraw this money. And why didn't I keep their cars, and fence them off? Also why didn't I take their master charge cards, buy stuff with em, and then fence em off?"

Brad King, Marion County State Attorney, told the press that he will seek the death penalty for Lee Wuornos.

For Lee, this is not a major concern.

"I hope I'll get the electric chair as soon as possible," she told the court. "I want to get off this planet, go to God and be up in heaven. I can't wait to leave."

Lee's moods pendulum back and forth. Some days she does not

want anyone to fight for her life. She is content to die. Other days she wants to live, if only for the sake of her adoptive mom. What she knows for certain is that she wants no more trials.

Steve Glazer, aware of the treatment that his client would receive in Marion County, asked Judge Sawaya to waive Lee's presence at the sentencing hearing.

"I did this for several reasons," said Steve. "First of all, I wanted to protect her from that treatment, and secondly, the jury will not have the opportunity to see her actions and reactions in court. How can they sentence a woman to death when they can't even see her?"

Tricia Jenkins had criticized Steve's involvement in the case because he had no "death penalty experience," but Steve says he is compensating for that.

"I've been reading everything I can get my hands on," he says, and he has determined his strategy. There will be no witnesses during the mitigation stage, Steve says, with the possible exception of Arlene Pralle.

"I'm going to appeal to the jury's sense of justice. Lee is saving the county money, she has taken responsibility for her actions by admitting her guilt and she does not ask for her life. She is prepared for whatever their judgment may be."

Steve feels that if Marion County gives her a life sentence, Pasco County will do the same. And Dixie County, scheduled to indict Lee on April 16, has already shown willingness to agree to a life sentence.

Meanwhile, Steve has been trying the case in the newspapers, sending positive messages to the public about Lee's desire to accept responsibility and ask forgiveness.

Using the press is "exactly what the state does," Steve says, "only Marion County is 80 percent Bible-thumpers and I'm hoping that will make a difference. If we can find a jury that is not contaminated."

In his private practice, Steve Glazer is known as "Dr. Legal." "Now they're calling him Dr. Lethal," said Billy Nolas, referring to Steve's handling of the case, which he felt paves Lee's way to the electric chair.

Billy feared that Lee would end up with death sentences in every county in which she was indicted.

"Why do you think Dixie County has finally indicted her?" he asked. "It would have bankrupted the county if they had gone to trial so they didn't indict her. Now that there will be no trial, just a sentencing hearing, they can go for a death sentence too. And if she gets other death sentences, who will bother with the Volusia appeal?"

On the lighter side, Billy lamented the fact that, without a trial in Marion County, Bruce Munster would not be forced to take the stand

and testify about his involvement with the "cop script" and Tyria Moore. "At least we could have had a little fun," he said.

For three days, a Marion County jury heard the evidence against Lee Wuornos in the murders of Charles Humphreys, David Spears and Troy Burress. In mitigation, Arlene took the stand to talk about Lee's childhood and to share a letter from Dawn Botkins. After four hours of deliberation, the jury returned with a 10–2 recommendation of death.

From her Death Row cell, Lee learned of the verdict on the evening television news.

For Lee Wuornos, it is only a matter of time.

"She could not bear the thought of telling any more lies," said Arlene. "People don't seem to understand how important it is to Lee to just tell the truth. She wants to make it right with God. The truth will set her free."

At The Last Resort Bar, an airbrushed portrait of Aileen Wuornos hangs above the grimy truck seat where she slept just before her arrest. During the Volusia County trial, a jail guard brought in an unflattering newspaper photo of Lee and placed it over the face in the portrait.

According to Cannonball, this was done because the girl in the picture looked a lot better than Lee actually did. The artist said she did that on purpose because everybody deserves a break.

The sign which accompanies the portrait reads: "Here Lied Aileen "Lee" Wuornos Her Last Night of Freedom January 9, 1991, At The Last Resort Bar."

Perhaps freedom, like Daytona Beach, is a state of mind.

Appendix
The Confession of
Aileen Wuornos

At approximately 10:15 on the morning of January 16, 1992, Aileen Wuornos met with with Marion County investigator, Bruce Munster, and Volusia County investigator, Lawrence Horzepa, in an office at Volusia County Branch Jail. Her intent was to clear the name of her friend, Tyria Moore, by confessing to the murders of six men along the highways of central Florida.

Portions of the three-hour confession have been used throughout the book. Following are further excerpts.

B. M.: *What I'm gonna do is I'm gonna preface the tape so that there isn't any doubt about anything that's going on. I'll be straight up front with you if you'll be straight up front with me, okay?*

A. W.: I would like to know if I wanted to...if I wanted to be straight up with one thing right here and now?

B. M.: *Sure.*

A. W.: The reason I'm confessin' is there's not another girl. There is no other girl. The girlfriend of mine is just a friend. She is working all the time and she...she worked at Casa Del Mar. She was always working. She was not involved in any of this...and the person that was murdered. She didn't know it was...until after the car was wrecked. See, she didn't know anything. She's really, really a good person, an honest person, a working person and she doesn't do anything wrong. She doesn't do drugs and all that stuff. She's just a real decent person that just works a lot. She was my...my...my roommate.

L. H.:   *Okay, so then what you're telling us is you're voluntarily coming forward to talk to us now.*

A. W.:   Yeah. To let you know that I'm the one that did the killings.

L. H.:   *Okay.*

B. M.:   *Okay. Now, let me read you your rights, okay? You have the right to remain silent. The Constitution requires that I so inform you of this right and you do not talk to me if you do not wish to do so. You do not have to answer any of my questions. Do you understand that?*

A. W.:   Yes.

B. M.:   *Do you want an attorney to be present at this time or any time hereafter you are entitled to such counsel. If you cannot afford to pay for counsel, we will furnish you with counsel if you so desire. Do you understand that?*

A. W.:   What does counsel mean?

B. M.:   *An attorney.*

A. W.:   Well, what's an attorney gonna do? I...I know what I did. I'm confessing what I did and go ahead and put the electric chair to me. (Inaudible sobbing)...I shoulda never done it. See, most of the times I was drunk as hell and I was a professional hooker and these guys would take my offer. I'd give 'em a little shit sometimes, you know, and so when they started gettin' rough with me, I went...I just like opened up and fired at 'em. Then I thought to myself, why are you givin' me such hell for when I just...I'm just tryin' to make my money...and you're givin' me a hassle.

———————

A. W.:   I don't understand why I would have...what would an attorney do? Help me from keepin'...gettin' the death penalty?

B. M.:   *I don't know that.*

A. W.:   I don't know. I don't know that either.

B. M.:   *It's your decision, Lee. I can't make it for you.*

A. W.:   If I did get the death penalty, do they stick you in a little room all the time?

B. M.:   *I don't know. I don't know.*

———————

A. W.: I'm a good person inside, but when I get drunk, I don't know what happens when somebody messes with me.....When somebody hassles me, I mean, I'm like, don't fuck with me.

B. M.: *Yeah.*

A. W.: I mean anybody would be like that. And...in other words, really deep inside I was gonna...when I was a little girl I always wanted to be a nun. And when I got older, I wanted to be a missionary, and I really got into....then I had some back problems. Then I fell in love with somebody and I had bad....when I love somebody, I love 'em all the way. But what I did, I don't understand why I did it. I just don't. I just know that they...they kinda gave me a hassle. When somebody gave me a hassle, I decided to whip out my gun and give it to 'em. Of course, I didn't really want to kill 'em in my heart, but I knew I had to. Because I knew if I left some witness, then they'd find out who I was and then I'd get caught. I have to tell. I have to tell the truth.

A. W.: And I just...I wanted to tell it....All I...I want to confess. I don't want my girlfriend in trouble. She doesn't deserve to go to prison or anything 'cause she doesn't know...she knows stuff of what I said in drunken spews, but she was not there. She did not know nothing and she did not...you know, she didn't...she couldn't believe me. I mean, if she...if she wanted to believe me, I'm sure she couldn't hardly believe me, is what I'm saying. And she loved me. And I loved her. And she was like, I can't believe you would do somethin' like this. So...I just want her to be very, very...I'm doing this because I don't want...I love her very much and she's so sweet and so kind and so innocent. She's just a real sweet girl. You know, I don't want her to get in trouble. 'Cause she didn't do anything. See, I was...she was at work. Casa Del Mar. While I was goin' out and hookin'. I would hitchhike. A guy would pick me up and I'd ask 'em if they were interested in helpin' me out 'cause I'm tryin' to make rent money, you know. And they'd say how much and I'd say thirty for head, thirty-five straight, forty for half and half, a hundred an hour. And they you know, then they'd say, Well, I'll take this or whatever and then, now...I'm telling you, I've dealt with a hundred thousand guys. But these guys are the only guys that gave me a problem and they started givin' me a problem just the...this year...the year that went by. So I, at the time, I was stayin' with some guy and I noticed he had some guns and I ripped off his .22, a 9-shot deal. And I carried that around while I was thumbin' around, which I couldn't believe the cops never searched me. I got...I got a message for the cops. You see a hitchhiker? Search 'em. They would never search me. And uh, uh, anyway, so when I'd get a hassle, if the person'd give me my money and I...I wouldn't do nothin' to 'em. But if the person gave me my money and then started hasslin' me, that's

when I started takin' retaliation. But I was...she was at work while I'd
be in Ocala or Homasassa or...or shoot, sometimes Fort Myers. I'd
leave for sometimes a couple days. It didn't happen too often. But I
would and I'd come back with a wad of money. She knew I was trickin',
but she thought I was doing it decently, honestly. And I'd say I made a
lot of money 'cause I was...been gone for a while. She didn't know I
killed somebody. See what I'm sayin'? And then when she found out
that I did, she left. She took off and went back home. I told her to go
home. You've got somethin' to do. Just go and leave. Get outta my life.
Because I don't want you involved. She didn't do anything. Yeah, she
said, yeah, and she started hatin' me. I don't blame her. She said, it's
easy to hate you. It's easy to get over you. And I lost someone very
dear in my life that I cared about. And I loved her with all my heart. I
just wish I never would've done this shit. I wish I never woulda got
that gun. I wish to God, I never was a hooker. And I just wish I never
woulda done what I did. I still have to say to myself, I still say that it
was in self defense. Because most of 'em either were gonna start to beat
me up or were gonna screw me in the ass...and they'd get tough with
me, so I'd fight 'em and I'd get away from 'em. And they I'd...as I'd get
away from 'em, I'd run to the front of the car or jump over the seat or
whatever, grab my gun and just start shootin'. Which they would be
out of the car. Most of them would be nude 'cause they took their
clothes off, see. And then they didn't, you know, didn't think about
runnin' back to the car or anything. I would start shooting out...
from out of the car, shoot at 'em. Did they find any prints on that car
that was, uh, the wrecked one?

B. M.:   *Yes.*

A. W.:   Did they find that Tyria's prints and my prints were on it?

B. M.:   *Yes.*

A. W.:   Okay. So that's why I'm confessing because, see, she didn't know it was
a car by a victim. She just thought I had...somebody loaned it to me.
And we just went around and drivin' around all the time and drinkin'
and drivin'. And then I told her I was too drunk and I asked her if she
wanted to drive and then she had a...she said, Okay, so she...we're
drivin' down the road and she was goin' a little too fast and I told her
to slow down and she couldn't control the curve and that's when we
wrecked. Then I went through the fence, got in back of the car after it
was wrecked, went through the fence, drove it down the road while it
was still smashed to hell. I had blood all over my shoulder and shit and
then I told her, I said, 'Listen, I'm gonna tell you somethin'.' She said,
'What?' I said, 'We can't let the cops know anything right now. This is
a cop car. I killed somebody, Ty.' She said 'What!' I said, 'I killed somebody.'

B. M.:   *...and I hope you won't lie to me. Okay?*

A. W.:   Oh, I'm tellin' you the truth all the way.

B. M.:   *So we can...we can sit here...we can sit her and wait till your attorney comes. We don't need to talk about the case or anything till y'all come to some decision.*

A. W.:   I don't care. I mean...I'm...like I been saying, I don't...I don't mind talking...I want this all...I'm telling you from the bottom of my heart, I'm telling you the truth about everything. I mean I can't be any truthfuller. I'm telling you, with...God by my side, I'm telling you the truth. So, don't worry. I'm telling you the truth, honest. I just got...I mean...this isn't a joke...I didn't mean to giggle there. I'm...I'm being very honest. That's all I can say. I...the only reason I'm doing this is because...number one, I'm guilty, number two, my girlfriend is not. She doesn't...didn't know anything. She never was around the time that I...hurt these people. She was at work. Er, she'd work, eat, sleep, come home and that was it. She's a very good person. She doesn't do drugs. She might drink a little beer now and then, but that's it. And she's a real sweet person and she doesn't deserve to be harmed in this because she didn't do anything. And that's another reason I'm confessing. 'Cause they were lookin' for two women and I wanna straighten it out that she was with me with the car but she didn't know the car belonged to somebody that was murdered...until after the wreck. And I told her, I said, 'Man, Ty, I've gotta tell you somethin',' you know in my mind. So I said, 'Ty,' you know, I said, 'get in the bushes, Man,' you know, 'cause I knew some cars were comin', and so she got in the bushes and she...she said, 'What the...what the fuck is the deal?' I said, 'I gotta tell you somethin',' and I said, 'I killed somebody.' She said, 'What!' I said, 'I killed somebody, man. This car is somebody I killed.' 'You idiot! What are you crazy! Why did you do that!' and all that stuff. So, anyway, I told her we gotta get outta here 'cause I don't want you to get into trouble, you know, you...you... know that you didn't do anything and, yeah, yeah, yeah, for sure, you know, and all this stuff. So I told her to hide in the bushes everytime a car went by. So finally, we started walkin' down the road and then those paramedics were tryin'...came by the road with a fire truck I think. And then we told 'em that we were hitchhikin'...two guys...I lied...I did all the talking. I said two guys picked us up and we got in a wreck and they...no, wait, no I didn't...I said two guys picked us up and they dropped us off and we're on our way to Daytona and they told us this is where, you know, you can get to Daytona...and this... but, it was the wrong road and all that stuff. And, uh, so then I told 'em, you know, we gotta get goin'...

L. H.:   *The only that that we can begin to talk to you again about the cases is if you wish to voluntarily come to us and say, Look, I no longer want an attorney. I want to go ahead and talk about these things. But since you have invoked your right to the attorney...*

A. W.: Yeah, because maybe an attorney can help me 'cause I know...

L. H.: *...and we can't talk to you.*

A. W.: Yeah, 'cause I know that it wasn't...I, in my heart, I know I self defended myself so maybe I need an attorney.

L. H.: *Okay.*

B. M.: *Did you contact one, Larry?*

L. H.: *Yes.*

B. M.: *One gonna come down?*

L. H.: *Yes.*

A. W.: Yeah, I know...I know that I have to defend myself because if I didn't, he probably woulda hurt me, killed me, raped me or whatever. 'Cause I'm tellin' ya, I'm serious. I have gone through at least 250,000 guys in my life. At least. And never hurt any of 'em. Matter of fact, I became very good friends with 'em, you know, and they really liked me. And they always wanted to see me again and stuff, but I always gave 'em the wrong phone number because I didn't really wanna always havin' calls, or I didn't even have a phone anyway. So I'd give 'em a wrong number and stuff so...but, I mean it, I...what I'm tryin' to say is I never woulda hurt anybody unless I had to and I had to at the time. So yeah, I guess I need an attorney.

A. W.: You know I really...I...I really suck.

A. W.: I'm very, very...I have to admit I'm scared about all this. I mean, I am very scared. I wouldn't of confessed if it wasn't for the fact that I don't want my girlfriend involved. I mean, I don't know, 'cause I've thought about it many times, but I don't want her involved. 'Cause she's not involved. I mean, you can ask her questions and stuff but she didn't know anything, she wasn't around and I'm telling you, I love her very much to the max, is what I'm trying' to say. I love her deep down inside very much. She's a Chr...well, she's not a Christian but she goes to...she used to go to a Church and she just worked, ate, and slept, and watched videos at home, or watched TV, Wheel of Fortune or Jeopardy or whatever and movies. She never did anything else. Have ...pop open a few beers 'cause she's not in...she's not guilty. And I'm willing to take the punishment because I'd rather confess that I did it so she won't have to...I...in other words, she doesn't deserve any

punishment. She didn't do anything. I don't know how to express myself on this. I don't want you to think I'm doin' it 'cause I love her and
am tryin' to protect her or something, 'cause I'm not. I'm doin' it 'cause
I love her and she's not guilty. She didn't do anything. I'm bein' very
wide open and honest. It's a very frightening thing for me to do...But
I told her I'm a bum. I don't...she was crying her eyes out. My family's gettin' all messed up. She...I didn't do anything. You got me involved in this jazz because of that car that you got wrecked. Um...
you need to go and tell 'em that you did it and get me straightened out
on this and I said, 'Yes, Ty, okay, I will.' And that's why I'm doing this.
Because I don't need her family or her gettin' messed up for somethin'
that I did. Hmmm. I know I'm gonna miss her for the rest of my life.
She's a real good person. So sweet and kind.

A. W.: Oh, you guys really...you can put me under hypnosis, you can take a
lie detector test, do whatever you can to make me show you that Ty
does not know...did...did not do anything. Honestly. I'm bein' so
honest, I can't be any honester than I am. She...she's just good a
good girl that met...got messed up with a creep like me. I met her at
Zodiac a long time ago. Three years of good friendship and bein' just
...lovin' each other and I screwed up the last year. I asked her, I said,
'If I never done this would you have stayed with me?' And she said
'Yes.' And so...I said, 'I guess you can...you can hate me now.' She
said, 'It's not hard to do.' I said, 'Do you love me a little bit?' She said, 'I
guess I do a little bit for ya' cause, you know, I guess after three years
you can still have a little love for me. I said, 'But, yeah, I guess, go
ahead and hate me 'cause it'll be easier for me to get over you and you
get over me.' But I don't have anybody, no family or nothin'. She was
my only friend in the whole world and that's why I loved her so much.
But I loved her because of her honesty. She never stole. My goodness, I
gotta tell you somethin'. She was workin' at a Laundromat, and she
found a $125.00 in quarters in the back of the washer, she coulda kept
the money, but, no, she gives it to the people, gives it back to 'em. And
we were hard up for rent then. We needed rent money real bad. So I
went out and made some money real quick. Then, I...when she was
workin' as a Manager in this Laundromat, I said, 'Ty, let me see fifty
cents'...'cause there's quarters in the laundromat, right? 'Ty, let me
see fifty cents. I'm gonna go get a soda.' We lived three blocks from the
place. She said, 'Hell no.' She said, 'Go home and get the money.' I'm
not gonna let you use any of this money. Would you believe that they
fired her, sayin' that she had taken six hundred some dollars. But there
was another guy that was workin' there and he died of Cancer. And
then there was another girl that was some kind of biker chick from
Canada that would take over...uh...little...you know, for an hour
or two...and I think they're the ones that stole the money. And she
got fired for that and she did not take it, 'cause, Honey, I...I mean, I

mean...I'm thinkin' of her...and when I talk to her...I'd be with here all the time and we needed rent money, I had to go out and hustle for it. There's no way she took it. You see what I'm sayin'? She's a very honest person. I guess 'cause we were Lesbians, they'd always mess with us. She got fired at the Casa Del Mar for (Inaudible)...'cause we were Lesbians. I know that's what the reason is. He's from Iran and, yeah. He didn't like the idea that he wouldn't...he couldn't get a piece of ass from her. Kept tryin' to get a piece of ass from all the girls at work. Yeah. He's the boss, you know. And, so, finally he said, Well I knew it was comin' to fire you. And she wouldn't give, you know, she's not gonna...she's real sweet and innocent. She ain't gonna...God, she's in love with me, you know what I'm sayin'? We didn't even have sex hardly. We had sex, I'd say, the first year, maybe three times and the next years, we didn't even have sex together. We were just friends. Just good friends. Huggin, kissin', but we were good friends. You know. So...that's why I'm saying...that's why I'm confessing because she's ...shit, she wouldn't deserve anything 'cause she didn't do anything, you know. I don't want her in trouble...for somethin' that I honestly did. I know right now, it's easy for me to confess. I know right now it's easy for me to say everything honestly now, when I get back to the cell I'll probably cry my eyes out. I'll go through a lot of hell, through Court and everything else. I'll take a major toll in this. I understand. So, I know it's very frightening for me to confess. 'Cause I know (Inaudible). I'm possibly lookin' at death, I'm possibly lookin' at life imprisonment. I don't know what I'm looking at, but I know one...thing, I just wanna get right with God again and give this...I'll put my trust with the Lord and with the people here so everybody knows. I am so sorry (Inaudible)...I mean I...I realize I don't have a family so I don't understand. But when I...after I'm...seein' Ty's family and everything...I have never met the family but noticing how Ty was on the phone and stuff, I realize now how badly I used to hurt some families. And the re...now...I...these...these men were older men...another thing after they were dead that didn't bother me 'cause I thought, Well, they're older. They probably don't have anybody hardly anyway so it didn't (Inaudible)...me too much. But I didn't kill 'em for that reason. I killed 'em because they tried to do somethin' to me. But I did think that. Well they're old, their Father and Mother's probably deceased and so why worry about it and stuff. I don't know. Creaky spots in my head, I guess, (Inaudible). I wish to God...I wish I hadn't done it. Not that I'm feeling sorry for myself for what I'm gonna pay, I'm saying I wish I never had the gun, I wish I never, ever hooked and I wish I never woulda met these guys. 'Cause I wouldn't of had to do what I did if I hadn't of been hookin', see. It's because of hustling, and the guy's gonna physically harm me, that I have to harm him back. You see what I'm sayin'? Yeah. 'Cause if I wasn't hustling, if I wasn't hooking around, I woulda never had a physical problem and I wouldn't of never had to hurt anybody. And I do have to say one thing, though, their families must realize that no matter how much they loved the people that died, no matter how much they love 'em, they were bad 'cause they were gonna hurt me. So they have to realize the fact, that this person, no matter how much they loved 'em or how good they felt that were, this person was either gonna physically beat me up, rape me, or kill me. And I don't know which one. And I just turned around and did my fair play before I would get hurt, see? So, I would love to say that to the families. I mean, that guy's gonna...You stupid Bitch. You killed my husband or whatever, you know. Or my brother or somethin'. And I'd have to...I'd just have to say to 'em, Listen, what they were going to do to me, I would be probably turning around if I had survived it, and say, You stupid Bastards. You almost killed me, you almost raped me, you almost beat the shit out of me. So, you know, that's how I have to look at it. I have to look at it like that, too. So I can't really say that they were sweet...

A. W.: You know, I know that these guys...one guy had a weapon with him. He had a .45 and I...it was dark and he didn't know where he put it ...this is the weapon that I sold. And, uh, I don't know where he put it. But I didn't know he had a weapon, see, I had no idea he had a weapon, but when he started shittin' me that's when I grabbed my gun and I started shootin'. And when I was done shootin' him, and I went through the car, and there was the .45 sittin' on top of the hood. I think he was gonna take the gun and blow my brains out. So that's... another case. And that's...I honestly have to say, If you're hooking, don't do it. I mean, I could help people out so bad because I think I had...I have six chan...I had six times I almost got killed. And I killed the person, see. And I'm being very honest. Now, to recollect all this stuff is gonna be hard. Cause a lotta times I was drunk...and after I'd done it, you know, I'd go and get drunk so, wow, to remember everything is gonna be a little bit difficult. I don't even know their names. I can't even remember their names.

L. H.: *...how many men have you actually shot and murdered? Shot and killed?*

A. W.: Six. All I can remember.

L. H.: *Six...six men that you remember?*

B. M.: *You forgot about the one that (inaudible). That makes seven.*

A. W.: No, 'cause I only did six.

L. H.: *Okay.*

B. M.: *Well, we'll go over those six first.*

A. W.: Right. I think there's only six.

L. H.: *Okay.*

A. W.: I know…I think it's six.

L. H.: *Okay, well, we'll…we'll go ahead now…*

A. W.: Okay, yeah, because…because if you showed me all the pictures of the guys, I can tell ya, and if you show me a picture of a guy that… you know, if there's a seventh guy, I can tell ya if I did it or not because …I'm bein' very honest with you, as much as possible. I mean I am telling you the absolute, honest to God, so help me Lord, strike me with lightening in my heart right now, if I'm not telling you the truth.

A. W.: I am willing. Okay, I know I'll be fine. I'm willing to tell 'em everything and I want them to understand Tyria is a very nice person, honest person, and she is not involved in this and she just worked, ate, and slept and stayed at home and she was never around the situations that I did except that when she saw any vehicles, I told her that I was borrowing the car. And everytime I told her that there was a murder victim in the vehicle after the situation after the wreck, and I had to tell her that because her life was in jeopardy in that situation, and after I told her that, she was all freaked out. She did not know what to do. She was willing…she was wantin' to turn me in and all kinds of stuff she wanted to do…she wanted to do all kinds of things, but then she loved me and she didn't know what to do. She was really hurt. She was really hurting inside. She did not know what to do. And I…I said to myself many a times…after I told her, I said, shoot, maybe I should have let her go ahead and turn me in.

A. W.: I think I probably…it was…I always shot somebody, if I could, you know, as fast as I could, it would always hit right around this area. Up here. Right over…I always aimed to the mid-section so I know I shot 'em.

A. W.: Usually it would be we both got naked and I was gonna do an honest deed but I had a big fight. They…they were either gonna physically fight me…either try to rape me or something or they were gonna try to…you know, so they wouldn't have to pay their…I don't know what they were gonna do. They just…started gettin' radical on me and I had to…do what I had to do.

B. M.: *Okay, the guy with the .45 that you told me about before, now is he before this or after this, do you remember?*

A. W.: I think he was before. He was the second guy.

B. M.: *Oh, the guy with the Cadillac was the second guy?*

A. W.: No, the guy with the .45, I shot more than...over nine times. 'Cause I was pissed when I found the .45 on top of the car. I re-loaded the gun and I shot him some more.

A. W.: And we were way out in the boonies there and that's where he [Charles Carskaddon] started getting physical...he said, 'You fuckin' bitch', and I said 'You fuckin' bastard you were gonna blow my brains out' and I kept shootin' him in the back seat of the car. Then I drove over to 52 and dumped the body out.

B. M.: *Was he still naked?*

A. W.: He was naked. I always stripped naked first. Mallory never stripped. He was just gonna physically fight me and get whatever he wanted. I don't know how without his pants off, but that was his trip.

A. W.: "...So I went to Tampa and I made a little money hustling. And I was hitchhiking home at night and this guy, he picked me up."

L. H.: *"Do you know what street or highway you were on?"*

A. W.: "I...I-4."

L. H.: *"You were on I-4? Coming out of Tampa?"*

A. W.: "Out of Tampa going to Daytona...."

L. H.: *"Okay. Uh. You get picked up. What happens then?"*

A. W.: "Alright...he asked me if I wanted to smoke a joint and said, 'Well, I don't really smoke pot.' He said, 'You don't mind if I smoke some?' I said, 'I don't care what you do. Do whatever you feel like doin'...it doesn't bother me.' So he's smokin' pot and we're goin' down the road and he says, 'Do you want a drink?' and he has, I don't know what it was, it was Tonic and some jazz. I don't know what kind of liquor it was. So I said, 'Sure, that sounds good to me.' So we're drinkin' and we get past Orlando and we're gettin' pretty drunk now. And we're continually going down the road and I...we're gettin' drunk royal. Then I asked him if he wanted to help me make some money 'cause I need some money for rent and everything. He was interested at the time. So we go out and we stop at this place on U.S. 1, but we spent the whole night drinking and...you know, havin' fun for a little while."

L. H.: *"What's havin' fun?"*

A. W.: "Like...just talking. He's smokin' pot and I'm drinkin' and we're talking. Then he said, 'Okay, do you want to make your money now?'..."

around probably 5:00 in the morning maybe. And I said, Okay, you know, so he's pretty drunk and I'm pretty drunk."

L. H.: *"Now describe this area where you're at."*

A. W.: "We're past I-95, about maybe a half a mile up the road. There was a little spot that went into the woods."

L. H.: *"And you're off of...which road?"*

A. W.: "U.S. 1."

L. H.: *"U.S. 1. Okay. Describe to me the spot in the woods, if you can. Was it small, large? Do you remember anything about it?"*

A. W.: "Well, it was dark. We couldn't really hardly see to get in."

L. H.: *"How'd you find it"?*

A. W.: "We kinda drove lookin' for this road to go in and we drove back around and we saw a road to go in."

L. H.: *"Okay, so you were looking for a cut-off in the woods."*

A. W.: "Right."

L. H.: *"...a spot in the woods that was..."*

A. W.: "Right."

L. H.: *"Already a trail?"*

A. W.: "Right."

L. H.: *"Okay."*

A. W.: "So we go into the woods...so he gives me the money and I start to disrobe. Now the guy's gettin' really...kinda startin'...now he's gonna start gettin' a little, you know, kissin' on me and stuff and... anyway, he hasn't disrobed himself at all."

L. H.: *"Do you know what he's wearing?"*

A. W.: "I think he was wearin' jeans and some shirt."

L. H.: *"Do you remember if it was long or short sleeves?"*

A. W.: "No, I don't remember at all."

L. H.: *"Okay."*

A. W.: "Okay, so, anyway, we're in the front seat. He's huggin' and kissin' on me and all this shit so then he starts, you know, pushin' me down. And I said, 'Wait a minute,' you know, get cool. 'You don't have to get rough, you know. This is...let's have fun. This is for fun, you know. And he's tellin' me, 'Well, Baby, you know I've been waitin' for this all night long' and stuff like that."

L. H.: *"Now where are you when this is occurring?"*

A. W.: "In the front seat of the car."

L. H.: *"Alright, and you're sitting where?"*

A. W.: "On the passenger side."

L. H.: *"And he is sitting...where?"*

A. W.: "In the driver's seat, goin' against me."

L. H.: *"Okay, he's behind the wheel of the car?"*

A. W.: "But he's comin' toward me."

L. H.: *"Okay."*

A. W.: "The doors are open. Okay. So then he's gettin' really heavy, you know, on me, you know, and stuff and I'm goin' like, now he's gettin' to where he just want to just, you know. Unzipped his pants, not take his pant off or anything, just start havin' sex and stuff. And I said, 'Well, why don't you just disrobe or something,' you know. 'I mean, whey do you have to have your clothes still on?' Then he started gettin' violent with me. So we're fightin' a little bit and I had my purse right on the passenger floor."

L. H.: *"What kind of purse did you have?"*

A. W.: "A...a brown purse."

L. H.: *"Is that the same purse that you..."*

A. W.: "Oh, no, wait. I didn't have my brown purse. No, it's not the one I had. I had a blue bag and it had a zip on the side. Okay, and it was unzipped 'cause I...I wanted to make sure if anything happened I...I could use my gun. Things are startin' to happen where he was gonna ...I thinkin he was gonna roll me, take my money back, beat me up, or whatever the heck he was gonna do. So I jumped out of the car with my bag and I grabbed the gun and I said, 'Get outta the car.' And he said, 'What...what's goin' on' and I said 'You Son-of-a-Bitch, I knew you were gonna rape me.' And he said, 'No, I wasn't, no, I wasn't.' And I said, 'Oh, yet, you were. You know you were gonna try to rape me, man.' So, anyway, I told him to step away from the car. Oh, no, no, no, I didn't. All this and another thing, okay. I know what happ...okay, I took...I got...I jumped outta the car, yeah, he was startin' to physically do stuff to me...aw, this is a different story. God. See it's so long ago."

L. H.: *"It's alright. Take your time."*

A. W.: "Yeah, Okay, I jumped outta the car. I pulled my gun out when he started to physically do shit with me."

L. H.: *"Now what type of gun did you have?"*

A. W.: "Nine. . .22, 9-shot, you know."

L. H.: *"Twenty-two long rifle?"*

A. W.: "No, it's a gun, like about this big. . ."

L. H.: *"Okay, why did you keep that gun with you?"*

A. W.: "I was keepin' it for protection."

L. H.: *"Where'd you get the gun from?"*

A. W.: "I stole it from a guy at a house."

L. H.: *"How long before?"*

A. W.: "Oh, God, I don't know. I think it was. . ."

L. H.: *"Months? Years?"*

A. W.: "I don't know, man, it might of been about, maybe a couple of months ago. . .I mighta got the gun just then. I don't. . .I can't remember. Like . . .like two days before or somethin'."

L. H.: *"Okay. That's no problem."*

A. W.: "'Cause I can't remember. It's such a long time. I did a lot of stuff in the time, you know."

L. H.: *"Okay, so you're back there. You jump outta the car. . ."*

A. W.: "I jumped outta the car 'cause he was physically starting to abuse me. And I remember now. He didn't even give me any money. This was another guy. This guy, he said, he said, 'Well, I'll give'. . .no, I said, 'Well, I always take my money first' and he said he wanted to see how the merchandise fit."

L. H.: *"This is what Mr. Mallory told you?"*

A. W.: "Yes."

L. H.: *"Okay."*

A. W.: "So, I said, 'Well, since I've been talkin' to you all night long, I think you seem like a pretty nice guy, you know, so okay, let's. . .let's go have fun. So I started to lay down and he was gonna, you know unzip his pants. And I said, 'Why don't you take your clothes off?' My God, you know, I said, 'Well, it hurt to do that.' Then he got pissed, callin' me. He said, 'Fuck you, baby, I'm gonna screw you right here and now'. . . somethin' like that."

L. H.: *"Now where are you?"*

A. W.: "I'm in the woods with this guy and the doors are open."

L. H.: *"Okay."*

A. W.: "I remember that. And I said, 'No, no, you're not gonna just fuck me.
You gotta pay me.' And he said, 'Oh, bullshit.' And that's when he got
pissed. Now I'm coming back to recollection. Okay, so then we started
fightin' and everything else and I jumped out. He grabbed my bag and
I grabbed my bag and the arm busted and I got the bag again and I
pulled it out of his hand and that's when I grabbed the pistol out. And
when I grabbed the pistol out, I just shot 'im in the front seat."

Later in the confession, she would say about Mallory:

"See, one guy, he was tryin' to screw me in the ass and stuff. . . he was gonna
try to a. . . anal screw. You know anal screw or whatever you call it. So I started
fightin' with him and I got to my bag and I shot him. And then when I shot
him the first time, he just backed away. And I thought. . . I thought to myself,
well, hell, should I, you know, try to help this guy or should I just kill him. So I
didn't know what to do, so I figured, well, if I help the guy and he lives, he's
gonna tell on me and I'm gonna get it for attempted murder, all this jazz. And I
thought, well, the best thing to do is just keep shootin' him. Then I'd get to the
point that I thought, well, I shot him. The stupid bastard woulda killed me so I
kept shootin'. You know. I other words, I shot him and then I said to myself,
Damn, you know, if I didn't. . . sh. . . shoot him, he woulda shot me because he
woulda beat the shit outta me, maybe I would have been unconscous. He
woulda found my gun goin' through my stuff, and shot me. Cause he probably
woulda gone to get it for tryin' to rape me, see? So I shot him and then I thought
to myself, Well, hell, I might as well just keep on shootin' 'im. Because I gotta kill
the guy 'cause he's goin' to. . . he's gonna. . . you know, go and tell somebody if
he lives, or whatever. Then I thought to myself, Well, this dir. . . this dirty bastard deserves to die anyway because of what he was tryin' to do to me.

"So those three things went in my mind for every guy that I shot. . . .

B. M.: . . . Did you watch TV?

A. W.: I watched TV all my life.

B. M.: Did you watch to see if the police. . .

A. W.: I watched TV all the time, but after the crimes, yes, I did.

B. M.: To see what the police were doing?

A. W.: To see if they had found the bodies.

L. H.: Okay, Uh, from all the, uh, shootings that you have told us about, uh, for
the most part, you've always gotten the drop on these guys. You've been able
to get your gun and point it at 'em.

A. W.: Uh huh.

L. H.:   *Right?*

A. W.:   Right.

L. H.:   *Okay. At that particular time, you were in control. Why didn't you just run? Why didn't you . . .*

A. W.:   Because I was always basically totally nude with my shoes off and everything and I wasn't gonna run through the woods. And briars and the . . .

L. H.:   *No, but still, like I say, you're in control. You got that gun. You could go ahead and get dressed while you had, you know, them do whatever you basically wanted. Why did you go ahead and . . . and shoot these people?*

A. W.:   Because they physically fought with me and I was . . . well, I guess I was afraid, 'cause they were physically fightin' with me and I . . . what am I supposed to do, you know, hold the gun there until I get dressed and now I'm gonna walk outta here? When the guy, you know, might . . . you know, run me over with his truck or might come back when I'm walking out of the woods or somethin' . . . uh, have a gun on him, too or somethin'. I didn't know if they had a gun or not.

L. H.:   *So was it . . . was it your intent, during each of these times, to kill this person so that they couldn't come back at you later?*

A. W.:   'Cause I didn't know if they had a gun or anything. I . . . once I got my gun, I was like, 'Hey, man, I've gotta shoot you 'cause I think you're gonna kill me.' See?

L. H.:   *What about the ones who didn't have a gun like Mr. Mallory?*

A. W.:   I didn't know they had . . . didn't have a gun.

L. H.:   *Okay, so you were taking no chances.*

A. W.:   Right. I did not know . . . what . . . had . . . they . . . what was in their vehicle. See?

L. H.:   *Okay.*

A. W.:   I didn't know if they had it under the seat, close by 'em. What. I didn't know if they were in arm's reach of another weapon or what. See?

L. H.:   *What made you take property . . . a lot of property or a little property from some and not from others? Was there anything there that . . .*

A. W.:   I guess it was . . .

L. H.:   *. . . motivated you to . . .*

A. W.:   I guess it was after, it was pure hatred. Yeah, I think afterward, it was like, You bastard, you woulda hurt me and, uh, I'll take the stuff and get my money's worth because some of 'em didn't even hardly have any money. They were gonna . . . they were . . . some of 'em didn't have

ANY money. Like that guy, uh, the Drug Dealer guy... he had twenty bucks and he was... he wasn't gonna give me any more money. The one with the .45 on top of the hood.

L. H.: *Mmm... mmm. So then you just started living off of the items that they had? Is that what you were doing?*

A. W.: No, I think I took 'em just for the fact that, you bastards, you were gonna hurt me, you were gonna rape me, or whatever you were gonna do, well, I'll just, you know, keep these little items so I don't have to buy 'em or somethin'. I don't know. I just...

L. H.: *It was like a final revenge?*

A. W.: Yeah. Okay. That would... that would do. Mmm... mmm.

B. M.: *Lee, after you shot one time, I mean you could've left. You could've taken their stuff and (Inaudible).*

A. W.: I didn't wanna do that because I was afraid that if I shot 'em one time and they survived, my... my face and all that, description of me, would be all over the place and the only way I could make money was to hustle. And I knew these guys would probably... would, you know, rat on me if they survived and all this stuff and... and I would... I was hoping that I... after what I had to do, that I wouldn't of had gotten caught for it because I figured that these guys deserved it. Because those guys were gonna either rape, kill... I don't know what they were gonna do to me. See what I'm saying'?

L. H.: *So you continued to kill these men to cover up, uh, when you when you shot these men. Mallory was the first. Is that correct?*

A. W.: Okay. You continued... you had to go ahead and kill these men so that they couldn't testify against you and have it back-tracked? From body to body then.

A. W.: Oh, no, I didn't even think that either. I... I shot 'em 'cause it was like to me, a self defending thing because I felt that if I didn't shoot 'em and I didn't kill 'em, first of all, if they survived, my ass would be getting' in trouble for attempted murder, so I'm up shit's creek on that one anyway, and... and... and... and if I didn't and if... and if I didn't kill 'em, you know, of course, I mean I had to kill 'em... or it's retaliation, too. It's like, you bastards. You were gonna... you were gonna hurt me.

L. H.: *So now I'm gonna hurt you.*

A. W.: Yeah. Mmm... mmm.

B. M.: *Yeah, all of... all of these guys that you shot, they seem to be older guys. Over the age of 40. What is that?*

A. W.: Because all of the guys that I dealt with were that age. Every... every guy.

B. M.: *You were dead wood for younger guys?*

A. W.: No. Every guy I dealt with on the road was anywhere from...let's see ...37 and up.

L. H.: *Was that your decision? I mean like the...*

A. W.: Yeah, because I...

L. H.: *...younger guy in his 20's would stop...*

A. W.: ...yeah, because, see, I don't do drugs or anything and I wanted to deal with people who didn't do drugs. I was lookin' for clean and decent people. But like I say, it just happened that the last...this following year, that I kept meetin' guys that were turning out to be ugly guys ...to me. That they were...fightin'.

L. H.: *Is there any property that you would have collected from any of these victims that may be stashed somewhere? You might have put it in the woods or behind an abandoned house or anything like that?*

A. W.: No. Uh uh. I just flung 'em out the window as I'm driving or...or stopped and threw 'em and stuff like that. I couldn't even tell you where because they were way out in the country somewhere where I didn't even know sometimes where I was at.

B. M.: *There's somethin' I forgot to ask you. There's another guy that's missing that we haven't found. A guy that worked for the Kennedy Space Center. A guy that worked for the Kennedy Space Center and there was a white Oldsmobile and the car was parked in Orange County off of Semmoran and 436. The guy had glasses on and this would have been right around the HRS guy's car.*

A. W.: Uh...

B. M.: *It was a white car and he was drivin' from Titusville to Atlanta...it was a white 2-door car...*

A. W.: Naw, I don't recall anything like that.

B. M.: *Do you have a picture of him, Larry?*

A. W.: Yeah, yeah, if you got a picture of 'em...

L. H.: *What was the name on that?*

B. M.: *Reid. Curtis Reid.*

A. W.: Curtis Reid. I don't know that one. I don't remember anybody like that.

B. M.: *He worked at the Space Center and he had a Space Center emblem on his windshield of his rear window and someone scraped it off. He had a lot of money. He just cashed his paycheck. You mighta had...*

A. W.: I never got anybody that had a lot of money.

B. M.: *He mighta had a thousand dollars, somethin' like that.*

A. W.: Oh, I never got anything like that. Uh uh.

L. H.: *No, I have a flyer of the emblem. I don't have that one.*

A. W.: I don't recall anything like that because I never...I never got a lot of money on it. The only money I got the most was that, uh, that I didn't know was a missionary dude, was like four hundred dollars.

B. M.: *Who's Susan Blahovic?*

A. W.: Oh, well, that's another fake I.D. I had.

B. M.: *How'd you get that one?*

A. W.: Oh, Lord, let's see, how did I get...oh, this guy in the Keys had a birth certificate and he told me to use it for...'cause I had a suspended driver's license and he told me I could use that I.D. Aww... because...and I had...I think I had a...that forgery warrant was at that time, I think. I had that on me. And he told me I could use this I.D., that it was his wife's I.D., that she had never...he hated his wife, big time. And that I could...she's never been in trouble and that I could turn that birth certificate and license, but don't get in trouble with it, you know, just use if for driving and stuff, so I did.

B. M.: *Alright. I think that's...*

A. W.: How in the world did you find out about Susan Blahovic now?

B. M.: *Oh...*

A. W.: And did I put my name on a motel as that or somethin'?

B. M.: *No, you got some tickets with it.*

A. W.: Oh, okay, I remember that. Alright.

B. M.: *I know about the time in 1974, you were arrested under the name of Sandra Beatrice Kretch.*

A. W.: Yeah.

B. M.: *Your neighbor.*

A. W.: Yeah. I was...I was young and she was 33 or somethin' and the Judge couldn't...I spent 10 days in Jail for that one. She got away with havin' to go to Jail on her damn ticket.

B. M.:   *Yeah. How far did you go in High School?*

A. W.:   Tenth and a half grade.

B. M.:   *Why'd you quit?*

A. W.:   Because my Mother died and my Father wouldn't let me stay at home and I was living out on the street.

———————

A. W.:   I just want...to know that I hope to God, that you guys do understand that Ty is not involved in this. She doesn't know. She thought that I had these cars either rented or...or borrowed 'em and all this jazz, and she wasn't too...too aware of what I was doing. I mean, she didn't know...exactly what was happening. I mean I...when I'd get drunk I'd say shit from the top of my head just to try to be a bad ass, 'cause I was drunk. And...but she didn't have anything to do with these murders. She didn't have anything to do with anything. She just worked, ate, slept, stayed at home, went to Volley Ball practice and was just a good gal.

B. M.:   *I know what I wanted to ask you. You said that you put the gun and a flashlight, some handcuffs into the water.*

A. W.:   Oh, yeah.

B. M.:   *Over by the bridge around Fairview. Now you walked to the...on the bridge there...were you in the middle or towards one side or the other?*

A. W.:   Oh, when you go to the bridge...

B. M.:   *Uh huh.*

A. W.:   ...there's the other little bank there...

B. M.:   *Uh huh.*

A. W.:   ...and it's right underneath the bridge there.

B. M.:   *Okay.*

L. H.:   *Is it actually in the water or did you hide it up underneath the bridge?*

A. W.:   No, it's...it's in the water.

B. M.:   *Okay. You took the gun and threw it underneath there?*

A. W.:   Yes.

B. M.:   *Now did you throw the handcuffs someplace else?*

A. W.:   No, I just dropped 'em along...

A. W.:   They're straight down?

A. W.:   Yeah.

B. M.: *Alright.*

L. H.: *Could you see 'em when they hit...hit the bottom of the...*

A. W.: No, but I know it's waist deep...around there. 'Cause some guy said he had cemented that part out there. And he had to get his net untangled from the crab trap and he told me it's about anywhere from here to there, in the water.

––––––––––

L.H.: *Lee, would you be willing, if we needed you to, uh, go out with us to try to locate that .22 that you threw into the water...if you can show us the exact location where you had tossed it? Would you be willing to do that for us, Lee?*

A. W.: I'm willing to do anything. I wanna just let you know I'm the only one involved in this deal...stuff...shit.

L. H.: *Also, too, uh, later on, would you be willin' to talk to other Investigators...*

A. W.: Oh, no problem.

L. H.: *...if needed, from the other counties that have cases involved.*

A. W.: I want this all out in the open and I want them to know that there's not two girls. Ty is as innocent as can be. There was only one person. It was me, 'cause I'm a hooker and I got involved with these guys because they were phys...it was a physical situ...'cause I'm telling you now, I'm serious, every day when I was hitchhikin', I would meet anywhere from five to eight guys a day and make...now, but some would say no, and some would say yes.

B. M.: *Mmm...mmm.*

A. W.: And I would make money. But they wouldn't abuse me or nothin' I'd just do my thing and make my money, stick it in my wallet and go.

B. M.: *Okay. That about wraps it up. Alright, now, I'm gonna turn the tape off and it is 2:21 in the afternoon.*

A. W.: Can I ask you somethin'?

B. M.: *You certainly can.*

A. W.: Do you mind if I keep these cigarettes 'cause I don't have any cigarettes at all?

L. H.: *You are quite welcome to them and I'm glad you didn't ask to keep my jacket.*

A. W.: Oh, yeah, that was warm. Thank you.

L. H.: *Sure, no problem.*

A. W.: I'm very sorry....

Bibliography

Chambers, Michael M. "Three's a Crowd." *CrimeBeat* (April 1992): 43.

Edmiston, Susan. "The First Woman Serial Killer?" *Glamour* (September 1991): 302–25.

Klinger, Rafe. "My Lover Is a Killer in Bed—and a Serial Killer Too—Say Cops."*Globe* (December 3, 1991).

Kunen, James; Grant, Meg; Dampier, Cindy; and Damman, Sara Gay. "Florida Cops Say Seven Men Met Death on the Highway When They Picked Up Accused Serial Killer Aileen Wuornos." *People* (September 1991): 45–48.

MacNamara, Mark. "Kiss and Kill." *Vanity Fair* (September 1991): 91–106.

McPherson, Malcolm. "Let's Make a Deal." *Premiere* (December 1991): 35–41.

Index